Born 1950 in Leeds, Jeremy Paxman's career in television journalism began in Belfast and has since taken him, as one of Panorama's team of investigative reporters, to most of the world's hot spots. In 1984 his investigation into the death of Italian banker Roberto Calvi won him the Royal Television Society Award for International Current Affairs.

Through the Volcanoes is Paxman's second book; in 1981 he published (with Robert Harris) a book about chemical warfare, *A Higher Form of Killing*.

JEREMY PAXMAN

Through the Volcanoes

A Central American Journey

PALADIN
GRAFTON BOOKS
A Division of the Collins Publishing Group

LONDON GLASGOW
TORONTO SYDNEY AUCKLAND

Paladin
Grafton Books
A Division of the Collins Publishing Group
8 Grafton Street, London W1X 3LA

Published in Paladin Books 1987

First published in Great Britain by
Michael Joseph Ltd 1985

Copyright © Jeremy Paxman 1985

ISBN 0-586-08572-6

Printed and bound in Great Britain by
Collins, Glasgow

Set in Sabon

For all of those who showed me kindness along the way, and for Elizabeth who put up with a lot when I returned.

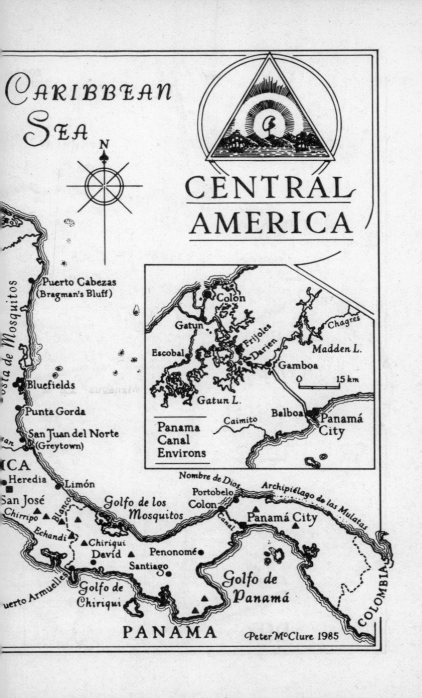

Contents

Introduction

The great bird turned lazily in the sky, swinging on the rising warm air. From this far below it seemed entirely black, an impression accentuated by the hard blue sky. The atmosphere was heavy and stale, and it was so hot that even to sit in the shade caused sweat to run in stinging little streams down my face. The bird was using the warm air current at the side of the volcano, sketching a slow circle out over the lake, across the foreshore and back to the volcano again. Further down the lakeside there were others making the same indolent motions, for the buzzards rarely hunt alone.

Close-up the birds had a satanic grandeur. At the tips of their broad wings the feathers ended in a serration like the teeth of a rusty old saw. Just before the feathers separated, there was a patch of white: the only touch of light anywhere, its effect was merely to emphasize the blackness of the rest of the bird. The legs trailed down below dark dirty fantails like the whips of a commercial sadist, idle but menacing. But the cruellest part was the head – sleek, black, and with a vicious hooked beak.

There was a youngish peasant sitting on the edge of the verandah: it was a Sunday morning and soon he would be irretrievably drunk on the fiery cane liquor which the cantina sold for a few cents a glass. The cheap alcohol smelt vile and had a paralysing effect upon the nervous system. It was one of the reasons there were so few genuinely old men to be seen. There were plenty who looked old and scarred and broken down, but usually they were not more than about forty, at the most fifty. Beyond that, those who survived the heat, the hunger and the *aguardiente* were freaks of nature. Here, the fortunate were young before their time.

Across the square the bell in the adobe church tower announced the consummation of the Mass. The man turned to me. The alcohol had not yet made a zombie of him, but there was putrefaction in his eyes.

'Something has died,' he said, nodding at where the buzzards had been circling a few minutes earlier. 'At least they'll eat well today.'

An hour later, I was travelling along the lakeside in the back of an open truck. With a couple of wooden benches tacked to the side walls, it passed for a bus in these parts. There were six other passengers, all in the same coarse cotton shirts and shapeless synthetic dresses of the truly poor. We were, I suppose, about two miles outside the village where the young man had spoken.

At that moment, at the side of a stretch of open road, a black mass flapped lazily into the air as the truck approached. It separated into ten or twelve of the buzzards, disturbed in their feeding and scattering unhurriedly as we passed. Even through the rushing air in the back of the truck, the stench of their meal was sweet and nauseating. I glanced into the ditch, curious to see what they had been eating, expecting the carcase of a dog or a pig. But the young man had been right: the buzzards had eaten well. On the ridge of the drain at the roadside were the feet of a man. The rest of the corpse lay head downwards in the gutter. The black trousers were unnaturally tight where his legs had swollen in the heat, and his stomach and chest had already been torn open. I was glad I could not see his face.

I turned quickly back to look across the truck at the woman opposite. If no one else had been inquisitive enough to look, she had certainly realized it was the corpse of a human being, for she fixed me with a hostile stare, forbidding me to say anything, making us silent accomplices. Then she made the sign of the cross over her chest. Whether she was praying for the dead or giving thanks for life wasn't clear.

The sight of those fat birds feasting on a human corpse haunted me. The old woman left the truck a few miles later, but she never looked back, never acknowledged beyond that first glance that either of us had seen anything out of the ordinary. She limped away in the dust, a woman who knew that the skill of survival was built upon an act of will and a sense of discretion.

Thinking about the experience later, it struck me that what I had seen that day was a metaphor for the whole of Central America: the towns, the villages and the churches consisted of no more than what was left when the scavengers had finished their work. They had come in a variety of forms, from the Spanish conquistadores of the sixteenth century to the twentieth century's procession of comic opera little dictators. Between them, they had stripped the countries down to a skeleton.

The idea of making a journey from top to bottom of Central America came to me the same evening. On a damp December night in London, the notion had a quixotic appeal. I had been to El Salvador and Nicaragua before, but much of the time on those visits I had been accompanied by a television crew or other journalists. Now I wanted to return alone.

To begin with, there was the fact that these tiny poverty-stricken little nations had been invested by the American government with such enormous significance. The Reagan administration had decided to take on its communist adversaries and Central America had been chosen as the battleground. But media reports of the area concentrated upon the generals, the politicians and the guns. The punchy minute-and-a-half stories on the television news showed plenty of firefights between the army and the guerillas in El Salvador or Nicaragua, but each event, an explosion here, an election there, appeared to have a vacuum-packed purity. They gave scant sense of what it felt like to be in the country, and made little connection between events. Perhaps there was none, but having heard the official views, I wanted to investigate further.

The trip would be different from the previous brief visits I had made to the region. For a start, I would travel through every country in the area. Secondly, I would not seek out the scenes of battles or elections: the journey itself and my own inclinations, rather than the demands of a news editor, would define the route. I thought – rather naïvely in retrospect – that this way I might get closer to a sense of how the local people lived their daily lives.

It was a perverse errand, but the idea of making a journey from Belize to Panama seemed that winter night to offer a way of satisfying my curiosity about the realities of life in Central America. I knew from the outset that parts of the journey might be dangerous, and others well-nigh impossible. It is not, after all, as if Belize or Honduras are on the way anywhere much: it would be a journey from nowhere to nowhere. Countries like El Salvador are usually avoided by all but the flotsam which wars wash ashore — arms dealers, mercenaries, aid workers, journalists, ideologues and missionaries.

Historically, once the Spanish had stripped the land of whatever they could carry away, the Central American isthmus had only impinged upon the thinking of Europe insofar as it represented the point at which the Atlantic and the Pacific came closest to one another: whatever significance the area had, it had acquired by virtue of its potential convenience as a transit point for world commerce. Its only contribution to the history of political thought had been to beget the term 'banana republic', and its rulers had tended to be funny little men with a taste for despotism and Ruritanian ceremonial.

What had changed now was not so much a result of developments within the countries themselves, although Nicaragua had undergone a successful revolution. The change, the reason why Central America had been invested with a newfound significance, had come about in Washington. For fifty years successive American and European administrations had tolerated, even encouraged, corrupt governments. We had been, as it were, passive accomplices. Now, suddenly, we were expected to show concern.

What Washington saw happening in Central America was Creeping Communism, the old Domino Theory from South-East Asia days dusted down and dropped into another corner of the globe. To try to stop the damage, the president had attempted one initiative after another: military advisers for El Salvador, clandestine financial support for guerillas in Nicaragua, new guns and planes, new ambassadors, economic assistance for friendly countries, economic pressure on unfriendly ones. The 'problem' of Central America had come to obsess the White House and the State Department.

Not long before I left for Central America, President Reagan explained the reasons for his government's preoccupation. Opinion polls had shown that most Americans had little or no idea which side their government was supporting in the wars in El Salvador and Nicaragua. So, reading from the transparent Idiot Board which makes him seem so natural on television, the president spoke in the slow, measured tones of a teacher spelling out *very important facts*.

El Salvador is nearer to Texas than Texas is to Massachusetts . . . Two thirds of all our foreign trade and petroleum pass through the Panama Canal and the Caribbean. In a European crisis, at least half our supplies for NATO would go through these areas by sea. It's well to remember that in early 1942 a handful of Hitler's submarines sank more tonnage there than in all of the Atlantic Ocean . . .

The national security of all the Americas is at stake in Central America. If we cannot defend ourselves there, we cannot be expected to prevail elsewhere. Our credibility would collapse, our alliances would crumble, and the safety of our homeland would be put at jeopardy.

The president was speaking about countries smaller than most American states, where wealth was measured by the number of times a month a family could afford to eat meat, and where to be well educated was to be crudely literate. The economic clout of their governments was less than that of a decent-sized American corporation. Now Reagan was claiming that unless the American design for these nations succeeded, 'our credibility would collapse', putting the safety of the most powerful nation on earth 'at jeopardy'. There were respectable American politicians who had not even seen the rise of Nazi Germany in such alarmist terms.

1
The End of the Earth

Before we had even seen Belize Bernie had tried to sell me part of the country. He was the sort of passenger you dread sitting next to, brimful of mindless bonhomie and crazed with a need to talk. He had introduced himself before the aircraft had taxied to the runway, given me his home telephone number by the time we were airborne, and ordered drinks for both of us before the stewardess had unbuckled her seatbelt.

Bernie was in real estate or, as he put it, 'rillestaiy'. And Belize rillestaiy was to Bernie what nirvana was to a Buddhist. Worse, he had all the missionary zeal of a new convert.

'Yeah, Belize is almost the only place left where a man can start out on his own, make a new life for himself,' he rhapsodized.

I had seen advertisements placed by people like Bernie in the back of obscure magazines. Poky little boxes buried away in the columns read by the lonely and the very bored. I guessed that as often as not the company cited was no more than someone like Bernie collecting his mail from an Albuquerque postbox and sending back a smudged brochure and a demand for an immediate deposit to secure the ranch of your dreams. The advertisements promised that for a few thousand dollars you could buy your own beach or plantation 'and a permanent escape from the pressures of city life'. And the FBI and nuclear war, they seemed to hint. Bernie was full of enthusiasm.

'A permanent holiday home, right there on the beach. The sea's clean, and you can get as much land as you want. And no one lives in the goddamn country – you can do what you want, and no one's gonna bother you. Know what I'm saying?'

His eyes hinted at orgiastic decadence.

'But it's just jungle you're selling, isn't it?'

'That land – see, if it'll grow all that jungle, it'll grow anything. Plant a few seeds and watch them bloom.'

I found it hard to imagine Bernie planting anything, far less clearing the jungle to create the field in which to plough the furrow. He had the sort of perfectly coiffed hair found only on predatory white males over forty, and his skin glowed with an unnatural tan. There were enough gold chains and rings about him to justify the employment of a score of South African miners. I could imagine him as the host at some wife-swapping party in a suburb in the Sun Belt.

'What about the Belizean government? – don't they have any restrictions on foreigners buying land? I mean, you make it sound as if the whole country's for sale.'

'Yeah, it is. Or most of it anyway. The government really want people to come in and open the place up. They got all this jungle, and no people. You want to think about it. I'm retiring to Belize in a few years.'

When you've managed to sell a few more hundred tracts of useless jungle, I thought.

'Well, I'm not planning to stay long in Belize. For me it's more of a departure point than a destination.'

Bernie was astonished, as if somebody had told him that he wasn't attractive to women.

'Where you heading?'

'I'm going to Guatemala first,' I said, wondering whether to tell him the truth. His evangelical certainty had made me feel decidedly eccentric. Then I rattled off the other countries in a quick mumble. 'And El Salvador and Honduras, Nicaragua, Costa Rica and Panama.'

'If you don't mind me saying so, Jerry, you're making a big mistake. Look, this is just about the only democracy around here. It's the only stable country in the area – the rest of them are just killing each other.'

Bernie's assessment of what was happening in Central America was a good deal better informed than most of his countrymen. To him the issue was simple.

'Communists could take over anytime. You could lose everything you got.'

Then came what he considered the most telling argument.

'Besides, they don't even speak English in those places.'

'It's OK, I speak Spanish,' I said, trying to make it appear that the language question was the only matter at issue.

Bernie had decided that it was time for straight talking. He tried to make it simple.

'Look, if you're keen on living, stay out of El Salvador. And Nicaragua. They've got it coming to them too.'

There was something so relentless about Bernie's warnings that when we arrived at Belize I walked as quickly as I could across the tarmac to escape him. It had to be said that the appearance of the airport did nothing to endorse his picture of a nation without a care in the world. At the sides of the runway, camouflage netting was stretched over anti-aircraft missiles, and along the edge of the airfield ran row after row of military Land Rovers, military barracks and military workshops. When the sun was out, the base was alive with pink-skinned British soldiers stationed in Belize to deter an invasion by the Guatemalans.

It was the rainy season, and outside the tatty little airport terminal the rain was coming down in sheets. Inside, the air was heavy with moisture and progress through customs tiresomely slow. A sign on the wall warned tourists (tourists?) not to try to smuggle out of the country archeological relics from the Mayan ruins. Whereas other countries tried to deter such pillage by issuing threats of prosecution and imprisonment, the Belize government had merely tacked up a polite little notice. 'BELI-ZEANS WOULD NOT CARRY PLYMOUTH ROCK OR STONEHENGE TO BELIZE. SO WE ASK ONLY THAT THE KEYS TO OUR PAST REMAIN WITH US.'

I could not imagine how a government which approached the theft of the national heritage in such a restrained manner would cope with predators like Bernie and his rillestaiy patter. I turned around and saw him standing near the back of the six or seven people waiting to have their passports stamped. Perspiration was making his shirt stick to his belly and his immaculate hair was beginning to fall apart. He waved laconically. I turned back to hand over my passport.

*   *   *

Belize is an aberration. Culturally, racially, linguistically, it has nothing in common with the nations which surround it. The fact that it is an aberration is the only thing which gives it a right to nationhood. The one hundred and fifty thousand people scattered about its jungles are fewer in number than in many an English city. It exists as a nation merely because it came about that the first European settlers spoke English rather than Spanish: it is in effect a part of the West Indies shifted by history to the American mainland. The official guidebook ('national tree: the mahogany; national bird: the keel-billed toucan; national animal: the tapir or mountain cow') claims that the first European settlement was established by ship-wrecked British sailors in 1638, but the Spanish – who had colonized the rest of the isthmus – never accepted the fact of British occupation, and the survival of the colony as a separate entity was entirely due to British *force majeure*.

Truth to tell, no one knows exactly how the British settlement came to be established, although the Belizeans themselves are fond of repeating the story that it was a home for British buccaneers raiding Spanish treasure vessels in the Caribbean. By the late seventeenth century its main importance to the British government was as a logging settlement for the production of mahogany and other woods, and as a centre of operations for whatever other meddling was to be done in the region. The Spanish periodically descended upon the primitive community and wiped most of it out, and the remaining settlers would then rebuild and await the next attack. They were never fully dislodged, and by the late eighteenth century the Spanish accepted that a separate settlement existed. Under the terms of the treaty ending the Seven Years' War, Madrid granted the British settlers the right to cut logwood, but not to establish permanent settlements. But as British power grew and the Spanish Empire withered, Spanish claims to the territory became empty boasts. In the words of a British minister who paid a visit to Madrid at the end of the eighteenth century, any mention of the British territories in Central America was likely to 'put the Spanish foreign minister into a passion', but by then the Span-iards lacked the power to translate rage into action.

Central America did not rank highly in the imperial preoccupations of the British government, and for the greater part of two hundred years Belize was never formally a colony. By the early years of the nineteenth century, the British government was describing the country as 'a settlement which for certain purposes is under the protection, but not under the dominion, of the British Crown'. In other words, the British were establishing a colony without taking on the liabilities of admitting that they had done so. The place was administered by a superintendent appointed by the British government, its laws were the laws of England, its language was English, its religion was Protestant and its protection was assured by the armed forces of the Crown. It was but a footnote to a footnote in the archives of the Empire when the territory was renamed the Crown Colony of British Honduras in 1862.

By the time independence was declared, Belize was identifiably different from the rest of Central America, not merely in its system of government but in the racial make-up of its population. When the Spanish colonized the rest of the isthmus they enslaved the indigenous Indians as a labour force to develop their settlements. The British settlers in Belize had no ready source of free labour, but solved their problem by buying black slaves at the market in Jamaica. By the end of the eighteenth century, out of a total population of almost three thousand, some two thousand were slaves.

In other settlements, the whites could only expect to keep the slaves under control with the whip, the gun and the vicious mastiff bred in Jamaica – a dog, it is said, which not only tracked down fugitive slaves, but would eat them if the owners did not haul it off when the exhausted runaway was cornered. But in Belize, the slaves seem to have been treated better. Conditions may not have been much more comfortable in the logging settlements in the jungle, but the work was not necessarily the mindless misery of the plantations, where the negroes were purely beasts of burden. And the persistent threat of attack by the Spanish obliged the whites to arm the slaves, which was a risk they could hardly have afforded to take if there had been a constant danger of slave uprisings.

In consequence, most of today's population of Belize look as if they really belong to an island in the Caribbean. But in addition to the black majority, other communities have developed in Belize, accentuating her separateness from the other Central American countries. Rebellious slaves, Indians fleeing the race wars in Mexico, Mennonites escaping compulsory education – all found refuge in the comparative tolerance of Belize. (The Mennonites, the men dressed in dungarees and straw hats, the women in long dresses and bonnets, are still divided into 'wooden wheelers' and 'iron wheelers', depending upon whether or not they have been corrupted by the internal combustion engine.) Most recently the refugees have come from Guatemala and El Salvador and, despite having been offered land by the government, are being blamed for everything from unemployment to the rising crime rate.

Belize City had the air of an African ground-nut port after twenty years of ground-nut blight. There was a lassitude in the air which was stale and infectious: Aldous Huxley, on a brief and bad-tempered visit, had remarked that 'if the world had an end, Belize would be it'. Fifty years later, the city had acquired no greater sense of purpose. It wasn't only that there were hardly enough citizens to justify a moderately sized town – it was that even Belize City, the largest settlement in the country, looked as if it had been exposed by mistake at a particularly low tide.

The sea was muddy brown, the streets were muddy brown, the tin roofs of the houses were muddy brown. The Caribbean ran into the city centre in a series of inlets the colour of strong tea and the houses perched along the water's edge on mouldering wooden stilts. It looked as if one reasonably high tide would wash the city away, the dirty clapboard houses bobbing off as a little flotilla of colonial relics.

The only edifice in the city which looked capable of withstanding the regular hurricanes was the cathedral, built of London brick in 1812. It was Aldershot in the tropics, a solid, unimaginative pile whose only concessions to the fact that it was not in Southern England were its corrugated iron roof and the hibiscus bushes in the graveyard. The bricks had been brought from Britain as ballast in the vessels which had called to collect the mahogany destined to become so many pieces of heavy English furniture. Black slaves had dragged the bricks from quayside to churchyard, and black slaves had laboured to erect the white man's temple. Inside the cathedral, simple plaques recorded the names of the soldiers, sailors, engineers and administrators who had fallen victim to the tropical diseases which regularly scythed through the expatriate settlement. They killed the blacks, too, but their only memorial was the cathedral they built for the white man.

I left the cathedral to walk back along the seashore. Mud crabs scurried down into the holes they had dug in the graves, their eyes bulging as they backed away from my footfall like tanks reversing into a trench. The only activity in the little port was where two British lorries were loading artillery shells on to a landing craft for transport to the army base in the south of the country. Three of the soldiers were leaning against a wall having a smoke and cursing their luck. I asked one of them what was happening in Belize.

'They're putting in a water and sewerage system,' came the surprising reply.

I laughed at what I assumed to be sarcasm. But I was wrong.

'It's the best thing that's happened in this country. Most of the stuff we have to drink is like that over there.' He pointed to an open drain filled with ink-black sludge.

'Is that all there is to do, watching the drains?'

'Well, there's one restaurant in town, but that's been off limits for weeks because so many people were getting ill eating there.'

'And there's the Rose Garden or the 102, if you're looking for a girl,' interjected the spotty one.

'Och, come on, he disnae wantae catch something,' said the third.

'No, it's OK, really,' the first one said. 'They're all inspected by the Medical Officer every week. You just ask to see their certificates. They keep them behind the bar.'

'Helps if you speak a bit of Spanish if you wanna be sure, though.'

'Spanish?'

'Yeah, all the girls come from El Salvador or Guatemala.'

'You'd have to come from somewhere like El Salvador to think this place was all right,' said the spotty one.

'You'd have to have a death squad after you,' the Scottish one grunted and stamped on his cigarette butt.

'I was just wondering if there was somewhere to eat,' I said.

'I'll tell you what,' said the first one. 'I wouldn't plan to go anywhere after dark in this town – not by yourself, anyway.'

I walked on past the harbour, skipping to avoid the potholes filled with rainwater. The city's paint supply had obviously never arrived as every building was bare wood turned grey by the sun and rain – or maybe it was just that people couldn't afford paint. Whatever the reason, the weatherbeaten wood contributed to the general aura of decomposition.

The harbour authority had posted a notice of regulations, safety precautions and conditions of employment at the main gate. It was the usual list, with one exception, appended at the bottom in bold capitals as an urgent afterthought: NO PERSONS UNDER THE INFLUENCE OF MARIJUANA WILL BE EMPLOYED. Talking later with a Belizean doctor I discovered that this was no more than a vain hope: his research showed that nearly half the population smoked dope regularly.

I stopped in a bar for a cold drink, and was standing at the counter when a lad of about eighteen came up beside me. He wore his hair in Rastafarian braids.

'Wanna buy some ganja?' His eyes were red and he held his face uncomfortably close to mine.

'No thanks.' Even had I wanted to, with thirteen customs inspections still to pass through, it hardly seemed a clever idea.

'It's good stuff,' he slurred, undeterred by my lack of interest.

'No thanks, I'm not staying long.' This was a foolish excuse to give, for it suggested that it was only the quantity that was in question. His response was predictable.

'OK, how much do you want?' There was something feral about his manner.

'No, really, I don't want any.'

'What's your problem, man?' he said. A tone of menace had entered his voice, as if in refusing to buy his drugs I had delivered a calculated insult.

'Nothing. I just don't want to buy any dope, thanks.' I turned away from him.

'Buy me a drink,' he said. I looked ahead at the rows of half-empty bottles at the back of the bar. I could tell by the smell of his breath and the warmth on my cheek that his face was no more than an inch or so from mine. He was trying to provoke me, and I was aware that the few other men in the bar had stopped their conversations.

'Look, I'm just going,' I said, deciding it was easier to leave than to get involved. I hadn't paid for the beer and the bartender was nowhere to be seen. I thought about how I might manage to leave a dollar or so on the bar and get out of the place without being seen to have given in, so making myself an easy touch for anyone who wanted to jump me on the way home.

'What's the matter? Don't you like drinking with niggers?' His question was intended for the rest of the bar as much as for me. Whatever answer I gave would be wrong.

'No, it's not that, but I'm just going.'

Through the swing doors I could see that the tropical twilight had already begun. Within ten minutes it would be dark. I wasn't sure I could remember the way back, and I recalled the words of the soldiers – 'I wouldn't plan to go anywhere after dark in this town by myself.'

'You know what you are? You're a fucking racist, man.' It was a denunciation for the benefit of the other customers.

'Look, that's got nothing to do with it. I've finished my drink, I don't want your ganja and I'm leaving. It's nothing to do with race.'

'You're a fucking racist,' he repeated, but slightly less insistently, as if he was merely disappointed that I hadn't accepted his judgement. Something of the tone of a child's 'I didn't start it' aggrievement entered his voice, as if the incident was my fault for not having discharged my social responsibilities and accepted his drugs.

I saw the bartender in the corner of the room.

'I've got to go to an appointment,' I said, wondering whether the youth would follow me out of the bar. 'How much was this beer?'

'Two dollars.' He was in no hurry to come to the counter and muttered the words reluctantly. Still no one in the bar was talking. The drug dealer was watching me with sullen contempt. I left the money on the bar and walked to the door, aware that everyone was watching, wondering whether anyone would say anything. As I pushed it open the drug dealer shouted out.

'Fucking racist.'

By then I was outside, walking briskly through the darkening streets, thinking how much easier it would have been to buy the ganja in the first place.

Belize's best-known hotel was a fading colonial relic called the Fort George. It effortlessly managed to reflect the country's three main cultural influences, combining the overcooked food of the worst English hotels, American pretensions and a Caribbean surliness. For seventy-five dollars the desk clerk booked me into a room in which the air-conditioning didn't work, the door wouldn't lock and the sheets were dirty. He was reluctantly persuaded to find me another. The lavatory flooded. Finally, after endless protests that 'the hotel is full', we found a room where everything seemed more or less in place. The shower didn't work, but since the room was on the top floor and the rain streamed through the ceiling into the bathroom, I decided it was redundant anyway.

An hour later I went down to find something to eat. Across the dining-room I recognized Bernie's unmistakably perfect apparel, and before I could pretend not to have seen him, he was calling me over.

'How you enjoying Belize? Incredible country, isn't it?'

'Yes, I suppose so. Someone just called me a fucking racist because I wouldn't buy his drugs.'

'Where that happen?' asked Bernie disapprovingly.

'Some bar in the middle of town.'

'That was your mistake. You don't want to spend time down

here in Belize City. You want to get out to the properties. Here, look at this.'

He handed me a little pamphlet advertising the Belize real estate for sale by an agent in Scappoose, Oregon. I noticed one reasonably typical item:

7000 ACRES. Only 25 miles from Belize City. 70 acres cleared and a fair set of buildings which would make a good headquarters for a cattle operation, cashew nuts, mangoes or pineapples.

Or, in other words, six thousand nine hundred and thirty acres of jungle. 'Would make' something or other seemed an appropriate promise.

Seeing Bernie in his polyester slacks and gold chains re-embarking on his sales pitch, I thought how understandable it was that the Belizeans should resent the brassy foreigners who were selling off the country or opening up holiday resorts for the unnecessarily rich. It denoted in effect a new colonization. And however much people in Belize might aspire to the American Dream, American Dreamers like Bernie, with their unassailable separateness, could hardly be more welcome than their European predecessors.

The national paper, published once each week, was full of news about a series of killings which had taken place in Orange Walk, a town with a population of no more than eight thousand. On a per capita basis Orange Walk must have rivalled Chicago during Prohibition: three people had already been shot dead and now a policeman had been murdered. The newspaper reports gave no explanation of motive, although a good number of Belizeans were blaming the violence on the refugees from El Salvador. Later I heard another account from a retired policeman I met outside the old wooden courthouse.

'It's the drug gangs,' he said.

'What kind of drugs?'

'Marijuana. They started growing it here a few years ago, when the Americans began cracking down on the traditional places. It's big business now – they say Belize is the third biggest producer in this hemisphere. It all goes to the US of course.'

I could see the attraction to drug dealers. It would be simple enough to conceal plantations in all those acres of jungle, and there were sufficient little airstrips around to make it easy for light aircraft to come in, pick up a few bales of marijuana leaves, and be on the way back to the United States before the Belizeans had noticed. What's more, there was no Belize airforce to worry about.

'It's big money. One acre of marijuana is worth about a quarter of a million dollars. You see, it beats growing bananas or pineapples or producing cocoa for Hershey Bars. So the growers need guards to protect the plantations in case someone else comes in to harvest the stuff or burn it down. That's why there are all these gunfights. In fact, you know the last time the British soldiers here fired a shot in anger? It was when one of the guards on a plantation fired a shotgun at an army patrol. He thought it was another gang coming to take over the field. The soldiers shot back, of course. Killed him, I think.'

Later that morning, as I was walking through the centre of town I came across another of Belize's less salubrious exports to the United States. There was a gaggle of glass-eyed men standing on the street outside a featureless concrete building. A small door in the wall opened and another man came out. Like the rest, he was holding a little swab of cotton wool to the inside of his elbow. Each time the door opened the heavy smell of blood and antiseptic drifted out into the street.

The men were frank enough about what went on inside the building: they were a small group who sold their blood regularly, receiving twenty-five Belize dollars for each 'donation'. The clinic would bleed them twice a week, so they could make two hundred dollars each month merely by opening their veins. The blood was turned into plasma at the clinic and then sold to American drug companies. When I asked one of the donors what he used the money for, he smiled, put his fingers in the shape of a V, inhaled deeply and blew imaginary smoke in my face.

The existence of the clinic, which was owned by the wife of a minister, was a deep embarrassment to the government. The national blood transfusion service, which was expected to supply blood to the Belize hospitals, relied upon free donations by the public-spirited and the relatives of the sick. Not only did the commercial operation, which was bleeding hundreds of people each week, detract from the national service, it also possessed facilities for turning the blood into plasma, which the state system could not afford. And each time the state system approached the International Red Cross for help in developing a proper national blood transfusion service, complete with plasma machine, the Red Cross replied that if Belize could afford to sell blood to American drug companies, then it didn't need the help of international charities. 'What they don't understand,' a Belizean doctor told me, 'is that if we need plasma, we have to import it from America. And it's plasma the blood bank is exporting from here in the first place. It's just ridiculous.'

Belize television has to be seen to be believed. Officially, the country has no television service. But a number of entrepreneurs, with the connivance of the government, have bought satellite-receiving dishes to latch on illicitly to the American network transmissions across the country. By some quirk of geography the transmissions most easily pirated in Belize seem to be those directed at the Chicago area. The consequence is that the people of Belize are treated to a torrent of advertisements for analgesics, laxatives, anti-flatulence tablets, plastic diapers and canine hamburgers interspersed with traffic reports for the Illinois suburbs. What is the average Belizean to make of 'The Newlywed Game', for example, in which three couples are pitted against each other to discover which knows the more embarrassing secrets about his/her partner's predilections? Or of the following extract from another quiz game –

'If the Prime Minister of Israel arrived unexpectedly for dinner, what would you serve him to make him feel at home?'

And the inexplicable (correct) reply from a Milwaukee blonde: 'Tacos'.

There is something quite ludicrous about the dissemination of this First World consumerist pap to an audience who have mostly never seen a McDonald's, let alone a Doggie Burger.

Belizeans supply Americans with their blood while America supplies Belize with dreams.

According to the map, the way to get to Guatemala City was to take the road west, cross the border at Benque Viejo del Carmen, catch a bus going further west to Flores, and then head south to Puerto Barrios on the Caribbean coast, from where there were good connections to Guatemala City. It would mean about three days' travelling, providing the roads hadn't been washed away in the rains. I began to ask about buses from the border into the interior of Guatemala.

'I wouldn't do that, if I were you. The road's been washed out,' said the first man I asked.

'There's fighting between the guerillas and the army on that road,' said another.

'The Civil Defence patrols won't let you through,' said a third, 'and anyway, I hear the bridges are washed away on the road from Flores.'

I suspected they were either lying or exaggerating, but it was impossible to know. There ought to have been a road from the coast of Belize direct into the heart of Guatemala, but the fact that it had never been built lay at the heart of the Belizean distrust of all things Guatemalan. Guatemala had recognized British rule in Belize in 1859 and in return the British had agreed to pay for the road. But the British never fulfilled the obligation, later claiming in justification that the Guatemalan government had failed formally to ratify the treaty within the specified time. Whereupon the Guatemalans claimed that as they had only ceded the territory in exchange for a road, they no longer recognized Belize as a separate state. From such small beginnings have national neuroses grown.

The wrangling over tracts of useless jungle has also provided Guatemalan governments with a useful distraction from their miserably oppressive behaviour at home. Guatemalan children are taught from infancy that '*Belice es Nuestro*', Belize is ours. Even the civil war in Guatemala has been blamed on Belize, and during one presidential campaign, a candidate actually declared that if the Guatemalan army wasn't prepared to recapture Belize he had enough hired guns in his own political party to do the job. However, in many senses Belize is more useful to Guatemala as a continuing irritant than it could ever be as a source of employment, wealth, or anything else.

In Belize, on the other hand, the fact that Guatemala not only has designs upon the country, but also possesses a human rights record which is grotesque even by the standards of Latin American dictatorships, has been sufficient to generate intense alarm.

'The American Embassy has got a Travel Advisory out warning people not to go that way because of the fighting,' said the man at the Post Office who claimed to know about the state of the war.

'Well, how am I supposed to get to Guatemala City then?' I asked him.

'You could try going south on the bus down to Punta Gorda. Maybe you can get a boat across to Puerto Barrios. That way you can find out whether the roads are open before you set off, and if you can't get through, at least you're stuck in Belize not Guatemala.'

'Where can I find a bus going south, then?'

'You want James's Bus Line.'

James's Bus Line didn't seem to have an office in Belize City, and when I saw the bus I understood why.

It had spent the best years of its life ferrying American children to school. James had not had either the time or the money to repaint it since buying it, and it stood there on the muddy little road in its fading yellow paint, with STATE LAW REQUIRES STOP WHEN BUS LOADING OR UNLOADING written in big letters across its back – a refugee from a leafy New England suburb.

James's ancestors had originally come from India, shipped in to cut sugar cane on the plantations in the south. At six-thirty in the morning he wasn't looking his best, sitting slumped behind the wheel as his assistant hustled the passengers on to the hard little seats. His comments throughout the journey were abrupt – as if words were something he'd spent a lifetime saving

and wasn't about to start squandering. I asked him how far we
were going.

'Two hundred and forty miles.'

'How long will it take?'

'Nine and a half, ten hours.'

'If we're lucky. Last week we set off at 6 A.M. Sunday and
arrived at 3 A.M. Tuesday,' said the conductor, butting in with a
laugh. 'Road was all washed out.'

There were ten of us scattered around the crude little bus
when the journey began, and although James was obviously
hoping for more, he finally bowed to the inevitable, closed the
door and started the engine.

The road started out through the jungle. On either side the
vegetation rose in an impenetrable green mass, removing all
sense of distance, like a tunnel. Soon, particularly when the
bus gained any speed, it began to feel claustrophobic. More
bewilderingly, the road, which I had assumed would run along
the Caribbean coastline from north to south, set off inland
towards Guatemala and then struck diagonally back towards
the southern tip of the country. Occasionally, the trees would
part to show the rusting bow of a freighter beached ten feet
from the roadside and we would realize how close we were to
the invisible sea. Then, just as suddenly, we were back to the
thick wall of green jungle. Miles inland, the road began to
climb towards the mountains of Guatemala, but then we turned
away, back across flooded rivers on makeshift bridges, around
the edge of swamps, and on through the flatness of the coastal
plain. Not only did Belize seem unsuited to human habitation,
most of it was demonstrably uninhabited. The map showed a
peppering of improbable place-names – Pull Trousers Swamp,
Wee Wee Cay, Teakettle Camp, Double Head Cabbage – but as
often as not the only sign of human life was a single hut twenty
yards from the roadside and enclosed by jungle.

The radio was playing a succession of Crystal Gayle songs,
interspersed with sermons from a fundamentalist preacher from
Birmingham, Alabama. It was Belize's national radio station
and occasionally the announcer broke in to deliver the news.

'Members of the Scottish Engineers and Star of Bethel

Masonic Lodges are advised of a Special Initiation tonight. Please govern yourselves accordingly.

'The death is announced of Lucy Whitty of Lucky Strike. She is mourned by her husband Moses, children Clinton, Easy, Clarence and Moses Junior.

'There will be an urgent emergency meeting of Rock Stone Pond Council tomorrow at 10 A.M.'

Not much happened in Belize without everyone knowing about it.

After a couple of hours we reached Belmopan, the new capital of Belize, modelled – if it's a dark night and you close your eyes – upon the idea of Brasilia in Brazil. The notion of building a new capital city had come after Belize City was hit by Hurricane Hattie in 1961 and wrecked for the second time in thirty years. The decision to build Belmopan away from the exposed coastal plain and up in the foothills towards the Guatemalan frontier probably looked impressive both to colonial administrators in London and to nationalistically minded local politicians, but the place was an absurdity. Twenty years on, all that had been achieved was the creation of a dozen or so concrete office buildings dropped into a clearing in the jungle, a corner of Milton Keynes deposited in tropical rainforest. Belize did not have the population to support one major city, let alone two, and the grandiose plans of the designers had already begun to mildew. Belmopan had, it was claimed, a population of four thousand, but where they lived was anybody's guess: in the natural scheme of things the jungle would swallow up the concrete in the space of a few years.

Three new passengers boarded at Belmopan. One of them fell asleep on the bench at the back at once. The second, an elderly white farmer with a broad-brimmed straw hat and threadbare dungarees, sat a couple of seats in front. His face was covered in sores and scabs, several of them bleeding – the effect was to make his lips seem like cicatrices too. He clearly wished to be left alone. The third passenger was a little old negro with straggly grey hair and a mouth with three teeth. He was travelling only part of the way, but I was glad of someone to talk to.

'Where you goin'?'

'Punta Gorda, and then to Guatemala, I hope,' I said. 'If I can get a boat.'

'Oh, you'll get a boat OK. Don't mean you wanna take it, though.'

By now I was familiar with the general Belizean hostility towards the Guatemalans, but even so I was unprepared for his next remark.

'The Guatemalans are the worst people in the world.'

'The worst in the world?'

'I tell you, I know, man. I been there, and I know. Maybe it ain't so bad for you if you're white, but if you're black and from Belize, brother, you better watch out.' And then he repeated himself. 'They're the worst people in the world.'

'What happened to you?'

'Never mind about me, that was years ago. Let me tell you what happened to my best friend last year.' He paused to check that I was paying attention.

'He went with his wife to Guatemala City to take some vacation, do a little shopping, see something new. It was their anniversary. He was a Carib, like me, same age as me, sixty-three. A little guy, quiet. He wouldn't hurt anyone.

'Well, they got to Guatemala City OK, same way you're going. They went to find a hotel. You know, somewhere not too expensive, because they wanted to save money. And they found somewhere they thought was all right.

'His wife went out to buy some fruit for them to eat in the room, to save going out to buy dinner somewhere. She was only gone ten minutes or something. When she came back she found him dead. Right there in the middle of the room, half on the bed, half on the floor. With all his guts hanging out. They'd shot him with a machine-gun.'

He stopped, distracted by the image he had conjured up, and stared out of the window at the rain falling on the jungle.

'Why did they do it?'

'I guess he liked to show his money off too much.'

'Did he have a lot of money?'

'I told you, he was like me. He'd got some savings with him, maybe a hundred dollars or so.'

'And you think they killed him for a hundred dollars?'

'Man, they'd kill you for ten dollars. Let me give you a piece of advice. Don't go to Guatemala alone. Take a friend with you.'

'I'm travelling alone,' I said.

'Well then, you'd better do some talking with the man up there.' And he raised his eyes, put his hands together, and smiled a smile of commiseration.

Somewhere out in the jungle — it was impossible to tell where since there was no hut or house or other sign of life — we stopped to pick up an Indian woman. The rain had let up for a minute, and she stood and called a couple of men off the bus. There was a figure lying crumpled up on the ground, sodden from the rain. His left arm and legs were inert. The two men lifted him up on the woman's instructions and manoeuvred him awkwardly up the steps of the bus. The man's hair was stuck flat against his forehead by the water and his eyes were rheumy. At first, he looked either simple or drunk. They manhandled him into the seat in front. His wife sat beside him and pushed a brown paper bag into his lap. Suddenly, in a terrifying demonstration of his sanity, he spat some words of Creole at her. She took the parcel from his lap with the look of a dog which has been beaten often enough to know its place.

They did not speak much, and what little they said I could scarcely understand. She would ask him a question, and he would bark back at her. The only words I could make out were 'bad' and 'bitch'. There was no reason for his viciousness, nothing she had done to deserve his vituperation. It seemed he was blaming her for his condition, for the fact that he was paralysed in both legs and one arm, was soaked and humiliated, and could look forward for the rest of his life to nothing but more of the same. She turned around only once during the trip.

'Is this your husband?' I asked.

She smiled a look of sullen resignation, a look that said 'it could have been worse.' That expression, of hope in the face of hopelessness and resignation before harshness, was one I saw all over Central America. It is bad. But it could be worse. It could be worse, because there's always someone, crippled, cut by a machete, maddened by liquor or blinded by grief, to compare with. It is terrible. But think, it could be worse. We're used to it.

When finally we stopped to let them off, I helped lift the man down the steps of the bus. He was still sodden, but there was another wetness in his trousers where he had been unable to control his bladder. As we lifted him his face was no more than an inch or two from mine. I caught his eye. Perhaps he'd say something, give a hint of explanation for his bitterness. He looked straight through me.

Punta Gorda was a frontier town without a frontier. It had that air of impermanence, of legal convenience, of places which exist by rendering legitimate or cheaper that which is illegitimate and expensive a few hundred yards away. The border here was the sea, but the same considerations applied. And there was something else that was distinctive about it: it was neither Latin American nor Caribbean but a mixture of the two. There was much the same mixture of black and white and Asian faces in the street as there had been in Belize City, although the Mayan features were commoner. The conversation was Spanish as much as English, and the music full of brassy Latin rhythms.

A couple of dugout canoes were tied to the little jetty, and a few fishermen were selling the morning's meagre catch. Three pelicans stood on piles driven into the seabed, motionless. I went into the little general store to see if I could change some Belizean dollars into Guatemalan quetzales. It was about ten feet square, dark and crammed with bars of soap, plastic hairgrips, clothespegs and cheap Chinese flashlights. The Indian proprietor was cutting open a stack of cardboard boxes stamped 'Hull, England', and pulling out bottle after bottle of Seven Seas cod liver oil.

'It's very popular with the Guatemalans who come over,' she said.

She told me I could buy a ticket for the boat to Guatemala up the muddy street at the Miramar Hotel. It was no more than a saloon really, three steps up to a darkened bar from where the Pointer Sisters racketed into the hot still air outside. It looked cool and sheltered from the muggy street. Two half-naked paratroopers were sitting on the steps, passing a bottle of rum from mouth to mouth. Their bodies were burned a deep red, and their eyes were lazy with drink. I had taken two steps across the verandah when a squat Chinaman came running towards me from the other end of the bar. He was screaming.

'You bastard. You get the fuck out of here.'

I jumped aside and he ran past, continuing to shout. I noticed that the veins on his forehead stood out, thumping. He stopped on the step above the two soldiers.

'You get out of here. I got a licence. I pay a lot of money for a licence.'

The two paratroopers turned around to face him. Their faces had taken on the drunken sneers of street corner toughs. The Chinaman continued to roar at them.

'You wanna drink here, you buy your rum here. You buy it somewhere else, you drink it somewhere else.'

'But we're not drinking,' said one of them, quickly handing the bottle to his friend. Something – the knowledge of the absurdity of his lie, some vestigial memory of orders about behaviour off-duty – stopped him going further.

'Get out of here.'

The two soldiers teetered on the edge of a decision to beat up the Chinaman, then thought better of it. They swaggered off the steps and sat down on a low wall three yards away. It was enough. The manager turned back inside, clenching and unclenching his fists as he walked and spat instructions to his daughter to serve me what I wanted.

There were still several hours before the ferry was due to leave, and the bar did have some rudimentary air-conditioning. It was a better place to pass the time than the jetty. Ten minutes later, having calmed down and smoothed his few remaining strands of hair with a lick of water, the Chinaman came back. He sold me a ticket for the boat, told me his name was Alexander, and grumbled about the price of a liquor licence. He

liked the British soldiers, he said. After all, without them the
Guatemalans could just walk in and take the place over; even if
every able-bodied man in the country was conscripted into
some kind of defence force, it would still be smaller than the
standing army across the border.

'And if they get out of hand, I just point to the notice,' he
said. 'THIS WAS A QUIET PLACE UNTIL YOU CAME IN. IF YOU
WANT TO FIGHT, FIGHT OUTSIDE.'

It seemed to work. Soldiers came in, sat beneath the grubby
pin-ups torn from *Playboy*, drank a coke or two, and ambled
off to kill time somewhere else. Sometimes they brought in girls
and fooled around, but even that was done with remarkably
little energy. Once, a thin old German with a deformed arm and
a thumb which looked as if it had previously been someone
else's index finger sat down and drank a bottle of rum, until his
Indian wife levered him to his feet and took him home. One of
the soldiers put a Boy George record on the jukebox at deafening
volume and danced with a bottle of beer. A bald European
farmer in a broad-brimmed straw hat asked for the key to
unlock the padlock on the lavatory door and drank a few
glasses in payment for the facility. A grinning drunk West
Indian shuffled into the bar, blinking in the dark. There was
blood caked across his nose, and his heavy serge trousers had
gone tubular with wetness. Alexander shouted at him, and
when the drunk stood still in bewilderment, grabbed his arm
and threw him down the steps outside. Another soldier put the
same record on the jukebox and held a girl close. She put an
arm around him, in the other holding a parcel of fish from the
market. It was the closest thing to excitement in town.

The Chinaman said that in another five years he'd have made
enough money to be able to retire. He was thinking about
somewhere on the English south coast, Weymouth perhaps. It
was so much quieter there.

When the time finally came for the boat to leave, I walked off
down the potholed street. I looked back to Alexander's bar. A
man had passed out on his back on the porch. And a dog was
retching on the steps.

2
Ancient Adversaries

The little boat was snub-nosed and canopied. Every five minutes the old black engineer would come up from below, stand at the top of the stairs and take out his battered silver pocket watch to compare it with the boat clock in the wheelhouse. Reassured that they were keeping the same time, he descended back into the engine room. There was one other crew member, also black, who manned the ropes when we left the jetty. The captain was old, bored and, inevitably, white. Once we had left the bay, he lashed the accelerator open with a length of string, stood at the wheel and took a swig of clear liquid from an old instant coffee jar. Possibly water, probably rum.

There were about twenty passengers, mainly Spanish-speaking Belizeans and black Guatemalans. We sat on wooden benches in the shade of the canopy behind the wheel; the deck timbers were either bakingly hot or too vulnerable to spatterings of spray. Soon it was clear that if it wasn't rum the captain was drinking, then he had drunk too much the night before. He was having trouble keeping his eyes open.

The sky grew overcast and the sea got rougher. Within an hour, the coast of Guatemala was visible in monochrome, black hills between a grey sky and a darker grey sea. Behind the hills was the misty outline of the mountains of the interior. Whereas Belize reached out to the sea in long low fingers of swamp, Guatemala plunged down to meet it. As we came closer to follow the coastline, the effect was spectacular: cliffs covered in jungle falling sheer into the ocean. I thought back to Belize and decided that on the whole I had quite liked the country – most people could read and write, and they didn't settle political differences by killing one another. In other places such phrases might have sounded as though they were damning with faint praise. In the context of Central America they meant a great deal.

The skipper had fallen soundly asleep, one leg wedged against a spoke of the wheel to keep the boat on course. Suddenly we came side-on to a particularly big wave, the boat rolled and a young half-caste woman with her elderly white husband shrieked and was thrown to the floor. The captain jolted awake and grabbed the wheel to bring the boat round so that she took the shock of the waves head on. By now several of the passengers on the windward side were soaked, two other women were screaming each time the boat rolled, and an old man was holding his hand over his mouth.

In the event, only two people were sick. A couple of hours later the captain gave up the unequal struggle with his own equilibrium and handed the wheel over to the mate. Now he sat glassily surveying the passengers, the night and the vomit.

We reached Puerto Barrios four hours after leaving Belize. As the little boat nudged its way into the harbour, the searchlight on the bow picked out seven men in green stetson hats holding rifles. Several more stood on the dock and in the customs hall in a variety of uniforms. In Belize the police had been unarmed bobbies. Here it looked as if it might well be illegal to be unarmed.

I found a hotel near the waterfront. It was not much more than a collection of stalls, a large room divided by wooden partitions with a piece of torn mosquito netting stretched across the top. None of the boards fitted properly, and through the gaps on three sides I could see into similar little cubicles, two of them empty with filthy sheets crumpled on the bed, one occupied by a fat man with three days' growth of beard who was lying snoring on his back. The place was alive with mosquitoes and cockroaches. I decided to escape for a while to get something to eat and made the following note in my diary.

'I suppose I must look an easy prospect for beggars. But even so, the change after Belize is astonishing. Throughout the meal, at a cheap roadside café, I was besieged by begging children. The worst was a boy of six or seven in filthy shorts and a torn T-shirt. He had no shoes, his head was shaved bald, and he was cross-eyed. I brushed him away, but no less than thirteen others followed in the following order: 1 little boy offering a shoe shine, 1 boy leading a blind old man, 1 elderly woman carrying a baby no more than six weeks old, 1 little girl carrying the same baby five minutes later, 3 little boys asking to eat the food off my plate, 2 other boys selling wooden model ships, 2 middle-aged male beggars smelling strongly of liquor, another shoe-shine boy, and another little girl. This last was the only one who managed anything approaching the beggars' wheedling smile. Perhaps the competition is too intense. After all, this was a cheap and undistinguished restaurant, so God knows what happens at the more expensive places.

'The moment I asked for the bill, all the children began to gather about the table. It had been an indifferent meal and I hadn't finished it. They could scarcely wait as I pulled a couple of notes from my pocket, although it was not the money they were after. These children were genuinely hungry. The moment I pushed back my chair, they stormed the table, grabbing chicken bones and fighting for the uneaten tortillas. I had been in Guatemala precisely three hours.'

The story of Guatemala is the history of the worst of Spanish America, the almost total extinguishing of a great native civiliz-ation by men whose avarice was bolstered by the almighty conviction of divine authority. For a start, the Pope himself had granted the Spanish exclusive rights to exploit and Christianize all the territories which might be discovered west of an imagin-ary line drawn down the Atlantic. Since the Pope was the Vicar of Christ, the Spanish believed their pillage to be sanctioned by God. When a Spanish expedition landed at an Indian settlement, the clerk would read out the curious legal-cum-spiritual argu-ment by which they felt entitled to seize the natives' land. Regardless of the fact that the bewildered Indians could not understand a word, the notary would begin:

We notify and make known to you as best we can that the living and eternal God, our Lord, created the heavens and the earth, and a man and a woman, of whom you and we ar.d all men are descendants, as well as all who shall come after us ... God, our Lord, gave the charge of all these people to one called St Peter, that he should be lord and superior over all men in the world and that he should be head of all the human race, and should love all men of whatsoever land, religion and belief; and he gave him the world for his kingdom, ordering his seat to be placed in Rome, as the place best suited for ruling the world.

Adding that they came with the blessing of St Peter's successor, they would slaughter all those who resisted. Soon the Indians began to flee at the first sight of any Spaniard drawing out a piece of paper.

The colonists were spurred on not only by a sense of moral legitimacy, but by greed and desperation. The discovery of the New World had been born of a European drive to find the route to the Orient and capture the trade and spice routes. When they realized that they had discovered instead an entirely new continent, new colonists were recruited to settle and claim the land for Spain. The men who sailed to the Indies were the predictable mixture of the adventurous and the hungry: Spain was a relatively poor, backward country, and the New World offered the hope of prosperity. The Indians they found in Central America – to their eyes primitive and uncivilized – wore breastplates, bracelets and anklets of pure gold. The reaction of these hungry men when they saw how casually the 'primitives' treated the most precious of metals may be guessed at. Inimitable pieces of statuary, jewellery and ornamentation were beaten flat and melted down to provide lumps of raw gold. And when supplies of the ornaments began to run low, they turned to prospecting and armies of Indians were sent to pan for gold. Successive armadas bumped along the coast, hoping to discover the source. The pervading, driving fantasy was El Dorado, the city of gold.

The Indians, by contrast, represented one of the last great aborigine cultures. By the time the Spanish arrived in Central America, the Maya civilization had declined from its peak. But its achievements had been staggering. By sophisticated astronomy and mathematics, the Mayas had devised an elaborate calendar, accurate even by contemporary standards. Pottery, sculpture and weaving were all in states of advanced sophistication. Pyramid temples had been built and towered above the surrounding jungles.

But they lacked the means to defend themselves against the Europeans. According to one of the colonists: 'They are naturally a lazy and vicious, melancholic, cowardly and in general a lying shiftless people. Their marriages are not a sacrament but a sacrilege. They are idolatrous, libidinous, and commit sodomy. Their chief desire is to eat, drink, worship heathen idols, and commit bestial obscenities,' he wrote.

There were others who took a kinder view of the Indians, but in the early years of the conquest, their ideas carried little force. Bartolome de Las Casas, a conquistador who later became a priest, described the Indians as 'humble, patient and peaceful', a Rousseau-like view which could hardly have been further from the general opinion held by the majority of his companions. The fatalism which Las Casas noticed damned the Indians to conquest and exploitation. The Spanish were aggressive and militarily sophisticated – among the weapons which they brought with them, for example, were horses, animals the Indians had never seen before. The Aztec king Montezuma wrote that they appeared to 'sit on deer as high as rooftops'. So far beyond the comprehension of the Indians were these fair-skinned foreigners that for a while Montezuma believed that the Spanish colonization marked the return of the bird god, Quetzalcoatl.

Central America was a disappointment to the Spaniards. To the north, in Mexico, Cortes discovered and destroyed the Aztec empire and created the Kingdom of New Spain. To the south, in Peru, Pizarro subjugated the Incas and discovered fabulous riches in the land where kings bought their freedom with rooms filled with gold.

Central America was colonized by expeditions coming south from Mexico and north from Panama, but by comparison it offered poor pickings. The Spanish troops who stayed in Central America were left with a place of mountain, lake and jungle. The commanders placated their disgruntled soldiers by granting them ranches known as *encomiendas*, and the Spanish crown gave, or 'commended', a certain number of Indians to each colonist. The *encomendero* then had the right to exact tribute and labour.

The argument for reducing the Indians to beasts of burden was seductive: white men were unable to work in the unhealthy climate and the Indians were too lazy to work by choice. Compulsory labour was therefore essential, otherwise there would be no income.

The greatest hypocrisy of this demeaning system was that the landowners were supposed to protect 'their' Indians, and to give them a Christian education. By 1528, the Franciscan missionaries in Mexico had become so outraged by the failure of the Spaniards to keep their side of the bargain that they informed their headquarters in Spain that 'it were a lesser evil if not a single inhabitant of the New World were ever converted to our Holy Faith, and that the King's sovereignty should be lost forever, than that these people should be brought to the one or the other by slavery'. But the view among many of the colonists seems to have been that the Indians were somehow less than human anyway. Bartolome de Las Casas had been sending back desperate reports for a number of years, including this account of what happened on the island of Hispaniola.

They made bets as to who would slit a man in two, or cut off his head at one blow: or they opened up his bowels. They tore babies from their mothers' breast by the feet and dashed their heads against the rocks. Others they seized by the shoulders, and threw into the rivers, laughing and joking, and when they fell into the water, they exclaimed: 'Boil, body of so and so!' They spitted the bodies of other babies, together with their mothers and all who were before them, on their swords.

They made a gallows just high enough for the feet to nearly touch the ground, and by thirteens, in honour and reverence of our Redeemer and the twelve Apostles, they put wood underneath and, with fire, they burned the Indians alive.

They generally killed the lords and nobles in the following way. They made wooden gridirons of stakes, bound them upon them, and made a slow fire beneath: thus the victims gave up the spirit by degrees, emitting cries of despair in their torture.

And there were many other testimonies to the brutality of the conquistadores – reports of mass reprisals against Indian villages if a single Spaniard should die in resistance, Indians executed by being tied to a stake and torn to pieces by dogs. In some places the main routes across country were said to be marked by the density of Indian bones at the roadside.

In the context of what the Spanish had done to the Indians during the 'pacification' of Central America, the failings of the *encomienda* system were predictable but – they argued – it was more enlightened than it might have been. The system which eventually replaced it as a result of the protests of priests like Las Casas, the *repartimeniento*, showed little improvement, however, giving Spanish settlers the right to exact labour from the Indians in exchange for money or food. It created a class of peons destined to a hopeless struggle out of debt bondage for the whole of their adult lives. Officially, the number of men working for a landowner was restricted, but the system was continually abused. Conditions were frequently so squalid and the work so exhausting that people took poison or hanged themselves to put an end to their miseries.

Although the system was modified, the existence of these labour practices corrupted the societies of Guatemala and much of the rest of Central America for hundreds of years. When European tailors clamoured for cheap dyestuffs, the plantation owners realized they could make a living producing cochineal or indigo, and since production of indigo was extremely labour intensive (it took up to two hundred pounds of plant to yield eight ounces of the dye), indigo mills were built next to the Indian villages, providing a constant supply of almost free labour. Similarly when countries like Guatemala and El Salvador took to the production of coffee or bananas, the tradition of cheap and abundant labour made harvesting easy.

The other catastrophe brought about by the Spanish was a medical one. Recent estimates by historians put the Indian population of New Spain (chiefly Mexico and Central America) before the arrival of the Spanish at some twenty-five million. Less than one hundred years later, the settled Indian population was scarcely more than one million and a quarter. The fate of the Indians in this area represents one of the great disasters of human history.

They were destroyed not only by hunger and despair but by

diseases from a Pandora's Box of sicknesses which the Spanish had brought with them, including smallpox, tetanus, typhus and VD. Other diseases like malaria and yellow fever, previously unknown in the Americas, were soon being spread by mosquitoes feeding on infected soldiers. The Indians, who had no resistance to these new illnesses, were swept down in swathes and the Indian population went into an accelerating decline, dropping by half in twenty or thirty years.

After the ravages of the new sicknesses came the destruction wrought by the Spaniards' horses, cattle, sheep and mules, none of which had previously been known in the Americas. They bred at prodigious speed and as there were no fences to hold them within the boundaries of the Spanish ranches, herds of sheep and cattle swept across Indian farmland, devouring the crops which formed the Indians' staple diet. Stricken by disease, driven from his land, hungry and enslaved, the Indian's traditional way of life in most of Central America was doomed.

In 1637 Thomas Cage, a Dominican priest, returned to England after several years spent travelling through Mexico and Guatemala. He described how, little more than one hundred years after the arrival of the Spaniards, the indigenous peoples had been reduced to servile misery. 'The condition of the Indians in this country of Guatemala is sad and as much to be pitied as of any Indians in America, for that I may say it is with them as it was with Israel in Egypt,' he wrote. The Spanish had attempted to stamp out all vestiges of the aboriginal civilization and the great cultures of the Mayas and Aztecs had all but ceased to exist. The vicious alcohol to which they now increasingly succumbed reduced them to 'drunken Indians'. They either accepted their status as 'half men', or they clung desperately to anything – including, on occasions, human sacrifice – which represented a link with the life which had gone before.

In the five hundred years since the arrival of the Europeans, their relationship with the Indians had improved very little.

Puerto Barrios had developed as a trade outlet for the bananas grown in Guatemala. If you were a banana, perhaps it wasn't such a bad town, but otherwise it had nothing much to recommend it. In order to get the fruit to the coast with maximum speed they had built a railway which went on to connect with Guatemala City, but no one I asked seemed very enthusiastic about it. 'Haven't you heard about the train? It's for freight, not for people,' they said, and I remembered the motto of the United Fruit Company fleet: 'Every banana a guest, every passenger a pest.' I was told that the journey would take anything from twelve to eighteen hours, but I had time to spare. 'Well, if you really want to go,' they said, 'it leaves at eight prompt.'

I arrived at the station at seven-thirty in the morning. The train had left at seven 'prompt', and the next was scheduled for three days later. I walked down to the street where the buses were parked and found one destined for Guatemala City leaving later that morning.

The journey climbing up to the central plateau of the country was pleasant enough. It was a Sunday and the only other vehicles were trucks packed with crescent-horned cattle. Occasionally one of them would stop, the driver would get down, and the boy who had been riding in the back with the cows would kick and tug at an animal which had slipped and caught its horns in the belly of another.

At each major intersection, the bus slowed down to look for more passengers. Immediately we would be surrounded by children selling drinks in plastic bags, old women with peeled fruit, and younger women with bowls on their heads filled with pieces of roast chicken, stringy beef and tortillas. Usually they thrust their wares through the windows, sometimes they came on board and rode a few miles to the next stop. Then the bus was so packed it was impossible to move, and the air was thick with shouting and the smell of food.

The houses here were different, mainly tatty little places with adobe walls and palm roofs. We passed the town of El Progreso, one of a dozen places with antinomic names like Democracia, Delicias and La Paz. The last thing any of them looked like was a place of progress, democracy, delights or peace.

Suddenly the bus pulled to a halt. Two army jeeps were slewed across the highway and a dozen short, wiry men in mottled reptilian uniforms and floppy canvas hats were standing along the roadside. Two of the soldiers pointed black Israeli rifles at the driver.

Nothing happened for a full minute. The soldiers watched the bus, we watched the soldiers. I tried to raise a smile from one of them. He was impassive. For the first time on the journey, there was silence in the bus. Finally, as if everything had been slowed down to half speed, a young sergeant – he could not have been more than seventeen or eighteen – walked to the door. He stood on the bottom step and shouted.

'Everyone off the bus with your papers in your hands.'

As we shuffled off, the soldiers separated the men from the women. I noticed that they were all Indians, broad-nosed and thick-lipped, faces almost like Halloween pumpkins. Their floppy jungle hats had been turned up at the brim and pointed at the front, looking like the beaks of birds. The worst thing about the soldiers was the terrible deadness in their eyes.

None of the women spoke to them as they were pushed back into a huddle. They stood silently together, exposed and vulnerable in their cheap nylon dresses, bare legs and bulging stomachs. The men they lined against the side of the bus, telling us to spread our arms above our heads, stretch out our legs, and lean inwards to balance on our fingertips against the side of the bus. I stood apart, unsure how to react. One of the soldiers pushed me against the hot metal and kicked my legs apart. Another frisked me, but failed to find the money belt under my shirt. Then the questions began, routine, like the search.

'Where do you live?'

'London.'

He had no idea where I meant.

'Where are you coming from?'

'Puerto Barrios.'

'Where are you going?'

'Guatemala City.'

'Why were you in Puerto Barrios?'

'I'd come from Belize.'

'*Belice es nuestro*,' he sneered.

'*Si, Belice es nuestro*,' I said, but my half-hearted joke was lost on him.

Several cars passed by, filled with people on Sunday outings. The soldiers waved them through with scarcely a glance, while they continued to search us. Those who could afford cars were their allies, as if their reasoning was 'the guerillas are poor, therefore the poor are our enemies'.

We were still standing in the sun when a dwarf jumped out of one of the jeeps. He wore a red shirt and his face was hidden by an absurdly large sombrero. There was a big pistol in a leather holster on his hip — its size turned his smallness from the benign to the sinister. He beckoned to the sergeant and drew him a pace or two away. The sergeant bent down so the dwarf could whisper in his ear. He pointed down the road. The sergeant stood up and shouted at us.

'Get back on the bus!'

There was a confused melee around the door. A fat old woman was having difficulty getting on to the first step.

'Come on! Rapido! Rapido!'

More confusion, and the sergeant struck the young man next to me with the butt of his rifle. He seemed on the point of shouting, then thought better of it and swallowed his anger.

'Rapido! Rapido!'

We scrambled up the steps. No one had said a word to the soldiers beyond answering their questions. And the soldiers had made not the slightest effort to be civil. Nor had they checked the women or the baggage compartment — there might still have been an arsenal on board. The whole exercise had been no more than a contemptuous demonstration of authority, of the power of the army. But then no one doubted that. They had the guns.

Guatemala City, high up on the central plateau and ringed by mountains, was smothered in a cloud of smog. It was Sunday afternoon and the streets were deserted. The city had a population ten times that of the whole of Belize and it was eerie to find it so quiet. The only people on the streets were the policemen on every corner, idling the afternoon away with their shotguns hanging loosely at their sides. The rest of the concrete city looked graceless and sad.

There was another bus standing at the street corner. On impulse I asked where it was going.

'Antigua, in five minutes,' the driver said.

On the map, Antigua – the old colonial capital – looked to be no more than a few miles away, and it seemed a better place to pass the night than Guatemala City. I would come back to the capital in the morning. It began to bucket with great cool drops of rain as we left the city, and it was still pouring when we reached the cobbled streets of Antigua forty minutes later. I was sheltering in a big stone doorway, wondering about finding somewhere to stay, when a series of what sounded like small explosions went off all over the town.

Around the corner of the cobbled street came an old Indian, banging a drum strapped to his chest. There was no sense of rhythm. Another Indian followed playing, tunelessly, on a thin cane pipe, and behind them came a dozen or so triangular-faced Indian women, their hair braided up on their heads with brilliantly coloured threads, their elaborately embroidered skirts and blouses sodden with rain. Each carried the banner of a different village church. Finally, wobbling on the shoulders of sixty-four Indian men in dark wet jackets, came a massive catafalque bearing the statue of a saint, glistening as the rain streamed down his gaudy wooden robes. The bearers were exhausted, and their faces had been jellified in the rain.

'It is St James,' said a little man huddled in the doorway next to me. 'Today is his Feast Day, and he is the patron saint of our town.' Nearly five hundred years after the conquest, and the Indians were carrying the image of the conquistadores' patron in procession around the town. The man pulled a plastic bag from his pocket, put it on his head and joined in.

I stood for a moment longer, then in a doorway across the street an Indian pulled a firecracker from his pocket, touched it with a match, and threw it at my feet. The man with the plastic bag laughed and shouted, 'You'd better come with us.'

At the steps of the cathedral, the women stood in a semicircle, fanning earthenware censers to keep the rain from extinguishing the incense burning inside. The pall-bearers manoeuvred the heavy dais up the steps, and a band in ankle-length brown raincoats began to blow at the plastic bags in which they had put their trumpets. The statue and its heavy wooden plinth were shuffled up the steps and through the great cathedral doors to the position it would occupy until the next procession in twelve months' time.

Antigua had been the seat of government for the Spanish Captaincy General of Guatemala from the middle of the six-teenth century until the town was shattered by an earthquake in 1773. The previous site of the colonial administration a few miles away had been abandoned when, after days of torrential rain, the crater at the top of the volcano above the town had filled with water and split its side. A tide of water, mud and rubble had swept down the hillside and engulfed the town.

The second colonial capital had been designed with one eye on the great natural catastrophes which might destroy it at any time, and the other on the urge to express in masonry the grandeur and permanence of the Spanish colonization. The architects had created a city of some elegance when the earth shook once more, the buildings cracked, and the citizens fled to establish Guatemala City in terrain they thought safer. Of the dozens of churches they had built in Antigua, almost all are still in elegant ruin.

At the back of the cathedral I found the ruins of its prede-cessor. The remnants of the several dozen cupolas lay on the ground, and the tombs of the conquistadores shone in the rain. In the crypt chapel the walls were black with candle smoke. There were nineteen candles burning at the altar and the ledge below was covered in the offerings which the Indians had left to propitiate the spirits – fruit, cakes and crudely shaped little cigars. The cathedral had been built in the hope that Indians would be attracted into the church and persuaded to abandon their native gods, and the figures of Christ, Mary and Joseph all had distinctly Indian features. Many of the Indians have never given up their original spirit gods and have integrated them with the images of Catholicism. As a consequence of the years of Spanish persecution, no Europeans have been able to penetrate the Indians' secretive religious beliefs. I was told of one priest in the northern highlands who had decreed that the Indians should abandon the custom of baptizing their children at a spring and conduct the ceremony inside the church instead. He was discovered chopped up into little pieces.

I walked back into the main cathedral building. The air was pungent with incense. The women were sitting in their brightly coloured dresses on the floor, talking and laughing together in a Mayan dialect I could not understand, overawed neither by the place nor the occasion. Perhaps they had come to pay homage to the patron saint of the people who had stolen their land, but who could say with any certainty who or what they worshipped? For a moment I thought how impressive it was that despite the terrible predations of the Europeans, the Indian beliefs were still somehow intact, secure in the recesses of their cultural tradition. Then I saw that the menfolk were standing huddled together in a deferential group listening to the mayor address them in Spanish. They were all soaked to the skin, their best dark jackets still sodden from the rain. The mayor was dry – an attendant stood behind him holding his umbrella. 'So kind of you,' I heard him say, in tones of patrician gratitude. The men stood in quiet respect. The most striking thing about the ritual so far had been the fact that everyone taking part had been Indian. But there was not a trace of Indian features in the face of the mayor.

To be Indian in Guatemala means to be relegated to the fringes of the society your ancestors owned. The Indians make up most of the population, yet according to a pamphlet produced by the American Embassy (the Guatemalan government does not make a point of emphasizing their plight), while the national literacy rate is forty-eight per cent, among the Indians it is under thirty per cent. The average Guatemalan might expect to live to fifty-five, but the average Indian dies at the age of forty-four.

It so happened that evening in Antigua that I ate in a restaurant owned by an American who had spent nineteen years in Guatemala, most of them among the Indians. He believed that their culture had survived mainly because the Indians live in isolated communities in the jungle and mountains. It was wrong to lump them all together as 'Indians', anyway – there were over twenty different languages.

'I worked on a project clearing the jungle,' he remembered. 'The only way you could get about was by boat. I used to go down the river and I'd come across a community of, say, six men and a dozen women. Then, I'd go on maybe another ten or twelve miles, and there'd be another settlement of three men and five women. You see, each community was self-supporting. Perhaps, if they needed a metal tool, they might go down the river to town, or buy it from a river trader, but the rest of the time they just lived by themselves. Didn't see another person.

'It was similar in the towns, even. This one town I lived in, there were eight thousand Indians living there. There were two women from outside. They were outcasts – the other women wouldn't let them wear the same dress as they did, wouldn't let them wash with them. You see, the local community is the strongest social unit. That's where you belong.'

The Indian areas of Guatemala are also the areas where the civil war is being fought. There is a simple explanation for this: the Indians live in the more mountainous, poorer districts because the better land has been seized for development by the mixed-race middle class and the big foreign companies. The two main guerilla groups, the Guerilla Army of the Poor and the Organization of the People in Arms, have their bases in the land left over for indigenous settlement.

It is hard to convey the pervasive sense of horror which underlies the war, and therefore everything else in Guatemala. This is the country which gave the world the term *desaparecido*, the soft, haunting word coined as the only way of describing a policy under which a government removes all trace of its citizens. Those who have never lived in an environment such as Guatemala lack even the mental frame of reference within which to begin to comprehend the atrocities that are committed.

A few incidents, taken at random from the newspapers, may perhaps give some indication of the horror. Two fourteen-year-old schoolgirls kidnapped on their way home ... A legless beggar machine-gunned from a passing car . . . The body of an unidentified young man found on the roadside, bound hand and foot . . . A university professor disappeared . . . Two male bodies and one female found in a cesspool, all showing signs of torture, faces disfigured to prevent identification . . . Thirteen soldiers killed in an ambush by guerillas . . . The body of a five-month-old baby discovered . . . Body found on roadside identified as that of trade unionist kidnapped nine months previously . . . Unidentified men abducted a family of four at gunpoint in the middle of the night . . . A decomposing human hand discovered when a dog picked it up from a garbage dump . . . Armed men attack the town of El Pico . . . Body of middle-aged man discovered with marks of pistol whipping . . . and so on, an endless nightmare which renders you sick with despair.

Not all the killings and disappearances can be the work of what in circumstances less nightmarish might be called the 'security forces'. But the arbitrary murders and tortures are so commonplace that the inescapable conclusion is that they are systematic; the list of victims includes anyone believed to be critical of the government – mayors, lawyers, teachers, journalists, over one dozen priests and nuns and up to ten thousand Catholic lay workers.

As president succeeds president, the tactics of the army change and the country rides a horrific see-saw as a policy of selective assassination alternates with a policy of massacre. One president discourages the army from razing Indian villages to the ground, then the bodies of former beauty queens begin to turn up on the streets with all their fingernails ripped out.

There is no possibility of redress for the poor people who are victims of these barbarities, for none of the normal conventions apply. In January 1980, for example, a group of *campesinos* decided to protest against the campaign of murder and repression in the province of Quiche, where hundreds of Indians had been slaughtered. They held press conferences, but they went unreported. They occupied a radio station, but still there was no official reaction. Finally they decided to attract attention by occupying the Spanish Embassy.

Perhaps they thought that by choosing the embassy of the

former colonial power, they would assure themselves of some protection. If so, they were sadly mistaken. The president ordered the police to attack. As they came through the gates, lobbing grenades, the peasants retreated to the office of the ambassador. Once they were inside, the soldiers padlocked the door of the room and set fire to the building. From the street, horrified bystanders watched as nearly forty people burned to death. The Spanish ambassador escaped with his life and one of the protesters was still alive when dragged from the ruins of the embassy. That night he was taken from his hospital bed by 'unknown men', and murdered.

Shortly before I went to Guatemala, I heard an account of how the army could behave in the countryside from an exiled Jesuit priest, Father Ricardo Falla. He was slight, bald and bespectacled, and spoke in a gentle, halting voice, at once sad and angry.

Six months after yet another coup had placed a born-again Christian named Efrain Rios Montt in the presidential palace (an act described by the founder of his mother church in Tampa, Florida, as 'the greatest miracle of the twentieth century'), Father Falla was visiting camps in Mexico for refugees who had fled from Guatemala. They were, without exception, poor, badly educated and frightened and the stories they told of their escape were often vague and confused. But in one of the camps, Father Falla came across a handful of survivors from one village, whose testimony enabled him to put together an account of the details of one particular atrocity.

In the border areas, where the guerillas were active, the Guatemalan army had adopted a policy of herding people into villages in order to gain more effective control. There was nothing unusual about this idea – it had become a more or less commonplace tactic since the British campaign against Communist guerillas in Malaya in the 1950s – but the Guatemalans applied it with particular viciousness and combined it with something akin to a 'scorched earth' policy.

In late June 1982, a large army patrol arrived in the village of San Francisco Nenton to search for guerillas. The local estate on which the villagers worked was owned – mere coincidence perhaps – by a colonel. The soldiers found nothing suspicious and seemed friendly enough to the villagers, even offering to arrange a supply of fertilizer for their crops. The army commander warned them to stay in their houses at night: 'If you leave your homes, then we will have to kill you, because you will be a guerilla.'

Three weeks later, the refugees said, the soldiers came back, about six hundred of them. After their previous experience, the villagers saw no reason to be suspicious, and even helped them unload boxes of equipment from a supply helicopter. But two things worried some of them: the expression on the faces of some of the officers, and the presence of a man 'on a leash like a dog'. Who he was – prisoner, guerilla informer or whatever – they did not know.

Late in the morning, the Colonel called all the Indians to the village square. They were expecting to be harangued again about their duties to the government, but instead the men were ordered into the courthouse and the women into the little village church. They sensed something terrible was about to happen and, led by the catechists, started to pray. The sound of children sobbing in the church rose over the murmur of prayer.

At about one in the afternoon, the soldiers began to pull women out of the church, taking them to empty houses where they raped and then either shot them or hacked them to death with a machete. They then set the houses on fire. Children who clung to their mothers were stabbed to death. One of the men in the courthouse saw the soldiers drag the last child out of the church. 'He was a little one,' he said, 'maybe two or three years old. They brought him out and stabbed him and cut out his innards. The little kid was screaming and because he wasn't dead, the soldier grabbed a thick hard stick and bashed his head. When he was dead, he just threw him away.'

With a calmness which suggests this massacre cannot have been an act of fury, the soldiers then began to prepare lunch. At about three in the afternoon, the killing started again: by now only the men remained alive. The soldiers began by dragging the old men from the courthouse, then cutting their throats with blunt machetes. One survivor noted how the soldiers

laughed when the old men screamed. Then they began on the
men of working age, making them lie on the ground and
despatching them with rifle shots. After killing one of them, a
soldier bent down, ripped open his chest and tore out his heart.

Those left inside the church knew that they now had little
chance of escaping death. As each group of victims was pulled
outside, those left behind would mutter another prayer. One of
the men managed to scramble out of a window at the back of
the courthouse, but when the soldiers realized that someone
had escaped, they began to shoot into the building. They killed
the sheriff, even the very civil defence patrol they had formed to
fight the guerillas a few weeks earlier. No one was to be spared.
The soldiers kept repeating that they would finish off the people
who supported the guerillas 'hasta las semillas' – until the last
seeds of revolution, by which they seemed to mean the children.

By six-thirty there were only seven men left, huddled together
in the dusk as the soldiers walked into the courtroom and
towards them. The soldiers pulled grenades and lobbed them at
the Indians. Miraculously, the grenade shrapnel missed one of
the men. He lay in the pile of corpses until late that night, then,
as the soldiers played with a radio they had looted, clambered
out of a window and escaped into the night. He had lost his
wife, his eight sons and some of their wives, his brothers and
his grandchildren.

By the priest's estimate, out of a village of about three
hundred and ninety people, three hundred and fifty had been
slaughtered. The atrocity was worthy of the Conquest.

The next morning, I understood why the Spanish had chosen
Antigua as the site for their capital: it was entirely surrounded
by the peaks of mountains and volcanoes, and sufficiently high
to have a cool European climate. The Feast Day celebrations
were still continuing, and in the town square a succession of
boys were skinning their shins trying to climb a greasy pole at
the top of which was a twenty-quetzal note. A few middle-class
Guatemalans, looking like extras from an imported American
television series in their designer jeans, sports shirts and Texan
boots, were watching. But there were no foreign tourists in

town, which was surprising, for it was a beautiful city and the selective vision of the tour companies would surely have ignored what was happening in the Indian villages in the hills.

I walked along the cobbled street and into one of the old churches. The religious statuary had a savagery about it which I assumed came from the Spanish influence in the country. Here Christ was not merely hanging on the cross: the blood streamed from the nails, his forehead was bleeding from the crown of thorns, and his side was torn open leaving the guts exposed. The church had been filled with fresh gladioli grown on the hillsides round the town.

Outside the church a middle-aged man tagged along.

'Want a guide?'

'Thanks, no.'

He was undeterred, pushing his bicycle along beside me. He said his name was Julio, and once he had been a radio announcer. Now he made a living taking tourists around the city. Except that there weren't any tourists these days.

'Four years ago, we used to have ten or twenty busloads of tourists every day, Americans mainly. Now, maybe there is one bus a day,' he said.

'Why is that?'

'People don't want to come to Central America any more. They think they're going to die if they come here.'

I was pleased to have the place to myself, but it was obvious that the drop in the tourist trade was hurting the town. The Indians who had walked into the square to sell their hand-woven cloths had a sales technique which bordered on the desperate.

There was something curious about Antigua, but I could not work out exactly what it was. And then suddenly it struck me. The town had no life of its own. It had great charm and elegance, and its ruins were clean and well-preserved. But apart from the Indians who came in from the countryside for the fiesta and the procession, the people lived off and for the tourists.

'Julio, how many people live in Antigua?' I asked.

'Oh, not so many now. The government built new houses for them elsewhere after the earthquake in 1976.'

At around three o'clock on the morning of 4 February 1976, the earth had shaken for half a minute. It was the worst time of day for an earthquake, for everyone was asleep. Those who suffered worst were the ones who always do the suffering, as the weak little adobe homes in the Indian shanty towns and villages collapsed instantly on top of their sleeping inhabitants. As survivors began pulling themselves out of the rubble, a series of after-tremors shook the country again. Twenty-two thousand perished; over one million were made homeless.

In Antigua, although the tremors did not kill large numbers, they finally created the opportunity to clean the city up for the tourists. Those whose homes had been damaged were moved out of the city to rows of neat little prefabricated dwellings in the next valley. From the top of one of the hills, you can see them laid out with a bureaucrat's precision, out of sight of the visitors.

In the main square, they were holding a little ceremony in honour of a local businessman who had paid fifty thousand dollars in order that the unsightly modern lampposts could be replaced with wrought-iron street lighting affixed to the walls of the old colonial buildings. As the tape was cut, the businessman and the mayor walked up the street on a carpet of fresh pine needles, followed by the town band. Fireworks went off all over the centre of town and the band struggled through a fanfare. I could think of a hundred things on which fifty thousand dollars might have been better spent. But they all involved helping the Indians. In spending his money on the glorification of the old colonial capital, the businessman had been making his contribution to the Conquest.

There had recently been elections in Guatemala, supposedly to mark the beginning of a return to civilian rule. The Americans had faith in elections in Central America – they were essential if Washington wasn't to be seen as bolstering up corrupt oligarchies, and like motherhood you can't be against them. But there was a fundamental flaw in the thinking: in a place such as

Guatemala, the theory and the practice of democracy are worlds apart. The State Department, however, seemed to think that the fact that elections took place was adequate evidence that a democracy existed.

The army's habit of systematically murdering those who dared to dissent had caused President Carter to put a ban on arms shipments to Guatemala. Now the Reagan administration was planning to give them ten million dollars' worth of military assistance and the elections were to provide proof that the country was worthy of the guns. In the fifty-six-page briefing document I was given by an American diplomat, it was stressed that the elections had been witnessed by 'large numbers of observers'. 'The extent of the turnout astounded both the Guatemalans and foreign critics of the process,' it said. The report played down the fact that voting was a legal obligation, and that nearly one quarter of the ballot papers were either null and void or blank. It would take a supreme effort of faith to expect 'democracy' suddenly to take root in a country where the majority had no stake in the society, and where violence was the previously accepted means of changing government.

At the time of independence, there had been a handful of revolutionaries in Central America who nursed the dream of a United Latin America, potentially as great as the United States, stretching from the Central American isthmus to the tip of Tierra del Fuego. But they were deluding themselves, for Central America was split by factionalism before it had even achieved its freedom. After twenty years of struggle, Simon Bolivar, the greatest hero of the independence campaign, came to a similarly gloomy conclusion about the impossibility of self-government in the former Spanish colonies. As he sailed for exile in Europe he wrote to a friend that 'the only thing to be done in America is to emigrate', before the mobs and tyrants took over.

Freedom came to Central America as a consequence of the Mexican declaration of independence in 1821. The following year the states of Central America thumbed their noses at Spain and declared themselves annexed to Mexico. Then in 1823 they released themselves from that arrangement and Guatemala, El

Salvador, Honduras, Nicaragua and Costa Rica formed the United Provinces of Central America. It was a pale imitation of the United States of America, but it began with high ideals: slavery was abolished, Indians were released from forced labour, elections were held. But Bolivar had been correct – the defeated candidate cried 'fraud' and took to the hills. The skirmishing continued intermittently for thirteen years.

The chaos was resolved in a manner that was soon to become the pattern throughout the region. What was needed was a *Caudillo*, a 'Strong Man', and in 1837 Rafael Carrera emerged as Central America's first dictator after the local clergy had persuaded him that an outbreak of cholera in the area was the result of deliberate poisoning by the Liberals. Carrera, a semi-literate former drummer boy, raised a guerilla army who proclaimed as their objectives the expulsion or death of all foreigners and the restoration of the temporal wealth of the church.

Carrera entered Guatemala City on horseback, wearing a straw hat into which, setting a pattern for his followers, he had stuck a sprig of foliage. According to the account of one John Lloyd Stephens, a visiting American, Carrera's men seemed

like a moving forest; armed with rusty muskets, old pistols, fowling pieces, sticks formed into the shape of muskets; clubs, machetes, and knives tied to the end of long poles. And swelling the multitude were two or three thousand women, with sacks for carrying away the plunder. Many, who had never left their villages before, looked wild at the sight of the houses and churches and the magnificence of the city. They entered the Plaza vociferating, '*Viva la religion y muerte as los extranjeros*' ('Long live religion, and death to foreigners').

Carrera entered the cathedral; the Indians, in mute astonishment at its magnificence, thronged in after him and set up around the altar the uncouth images of their village saints ... A watch was brought him, but he did not know the use of it. Probably, since the invasion of Rome by Alaric and the Goths, no civilized city was ever visited by such an inundation of barbarians.

Carrera, Guatemala's first dictator, abolished elections and became the progenitor of a tradition of crude semi-fascists who ruled the country for one hundred years. By the early years of the twentieth century, the system of government had given rise, inevitably, to corruption on a gargantuan scale. In the 1930s, one of the more ludicrous of the country's presidents, who believed himself to be something of a reincarnation of Napoleon, set about attempting to root out corruption by touring the country with an orchestra. While the band played outside regional government offices, the president would slip inside to inspect the books personally. Not surprisingly, in common with most attempts to prevent officials using their position to buy themselves a pension, this campaign, such as it was, failed.

By the 1950s, President Jacobo Arbenz was the inheritor of the unfulfilled yearnings of a people who were increasingly questioning why the notions of freedom, justice and liberty they heard articulated elsewhere didn't seem to apply in Guatemala. Arbenz had been a largely apolitical army officer until driven to devote himself to political reform. He was blessed with good looks and cursed with the ability to make the declaration of even the most exciting political adventure sound like the recital of a shopping list. He had succeeded to the presidency in the wake of Guatemala's first free elections, but his reforming policies meant that the United States soon began to accuse him of being a communist.

The project which led to Arbenz's downfall was a proposal to buy from the American banana company, United Fruit, several hundred thousand acres not currently in use, and to redistribute them to landless peasants. But he had reckoned without the might of the United Fruit Company and, more specifically, without the fact that John Foster Dulles, then running the State Department, and his brother Allen, chief of the CIA, had been closely associated with the company for years.

The plan the Americans devised to topple Arbenz depended upon two lynch-pin figures, one to lead a 'spontaneous revolution', the other to ensure that the revolt followed the plan drawn up in Washington. For the first job they selected the closest thing they could find to a folk hero with supine ideology. One contemporary observer was sufficiently baffled by Carlos Castillo Armas's intellectually muddled view of the world that he remarked, 'He had a dreamy air about him, almost mystical, or perhaps just plain dopey.' Against this apparent disadvantage, there was the fact that he had previously been wounded (a difficult feat in an army which rarely saw combat), had faced a firing squad and survived, and had subsequently tunnelled his way out of a prison cell. Having chosen their man, the CIA then flew Castillo Armas to Florida for secret meetings which made him leader of the 'political party' they had created.

For the task of ensuring that the newly created national hero did not do anything too nationalistic or potentially damaging to American interests, the State Department posted John Peurifoy to Guatemala as ambassador. When he arrived in Guatemala in the autumn of 1953 he spoke not a word of Spanish, and in his loud check jackets, gaudy ties and brilliantined hair he might have been a model for other political meddlers who followed in his footsteps years later in places like Vietnam. Within weeks of his arrival in the country, Peurifoy had delivered a sermon to the Guatemalan president on the evils of communism and begun a clandestine campaign in the newspapers to discredit the government.

The opportunity came in May 1954. In the early morning of the 15th, a Swedish freighter, the *Alfhem*, docked at Puerto Barrios. Ten trains set off in procession for Guatemala City along the old banana railway. They carried fifteen thousand crates, mostly labelled 'Optical and Laboratory Equipment'.

Washington was certain the crates contained guns. The ship had been tracked almost the whole way since it left the Baltic one month earlier, apparently bound for West Africa. The orders given to the vessel, supported by other intelligence, indicated that the ship was really carrying Czechoslovakian weapons. The CIA ordered in a group of guerillas from Honduras to ambush the train, but in the pouring rain their detonators got wet, there was a confused gun battle, and the mission failed. In a speech prefiguring many later comments about Nicaragua, Eisenhower then announced publicly that the weapons were more than the country could possibly need for self-defence and could easily lead to the creation of what he called a 'communist dictatorship'.

The CIA's clandestine radio station, 'The Voice of Liberation', now increased its propaganda and alarm-inducing broadcasts 'from somewhere inside Guatemala' (actually Nicaragua and Honduras, as substantiated by Stephen Kinzer and Stephen Schlesinger in their book *Bitter Fruit*). Arbenz grew increasingly nervous, ordering the arrest of suspected 'subversives' and declaring a virtual state of siege, and this had the effect of making the disinformation spread by the CIA radio look increasingly plausible. Meanwhile, American arms supplies began to arrive in Honduras, supposedly destined for the Honduran army, but in fact delivered to the forces of Castillo Armas at his base near the Guatemalan border. Mercenary pilots in CIA aircraft began to fly over Guatemala scattering leaflets demanding the resignation of the president, as Castillo Armas's group of a few hundred disorganized rebels trekked across the frontier.

It was a war of illusion. According to 'The Voice of Liberation', which increased its transmissions as the campaign went on, there were thousands of well-armed 'liberators' marching on the capital. It was nonsense, but it was sufficient.

After two weeks Arbenz had had enough. His voice came crackling over the radio from the presidential palace with the announcement of his resignation. Just before twelve on a warm July night he crossed the street, walked into the Mexican Embassy and begged for asylum.

A caretaker president succeeded Arbenz, in the hope that the programme of reform and land redistribution might continue without him, but the CIA decided that he had to go too. Peurifoy was later said to have demanded that in order to demonstrate his good faith and trustworthiness, the new man should order the execution of a number of named communists. When he failed to measure up to expectations, an American pilot flew over Guatemala City and bombed the main army base. The counter-revolution triumphed.

Castillo Armas and Peurifoy travelled to the capital in the embassy aircraft. The American ambassador had spent much of the previous few days wandering around with a revolver in his shoulder holster and, as the pace of the coup quickened, he had abandoned his garish suit and tie for a zip-up one-piece flying suit. Castillo Armas in turn removed his check shirt and leather jacket, and arrived in the capital looking fit to play the part of a statesman. The two men were joined in their triumphal entry by the Papal Nuncio. Guatemala's brief flirtation with reform was over.

After the coup, the ambassador's wife Betty Jane Peurifoy penned a few lines of patriotic doggerel:

> Sing a song of quetzals, pockets full of peace!
> The junta's in the Palace, they've taken out a lease.
> The commies are in hiding, just across the street;
> To the embassy of Mexico they beat a quick retreat.
> And pistol-packing Peurifoy looks mighty optimistic
> For the land of Guatemala is no longer Communistic!

As the poem indicates, the plan had been for a junta, mildly reformist – no threat to either the United States or the United Fruit Company – to rule after the coup. In the event, it was Castillo Armas who succeeded to the presidency. He declared three-quarters of the population disenfranchised by virtue of their illiteracy, cancelled the land reform programme, banned trades unions, revived the secret police and burned 'subversive' books. And his coup sowed the seeds of all that has come since: security of investment for foreign companies, the dictators, the guerillas, the war and the hideous brutality. Over the ensuing thirty years, according to human rights groups, one hundred thousand people were killed and nearly forty thousand disappeared.

The man I spoke to at the American Embassy in Guatemala assured me that the elections which had just taken place were the first to be genuinely free for as long as he could remember. Or perhaps he meant since the coup which toppled Arbenz. According to the potted history of Guatemala he gave me, 'Arbenz's policy of open arms to the communists alienated many key sectors of Guatemalan society, including the military, and an invasion by Colonel Carlos Castillo Armas in June 1954 was successful in ousting him.' It made no mention of the State Department, the CIA, mercenary pilots, American arms supplies, or indeed, of the fact that Castillo, the 'anti-communist exile', had been a furniture salesman until the CIA selected him for the role of national hero.

Like every other bus I had come across, the bus for Guatemala City was an old American schoolbus, leaving 'in five minutes'. And the crew, like others I had encountered, consisted of a middle-aged driver and a teenage conductor. Since there were no official stops, the driver hooted the horn at any likely-looking pedestrians, while the conductor hung out of the door and shouted the destination at them. When potential customers were sighted the bus slowed, he jumped off and began simultaneously pushing the prospective passengers towards the door and wresting their baggage from their hands, swinging it up on to the roof. By this time the bus was moving again and the conductor would have to sprint to grab the door handle before it left him behind. It was a job for fit and young hustlers, and I never saw a conductor over thirty. By that age, I guessed, they had either saved enough money to become a driver, or they had raced for the door once too often.

Since the buses had originally been designed to deliver American adolescents short distances to neighbourhood schools, the seats were unpadded and the aisle between them was wide enough for a child, but not an adult, to pass. As, in this second incarnation, they never began their journeys until they were at least eighty per cent full, and then stopped to pick up more passengers along the way, the next job of the conductor was to organize, in a series of abrupt shouts, the rationing of seats to backsides. Once all the seats were occupied, passengers wedged themselves across the aisle, and when both the seats and aisle were full, the children got parcelled out, usually on to the laps of those sitting across the middle. So long as no one got on or off, the system was uncomfortable but tolerable. Unfortunately, not only did passengers want to alight and descend with irritating frequency, but the conductor insisted upon clambering down the bus, first to issue tickets, and then, for some inexplicable reason, to collect them back again.

I found a hotel in the centre of Guatemala City. The room looked directly into an office over some six feet of noise and exhaust fumes, and smelt of stale greasy food from the kitchen. But something had upset my stomach, and at least there was a convenient lavatory. I swallowed half a dozen Lomotil and went to bed.

The following morning I felt better and set out to explore the city. Not even many Guatemalans will say much for the place: it is dirty, the reputation of its thieves is legendary, and its atmosphere is dangerously polluted. But by comparison with life in the countryside, the city represents hope for the poor and each day dozens of families arrive with their pathetic bundles of belongings, unable to find work at home. With the national population growing at the rate of three per cent each year, and the economy declining by two per cent, the flight to the city is often the last hope. Many of the Indians also believe that by coming to the capital, they will find a place in a society which up to now has disregarded them, that by adopting the dress and language of their rulers they will become creoles overnight.

There was a cluster of homes which had sprung up at the edge of town, called El Exodo, unusual in that normally the army move in and demolish the shanty towns before they have become established. This one was four months old, a smelly sordid collection of hovels of wood, cardboard and beaten old oil drums. Forty-five thousand people lived in the place and new families were arriving every day. Those who could not find work were making do as best they could, thieving, begging and selling their bodies. Pigs, dogs and disease wandered the streets.

The taxi-driver who picked me up nearby said, 'It is lucky it is the rainy season – it keeps down the flies. The army will pull it down when the rains finish, it is too bad.'

'And what will happen to the people?'

'They will go somewhere else.'

The driver had an old Buick – 1959 he told me proudly when I asked – and with one step up the ladder he had no room for sympathy with the people huddled into the sordid little shanty town. I asked him what there was to see in Guatemala City. He thought for a while.

'Nothing. Why don't you go to Lake Atitlan? All the tourists go there.'

'I'm not interested in tourist activities. What do Guatemalans do on a day like today?'

'On a day like today, señor, Guatemalans go to work.'

'But if they don't have to work?'

'Ah. If they don't have to work, they are not looking for something to do in Guatemala City. If they don't have to be here, they aren't here. You American?'

I told him I was English.

'Have you been to Belfast?'

'I lived there for three years,' I said.

'Who is winning the war between the Catholics and the Protestants?'

'Well, it's not really a war between the Catholics and the Protestants — it's more about the country they want to belong to.'

'Same thing here,' he said with a knowledgeable nod. 'The Catholics want us to belong to Russia and the Protestants want us to belong to the United States.' He laughed.

'You're a Protestant, I suppose?'

'Of course. I'm born again.' The taxi-driver launched into a diatribe against the Catholic church. The faith had been betrayed by all the communist priests who were no better than the guerillas. If they preached about revolution, they deserved to die. And he hoped the army killed a lot more of them before they corrupted any more Indians. The Indians were simple people, the priests were clever, and telling them they could create heaven on earth by supporting the guerillas just made the war worse.

We had touched on a resonant issue. It was true that a good number of priests had taken sides with the guerillas in Central America. In Nicaragua, priests had fought with the Sandinista rebels during the uprising and were now serving in the revolutionary government. In El Salvador there were at least two priests serving as guerilla chaplains and many more who believed in their struggle. And in Guatemala there was a priest from Belfast living in the hills, the story went, with a rifle and even a girlfriend.

By no means all of the Catholic church shared this identification with the cause of revolution, however, and in Nicaragua
in particular there was open conflict between the leftward
leanings of the government and the more conservative dispo-
sition of the hierarchy. But to the extreme right wing, to be a
certain kind of priest, particularly a Jesuit, was equivalent to
taking up arms with the rebels. The people they condoned were
those like the taxi-driver, who joined Protestant sects to be
born again and receive the message about the road to earthly
prosperity through the work ethic and teetotalism – a message
which included a good deal of advice to 'stay clear of politics'.
As a consequence, the governments in countries like Guatemala
and El Salvador had encouraged an assortment of fundamentalist groups to come to their countries and proselytize. Their
growth had been phenomenal, and just recently the Catholic
church had begun to fight back. I had seen several little cards in
shop windows designed to keep out the Protestant evangelists:
'Whoever does not believe in the Virgin does not believe in
Christ,' they said, or, more bluntly, 'We are Catholics, we do
not allow visits or propaganda from Protestants.'

We passed a Drive-In McDonald's in some smart area of
town. There was a line of Japanese and German cars waiting at
the collection window. A little boy in bare feet was standing in
a puddle tapping on the window of a white Subaru, trying to
sell a plastic bag of fruit. I guessed it would cost less than a
single cheeseburger. The seven-year-old girl inside the car looked
at him curiously, then turned away as her mother handed her a
milkshake and a hamburger. The mother glanced at the little
boy, gunned up the engine and sprayed him with water from
the puddle as she drove off.

I paid off the taxi and walked through the central square.
The cathedral and the national palace were undistinguished
buildings, although the palace was certainly eye-catching – in
parts it had more colours than a Neapolitan ice cream. I
wondered whether it was because no president could stay in
power long enough to complete the redecoration. The park in
the square was shuttered off because, they said, the government

was building an underground carpark. It seemed symptomatic of local priorities.

In the market a drunk accosted me, trying to sell a grubby dog-eared guidebook.

'No, thank you.'

'But issa goobook,' he said.

'I don't want it.'

He followed me from then on, occasionally gesturing at stalls or hissing at stallholders to serve me. I had broken my shoelace that morning and I bought another.

'Goolaishes,' said the drunk, in an unwelcome, tipsy chorus.

For the next half hour, as I walked through the market, he followed. As I turned left, a voice behind would say 'To delefft.'

I turned around and walked back the way I had come. 'Gooidea,' I heard over my shoulder. Finally, when I stopped outside a shop selling plaster Baby Jesuses, he pressed his face to the glass and slid to the ground.

Ten minutes later a street urchin sidled up to me.

'You got dollars? You want to change?'

The Guatemalan quetzal is in theory of equal value to the dollar, but this is a polite fiction maintained by the Central Bank to preserve national pride and exploit the tourists who still visit the country.

'I'll give you one thirty-four to the dollar,' the boy whispered. Such a profit was not to be dismissed lightly and I agreed. We walked down the street, then he ducked into an alley. We emerged at the back of an office building and found ourselves facing an arcade of shops. The boy made for the last one in the row. The sign outside offered 'Flowers for Every Occasion', but even though it was the middle of the day, the door was locked and there wasn't a single flower in the window. The boy knocked on the window, a youth appeared from the back of the shop, opened the door a crack, scrutinized us and let us inside. Another youth tapped on a door in the wall at the back of the shop and a female voice cried 'Come!'

There were three tables along a wall, a woman behind each of them. In the corner were two guards. The room was small and smelt of perspiration. It had a temporary air to it, as if the whole place could vanish without trace within three minutes. I sat down at the first of the tables and handed over a fifty-dollar bill. It was a new note and the woman stuck her fingernail into it, turned the note back against her finger and rubbed it against a sheet of white paper, testing to see if it was a forgery.

'Is it OK?' I asked.

'A good factory,' she said, and smiled.

Within a minute it was all over. She had my fifty dollars, I had seventy-seven quetzales.

I discovered later that the banks allowed foreigners to change up to one hundred quetzales back into dollars at the official rate of exchange. Presumably, then, if you were sufficiently dedicated you could live free by changing one hundred dollars back and forth every day and living on the extra thirty or forty quetzales.

That night I was the only guest for dinner in the echoing hotel dining-room. I read the newspaper. A spokesman for the foreign minister was expressing the hope that diplomatic relations might be restored with Spain, 'on conditions which do not involve any humiliation of national dignity'. There was no mention of the circumstances under which diplomatic relations had been broken and thirty-seven unarmed people incinerated. I started my dinner, but just as I took my first mouthful the lights went out.

The guerillas were burning buses in El Salvador, and not surprisingly, the bus companies didn't like to use their best vehicles for the run over the border. Still, I was pleased to find that I could travel overland as I had half expected to have to fly. I bought a ticket on a vehicle which advertised itself as an express, a Japanese minibus which left at six in the morning with twenty-eight of us crammed inside.

I was not sorry to be leaving Guatemala City. It was choking, congested and noisy, but as we climbed through the amphi-theatre around, it had the charm of distance. From the hillside the kind morning light made it look as cultivated as many a European city. This time of year, the rainy season which many Central Americans called winter, was the best time to see the country. The wind blew in the rain, which kept temperatures bearable and turned the hillsides from sunburnt brown to lush green. In places the plain was pockmarked like a cauldron of pea soup at the moment of boiling. High on the hillsides above, on slopes so sheer they seemed unwalkable, patches of paler green stood out where the Indians had cultivated fields of maize.

The passengers on the bus were almost all lower-middle-class Salvadoreans, returning from work or visits to friends in Guatemala. When we stopped on the edge of town to collect a blowzy grandmother and her maids, the two men who had been sharing the front seat gave it up to her and crammed themselves into the aisle, less out of courtesy than a deeply ingrained sense of social order.

WELCOME TO MILITARY ZONE NO. 10, it said in Orwellian print on the outskirts of a Guatemalan border town. There was a self-assurance about the army in Guatemala which I didn't much like. They had fought the most successful anti-guerilla campaign of all the countries in the area. And they had done it without American support because of the whimpish worries of American politicians about their human rights record. The Guatemalans' military pals were the Argentinians and the Israelis. The American army they regarded as soft, badly trained and overequipped. But they had the further assurance of knowing that if things should ever get really serious – if the guerillas were to win in El Salvador and open a second front in Guatemala, for example – the United States would come marching in, human rights or not. It was a comforting, unstated safeguard which gave them a licence to do exactly as they pleased.

As we approached the border, the conductor on our little bus began shouting.

'We're almost there. We're almost there.'

He and the driver were both Salvadoreans, and there was pleasurable anticipation in his voice.

'Get your papers ready! We're only waiting twenty-five minutes! Anyone who doesn't make it gets left behind!'

When we reached the border post the portly grandmother was ushered through the long lines of patient peasants as if bypassing obstacles was part of her birthright.

'Come on! Come on!' An hour later the driver was calling us back to the bus with unnecessary frenzy. 'Let's go! Who wants to stay in Guatemala?'

Something changed when we crossed the border, and for a while I could not work out exactly what it was. The countryside was much the same, although soon the little patches of maize gave way to extensive groves of coffee. The change was in the people – not so much in their physical appearance as in their numbers. El Salvador is the smallest of the states in the old federation of Spanish Central America, but it is by far the most densely populated. The country's borders form the sides of a pen within which the people are crammed in uncomfortable, jostling closeness: although no bigger than Wales, it has twice the population.

In Guatemala City we had joined the Pan-American Highway, the great project initiated to provide a road from Alaska to Tierra del Fuego. Except for a section in Panama, the road was now more or less complete. But since responsibility for construction rested with the individual governments across whose territory it passed, in some places it was broad highway, in others no more than a potholed track. The government of El Salvador had obviously taken its responsibility seriously and somewhere around Santa Ana it turned into a dual carriageway, empty but for our little bus and the occasional truck loaded with sugar cane and, perched on top, the cane-cutters, their flat faces drawn even flatter by the wind. Once we passed the carcase of a horse in the road. Its stomach had been squashed flat on to the tarmac but its ribs had somehow remained intact. Even at fifty miles an hour, the stench drifted in through the windows and the fat lady in the front seat pulled out a handkerchief and held it to her nose.

In Guatemala the war had been remote from most of the country, fought in the Indian villages in the north. But in El Salvador it seemed to be everywhere. Even the policemen wore army fatigues and directed traffic with automatic rifles hanging from their necks. We were coming into the country from the north-west and most of the fighting was in the east and north-east, but the country was so small that it was almost impossible to tell which areas might or might not be affected on any one day.

Approaching the capital we passed convoys of troops heading past us on their way to the war, their rifles sticking out of the sides of the trucks like the back of a porcupine.

On the edge of town a massive hoarding straddled the road and a tin-helmeted soldier cradling his rifle looked down on us. I AM WITH OUR COUNTRY AND MAY EVEN OFFER MY LIFE FOR YOU. AND YOU, WHAT ARE YOU DOING FOR YOUR FATHERLAND? I couldn't imagine what effect the advertisements had upon the people of El Salvador. But they were enough to worry the casual visitor.

3
A Page Two War

San Salvador managed, impossibly, to combine the normally mutually exclusive qualities of menace and absurdity. In the newspaper that morning the front page was dominated by a photograph of the contestants in the 'Miss Photogenic' competition, posed by the pool of the Sheraton Hotel. The Sheraton was the place where men of unmistakably military appearance had shot dead two American trades union advisers and a Salvadorean colleague as they ate dinner. The newspaper picture showed the contestants standing in bikinis, one leg coyly tucked around the other, smiling the smile of the pliant. When I turned to page two of the paper I discovered from a short paragraph that while the elite of the local press corps had been at the Sheraton salivating over Miss Photogenic, guerillas had attacked a town in La Libertad. Thirty-seven people had been killed in a battle which lasted for hours. Not front-page news, apparently.

The city itself had a brisk, almost cosmopolitan air to it. The Salvadoreans are said to be the most industrious of the Central Americans, a reputation they are proud of, and their capital looked at first sight to be a place of broad boulevards, clean white office blocks and great advertising hoardings. The stores in the shopping malls were well stocked with sports shirts and tennis rackets and every conceivable kind of consumer goody. In these districts, the city was a monument to the dreams of the rich. But it was a deceptive appearance, a testament to the uncaring folly of a tight little coterie of rulers who worried a great deal about the semblances of sophistication and little for decent drains, hospitals or schools. It was a phoney city with as much authenticity as the fake-fronted townships Potemkin erected across the Russian steppes when Catherine the Great travelled her empire looking for reassurance of the modernity and stability of her kingdom.

The majority of San Salvador's inhabitants lived in the slums scattered along the ravines on the edge of the river, or in the shanty towns at the fringes of the city. There I saw naked children playing in open sewers, and red-eyed, stupefied men wandering the dirt-track street. The houses were all little wooden shacks with tin roofs; a few of them had managed to obtain an illegal electricity supply by connecting themselves to the overhead cables.

The men were drinking *aguardiente*, a clear liquid which smelt like rocket propellant. It was called Muneco, or The Doll, and it came in little bottles with a label showing a cowboy in a blue shirt. Inside the cantina there were wooden bars across the counter, in case the customers became violent, and a saucer filled with salt and bitter little plums. Behind the grille, the bartender was a young man of perhaps twenty, naked to the waist for relief against the sweaty heat. Pictures torn from pornographic magazines were tacked to the wall.

Outside the cantina a little girl was standing in the drain holding a plastic doll by one foot. The other leg was missing. The doll was almost as big as the girl, but while its face was round and pink and well-nourished, hers was thin and dark and hungry. There was a dog cowering in a corner across the alley. It was covered in scabs and sores, and it stood in red and pink nakedness where the hair had been rubbed from its back.

'Who lives here?' I asked a woman washing clothes in a bowl over the drain, expecting to be told that they had all recently arrived in San Salvador from the countryside.

'The poor people live here,' she said. There was a defiance in her face. Then she amplified her answer.

'Yes, the poor. Thieves, soldiers, guerillas. The poor.' She threw her head back and laughed toothlessly, as if they were all more or less identical, part of the same great horde travelling separate routes to the same meagre objective.

I heard later that one of the ways the government was trying to reduce the population in the shanty towns was by a programme of sterilization. The scheme was supposed to be voluntary, but hospitals were in fact being used to recruit candidates. Since the monthly allocation of drugs to a hospital was dependent upon the number of sterilizations they performed, women who were admitted towards the end of the month to have a child delivered would sometimes find themselves involuntarily sterilized at the same time if the quota for that month was unfilled.

On the way back into the centre of town I stopped to rest on the greenest area of grass I had seen since leaving England. I had walked twenty or thirty yards, past a fountain and a couple of men trimming the lawn with machetes, when a fat woman with heavy make-up came waddling up the drive behind me.

'Can I help you?'

'Is it private here?'

'Yes,' she said. But it was not the reply of an offended proprietor.

'We have facilities here to suit everyone, and our terms are most convenient.' She was pulling at one of her dollopy gold earrings.

I noticed each little manicured lawn had a stone name-plate, with words like 'Serenity', 'Hope' and 'Eternity' embossed upon it. I was in a newly established Garden of Remembrance.

'Take this model, for example.' She opened a folder she was carrying and pulled out a picture of a tomb, complete with the statue of an angel.

'This plot has accommodation for twelve to eighteen family members and comes with a likeness of one of the apostles.'

It was a well-rehearsed patter, although I doubted whether she could seriously believe I was a potential customer. I noticed she had not mentioned anything about the price.

'How much would that cost?'

'That, sir,' she drew a paper napkin from her brassière and wiped her lips, 'would be forty-five thousand colones.'

'Have you anything cheaper?'

'Well, the cheapest we have is this one, sir.' She handed me a leaflet which showed four coffins piled on top of one another in the earth. 'That one will cost only six thousand colones.'

I had to admit that by comparison it was a bargain. She guessed I had reservations.

'You get a ten per cent discount for cash.'

I said nothing.

'Or, if you prefer,' she dabbed her red lipstick again, 'you could put down a twenty-five per cent deposit and pay the rest off over thirty months.' She looked at me in a final burst of optimism, then said, 'Well, take the leaflet anyway.'

I turned to walk down the drive, glancing at the paper she had given me. At the bottom I read in Spanish the words of 'the well-known cleric and writer, Dr Frank Crane': 'Death is as natural as life. It is an obligation to prepare ourselves for it, like other inevitable realities.'

'Here,' the woman cried, running after me, 'take my business card. We get paid on commission.'

The vehicles which came to epitomize San Salvador for me were the armoured Cherokee jeeps which the rich used to travel to and from their homes. With their darkened, bullet-proofed windows it was impossible to see the driver or passengers, which gave them an inhuman appearance, almost as if they had a life of their own. The irreverent called them 'garch-mobiles' because no oligarchy home was complete without one. They cost fifty thousand dollars each, and the particularly well-heeled bought a second in which their bodyguards followed, rifles sticking out of the open windows. They said that before the company handed the cars over, they test-fired a submachine-gun at them in the showroom for you. It was an open secret that many of the death squads were financed by wealthy exiles in their Miami condos. Numerous witnesses reported having seen a garch-mobile the previous evening in the place at which the mutilated body of a death squad victim was discovered the next morning.

The police, by contrast, made do with black and white American saloons, in which they cruised the streets with their rifles poking out of the windows. Even by Guatemalan standards, some of the officers in the Salvadorean police and army were spectacularly venal. In the mid-seventies, the army chief of staff had been arrested and charged with preparing to sell the country's stock of machine-guns to the American Mafia. The normal military progression, they said, was 'Lieutenant, Captain, Millionaire'.

El Salvador had a motionless feel to it. At the same time as the American government was pouring unprecedented amounts of money into the place, it had applied to the United Nations for the status of 'least developed nation', a distinction it would share with countries like Haiti and Upper Volta. At the same time as more money was being spent on the army, they talked about the guerillas growing stronger. At the same time as the country was being pacified, more and more people seemed to be talking about their escape routes if things got much worse. All that was changing was the speed at which the country trod water.

The cathedral in the centre of town typified the way the place had been arrested in mid-history. It was a modern building, of concrete and brick, but it had never been finished: the steel reinforcing beams and wires hung out of the side, rusting away; the window-frames were filled not with glass but with transparent corrugated plastic; the main gates were locked shut and entry was by the side doors, as if religion was something to be practised in secret, despite the Catholic pretences of the institutions of government. It was mid-morning on a Monday, yet the building was packed with poor people praying in the bustling echo which passed for silence. The base of the walls had been daubed with a coat of white paint, but high above, corroding wires dangled over the worshippers from the unpainted grey concrete. It had been like that for years, ever since the archbishop ordered the construction work to be halted, saying 'We must stop building the cathedral and start building the church.' No one knew when, if ever, work would recommence. A group of musicians were pulling at violins in a corner of the nave. On the back of the pew in front of me, someone had scrawled 'FMLN', the initials of the guerilla front, and beneath that, 'God is with the poor'.

From the earliest days of the Spanish Conquest in Central America the three institutions which mattered in society – the church, the army and the oligarchy – had coexisted in a state of tacit conspiracy. But the 1968 Episcopal Conference in Medellin,

Colombia, split the cosy alliance by committing the church to the support of the hungry and the dispossessed. This radical change was of particular significance in El Salvador, where the rich began to fear a church they no longer controlled.

By the mid 1970s, priests and nuns were at work all over the country establishing Christian 'base communities' among the poor and landless. These communities were essential to the development of a 'People's Church', but they also provided the first focus for organized demands that the poor be given a share in the wealth of the country. Not only the local landowners but senior members of church hierarchy became alarmed at the speed with which the ideas of the radical priesthood were taking hold. In an apparent attempt to regain control, in February 1977 the Vatican appointed Oscar Arnulfo Romero as archbishop. Romero was thought to be a conservative and it was expected that he would begin to haul the left-wing clergy back into line.

But within five weeks of his appointment, the assassins had begun to exert influence over the new archbishop. Late one afternoon in March, a Jesuit priest, Father Rutilio Grande, was driving out to say Mass at a village north of San Salvador. As his Land Rover passed a group of men standing at the side of the dusty road, they levelled automatic rifles at the vehicle and opened fire. The priest was hit in the throat, skull and back, and died instantly. There was no doubt that the killers, like most of the death squads, were members of the police or army, but if they sought to intimidate the church into submission, they achieved the reverse. The archbishop closed all Catholic schools in mourning, called for an investigation, and encouraged demonstrations defying the state of siege. As Romero began to attack the repression of the state, opening an office to investigate the ghastly catalogue of disappearances, tortures and murders, and speaking out against the behaviour of the government in his sermons, he developed into the most popular figure in the country. At the same time, the hired guns of those who felt threatened by the clergy's independent leadership responded characteristically. Two priests were murdered, two tortured, fifteen driven out of the country, and the entire Jesuit community of thirty-three men was warned to leave El Salvador within one month or face 'execution'.

There were many other incidents which had helped to turn the supposedly conservative archbishop into the champion of the poor. He asked the Americans to cut off military aid to the government, supported protest strikes, and spoke out incessantly against the violence which corrupted every aspect of national life.

At the beginning of Holy Week 1980, Romero ended his sermon with an appeal to the soldiers, police and National Guardsmen:

'Brothers, each one of you is one of us. We are the same people. The *campesinos* you kill are your own brothers and sisters.

'When you hear the words of a man telling you to kill, remember instead the words of God, "Thou shalt not kill." God's law must prevail. No soldier is obliged to obey an order contrary to the law of God. It is time that you come to your senses and obey your conscience rather than follow sinful commands.'

This was too much for the army High Command, which considered the sermon an incitement to mutiny. The following evening the archbishop was celebrating Mass. As he raised his arms to invite the congregation to pray, a sniper at the back of the church shot him through the heart. At the funeral, bombs, sniping attacks and the ensuing panic-stricken stampede took the lives of nearly thirty of the mourners. After that experience, it looked unlikely that peaceful demonstrations would change anything. Whoever had secretly etched the initials of the guerilla group into the cathedral pew had evidently reached the same conclusion.

Although the war was being fought mainly in the north and east, its influence permeated everywhere, intruded upon each waking thought. And it wasn't merely that there seemed to be men in drab olive uniforms all over town. The war was like a lunatic relative which had once been locked up, but was now on the loose. What would he do next, and how much longer was it possible to deny the fact that he was their flesh and blood? Rumours of the latest offensive or atrocity were passed on quickly. It didn't matter whether the stories were factually accurate or not, for the existence of the uncaged beast was not in question and precision was unnecessary. Hearsay was the common currency.

I had first visited El Salvador at the beginning of 1981. The guerillas' 'Final Offensive' was still offensive but nothing like final: there was a curfew every night, and every morning a fresh crop of disfigured corpses on the streets. I had covered several wars before, but El Salvador struck me as the foulest, most hopeless place I had seen. Radical theologians talked of 'institutional violence', but it seemed more accurate to talk of cultural violence, or a culture *of* violence, so little did human life matter. At night I had lain awake in my room, terrified and unable to erase the grotesque faces on the corpses I had seen each day.

'Ah, it was worse then,' said the businessman in his hammock, 'those were the worst days. In our neighbourhood we were expecting the guerillas to come down the side of the volcano and into our homes. We had organized secret defence committees and we, the people who lived there, were going to fight them house by house. Yes, it was worse then.' Those who lived through the wars are always making judgements of this kind – it was worse then, but now isn't as good as it was another time. His wife, moulded like a ball of lumpy plasticine into a shiny swimming costume, interjected.

'But things are bad again now.' She turned to me. 'You shouldn't try getting from here to Honduras. The guerillas are burning the buses. Last week they cut the road for four days! Imagine! Nothing moved from San Salvador to San Miguel or the frontier! And the army didn't do anything about it, just let them set fire to anything that tried to go through. Maybe you think they won't touch you because you're a writer, but last week they machine-gunned a whole bus – I don't know why – and killed seven people.' This last comment was typical of the El Salvador rumour machine. I found no one who could confirm the machine-gun attack, although it was true that the guerillas had cut the road for four days. In a place where the newspapers were political tracts and the radio stations aerosols of propaganda, gossip soon acquired the status of fact.

It was a Sunday afternoon and the Pacific surf was crashing on to the beach in great grey rollers, so powerful that it was dangerous to venture out more than a few yards from the shore. It was the first time I had seen the Pacific since leaving Belize, and it had come about as the result of a happy, spontaneous invitation to accompany a family going down from San Salvador for a day at the beach. We had driven from the capital on a great highway with tollbooths and storm drains and scarcely another vehicle. We passed the glistening concrete and glass airport building, part of the same monumental folly, and dropped down to the sea near the Treasure Beach Hotel. The airport, the road and the hotel had all been part of a scheme to attract tourists to play in the Pacific surf. By building the airport halfway between the capital and the coast, visiting American holidaymakers en route to a week of waterskiing and scuba-diving would be sheltered from the disturbing sights of the sick and stinking shanty towns around the capital. Unfortunately for the visionaries, the war meant that the idea had been still-born, and the road was empty, the airport underused, and the hotel closed down.

Rodrigo and Clara's beach house was a few miles further up the coast, through several cotton plantations which had recently been given by the government to the *campesinos* who worked them. Rodrigo, who was an intelligent, tolerant man, thought this was a good policy, but now the guerillas had said they would burn the plantations down. The newly-enriched share-croppers worked on in apprehensive faith, because they had no choice: if they stopped work they wouldn't eat and the army would consider them guerilla sympathizers, but if they continued to cultivate the cotton the guerillas would accuse them of supporting the government and come and put the fields to the torch. A little further on we passed through a palm-thatched fishing village, stopped and got out – mother, father, children, maid, dog – at the beach house. It was two or three times larger than the homes of the fishermen, but modest by the standards of the local business class. The gates were opened by a very thin old man.

'You know, I used to worry about coming here,' Rodrigo said. 'I asked Pedro', he nodded at the old man, 'if "the boys" were around. He told me they came down to the beach in the evening with their guns, but apparently just for a swim. I gave him a pistol once, for protection in case they decided to attack the house, but next time I came down, he'd sold it to someone in the village.'

'Do you think he might have sold it to the guerillas?' I asked. Rodrigo smiled.

'Who knows?'

There was a hooting of car horns and another family arrived. A second man with the look of affluent good health, another wife with too much make-up, hairdye and stomach. We were introduced and drank a couple of 'coco-locos' of rum and coconut milk. Someone handed round little squares of bread spread with indifferent caviar. Beyond the fence two little girls and a broken old woman in a threadbare dress came along the beach, gathering coconuts and maize cobs washed down in the storm.

By the standards of Europe or North America, these were not particularly wealthy people (indeed their recurrent nightmare was how they might scrape by if the worst came to the worst and they had to flee to the United States). The truly rich in El Salvador, the oligarchy families, have no worries about making ends meet anywhere in the world, and most of them have had ample illicit foreign bank accounts for years. Rodrigo was, I suppose, as close to a bourgeois liberal as is possible in a semi-feudal state. He ran a small engineering factory.

'Not long ago we had a couple of kids come into the factory. I saw them from my office, about thirteen or fourteen years old. It looked as if they were collecting for the local football team. The next thing I knew, I felt a gun just here.' He patted his kidneys. 'Well, I emptied the safe deposit box, the petty cash, everything. Now I have an armoured car come to collect whatever cash I have at the end of the day.'

'You know,' I said, 'that kind of thing can happen anywhere.

Except maybe it's easier to get a gun here. Have you had any trouble specifically as a result of the war?'

'Well, I started getting phone calls telling me I had to give money to one of the guerilla groups, the FPL, and that if I didn't, they'd kill me.'

He spoke matter-of-factly, as if it was as common a business inconvenience as completing annual accounts. I asked him how he reacted.

'I built a bunker in my office.'

'A bunker?'

'Yeah. As soon as I get to work, I lock myself inside it. It's got concrete walls and there's a window with bullet-proof glass so I can see out. The door's made of bullet-proof steel and there's a hole in it I can stick my gun through. My legal gun, that is, the Browning.'

'You have any other guns?'

'Just a couple, a shotgun and a forty-five. The government's beginning to tighten up on things now, and I don't like to have too many illegal ones around.'

'What happened with the threats?'

'They started calling me at home, saying if I didn't pay, they'd kill someone in my family. They said they knew where my kids went to school. It was a bad time, you can imagine. I changed my number, went ex-directory, and after a while the calls stopped.'

'Have you had much trouble with the army?'

He misunderstood my question at first, thinking I was talking about the army's habit of forcibly conscripting young men.

'No, I meant security problems with the army at your factory.'

'Not really. My best manager — a young guy, thirty-three, really first class — was taken away by some men and shoved into a car. They were all in civilian clothes, but it must have been the army.'

'How do you know?'

'Because the guerillas don't do that kind of thing in broad daylight. The army shot him and then buried the body. Luckily someone found the place, and even more luckily, someone recognized him — lots of times they do things to the faces so you can't recognize them, and other times there are so many bodies, and everyone's so frightened the same thing will happen to them, that you never hear anything more. So it was lucky – if the body hadn't been found and identified his widow couldn't have collected the insurance.'

Some luck, I thought. Some army.

We joined the others and set off for a walk along the black volcanic sand. The sun was hot, and the coco-locos had loosened our tongues.

'Who joins the army here?'

'Oh, "they" join the army. People like us – people with a bit of money – don't join up. No, "we" pay "them" to fight to protect us.'

'But I thought there was conscription.'

'Not if you've got any money there isn't.'

'So the people who are doing the fighting are basically the same on both sides?'

'Yes, the soldiers are poor on both sides. But this is a small country, you know. Carlos here has a brother fighting with the guerillas.' He gestured at the man who had arrived at lunchtime.

'He was educated by the Jesuits,' Carlos said, as if that explained everything. 'Then he finished his studies in Europe,' he said by way of amplification.

'The other day, they found some *guerilleros* in a house just a couple of hundred metres from where I live,' said Carlos. 'There were three of them. Funny thing is, the house is owned by a colonel in the army. They say he's a bit of a leftist.'

'What do you mean, he believes in elections?'

'That sort of thing.' He smirked.

'What were the guerillas doing in the house?' I asked.

'Just living there and, I guess, going down and robbing the odd bank. I got held up by a couple of guerillas last year. Came up to me when I was stopped at a road junction, pulled out machine pistols, and stole the car and my money.'

'Funny to think they might have been your neighbours.'

'El Salvador's like that. Duarte's right-hand man has two sons with the guerillas, I've got a brother with them. And anyway, communism's nothing new here. We had a communist revolt fifty years ago, and after that things got better for a while, and then they got bad again. There's another thing, too. Fifty years ago, people here didn't know too much about the outside world. When my father went on business to Europe, he'd be gone for months, because the boat trip took over a month. In those days we could get away with telling people that things were difficult for them because that was how it had always been. Now they've all got radios – they know there's a better life available. So when coffee prices drop and people lose their jobs, the guerillas tell them it's because of the system here, and that if they fight, they can get what they want.'

'But maybe they're right,' I said. The rum and their frankness had made me argumentative. 'They can't vote for a communist in the elections, can they?'

'No, but they can vote for other parties, socialists for example, if they want to change things.'

'But there weren't any socialists standing in the last election.'

'I know,' he said.

Rodrigo told me his theory about why the war had started.

'We've had all the present problems in El Salvador for generations, of course,' he said, 'but we had a real chance to start solving them in the 1970s. The traditional industries here used to be indigo and balsam for Europe, but when the market began to collapse – after they developed chemical dyes, for example – we started into coffee. Of course, coffee needs big plantations and a big workforce, so they took the land the peasants were using to grow food to feed themselves, consolidated it into big plantations, and then the peasants were available as the workforce. Because Salvadoreans work hard and the soil is rich, the plantation owners began to get very rich. The *campesinos*, well, not much changed for them, because there was never enough money left over to build the schools and hospitals and things they needed.

'In the 1970s, you remember the big coffee price explosion? There was a bad winter in Brazil in 1973, half the Brazilian coffee crop was destroyed, and the price for the rest went through the roof. Well, El Salvador had a lot of coffee to sell and we made a fortune. But the government started to get greedy. Instead of spending all this new money on doing things for the people – because it would have taken some windfall like that to provide enough money to start doing anything substantial – the government decided to try to keep the price high, started dealing in coffee futures. Then, overnight, the market changed the rules, the price collapsed, and all the money had been lost. It was inevitable that the war would get bad.'

I had no idea whether this was an accurate version of what had happened, although it certainly contained a credible mixture of greed and incompetence. It was undoubtedly true that fluctuations in the price of coffee had precipitated unrest in El Salvador before. In 1932, with the price of coffee forced down by the Depression, and thousands left without work and sufficient food to eat, the Communist Party had called for a popular uprising.

The social circumstances could hardly have been better suited to revolution. Less than half a per cent of the population owned ninety per cent of the wealth of the nation, and there was virtually no middle class. A visiting American military attaché wrote: 'I imagine the situation in El Salvador today is very much like France was before its revolution, Russia before its revolution, and Mexico before its revolution. The situation is ripe for communism, and the communists seem to have found that out.'

The military government had come to the same conclusion and the Communist Party had been declared illegal. A young Marxist, Farabundo Marti, took advantage of the situation to organize an uprising by poor Indian peasants who were desperate for any improvement in their conditions. Although born to a family of big landowners, Marti had spent the last few years travelling Central America, working as a labourer and promoting the idea of revolution in Guatemala, Honduras and Nicaragua.

But the El Salvador revolt was preordained to fail. Marti himself was arrested at a clandestine meeting three days before the uprising was due to begin, but the news of his capture was not passed on to the peasants who were to spearhead the revolution. An uprising of sorts began on the night of 22/23

January when the Indian labourers, armed only with machetes, set upon selected landlords. Their wives were raped in front of them, and they themselves were tortured, dragged around town, and finally hacked to death. Later, when the time came to bury many of the corpses, vital organs could not be found and were presumed to have been eaten by pigs or dogs. But after the initial orgiastic violence, the uprising was doomed, for it was disjointed and leaderless, and the rebels did not have the weapons to defend themselves against the guns of the army. Within three days the revolt had collapsed. A humane government with any sense of political foresight might have treated the rebels with compassion and good sense, but in El Salvador such commodities were in short supply.

Wholesale slaughter followed. Groups of peasants were tied together by their thumbs and machine-gunned against church walls. Others were shot by firing squads so badly managed that in order to kill all the victims, the soldiers had to reload their rifles halfway through. The ditches at the roadside were used as makeshift graves. No official records were kept of the number murdered by the army, but estimates range from a lower figure of six or seven thousand people to an upper estimate of fifty thousand. The military ruler, General Martinez, a prize lunatic who believed he was guarded by 'invisible legions', justified the massacre by saying, 'Killing an ant is a greater crime than killing a man, because a man is reincarnated after his death, while an ant dies once and for all.'

With Marti, they went through the motions of a trial by military tribunal. The young communist was scornful of the whole proceedings, describing them as the trial of one class by another and refusing to ask for clemency. He spurned the opportunity to confess to the prison chaplain and died bound and gagged, facing a firing squad beneath the old stone cemetery walls.

The issue upon which the mad dictator and the young fanatic had faced each other is still the dividing-line in El Salvadorean society, forty years later. Both individuals have their memorials. The Farabundo Marti Liberation Front, or FMLN, is the

coordinating group of guerilla organizations. General Maximil-
iano Martinez is immortalized in the name of a death squad.

I was apprehensive about continuing my journey to the Honduran border. It was impossible to get reliable information, but
according to rumour, the guerillas had said any public transport
on the highways would be attacked, so the buses weren't
running. There was no railway line and every Salvadorean to
whom I mentioned my plan condemned it as foolhardy and
suggested I take the plane direct to the Honduran capital,
Tegucigalpa. However, as I wanted to avoid travelling by air, I
decided it would be easiest to hire a car with a local driver and
see for myself if we could get through. I went in search of one
at the Camino Real Hotel.

Every city in every country at war has a hotel favoured by the
press corps. In El Salvador it is the Camino Real, a characterless
modern building on one of the boulevards close to the city
centre. Everyone seems to have forgotten how it came to be the
home for visiting journalists, but now the press keeps the hotel
in business. After the initial influx of journalists realized that
they weren't going to see the war fought to a resolution within
the next few weeks, the news agencies and television networks
took long leases on suites of rooms, turned them into offices
and rotated staff through them. At times of increased interest
among the networks in New York, the place fills with platoons
of correspondents, engineers and camera crews, plus baggage
trains of several dozen cases of equipment. Then the hotel
personnel abandon the last pretence of service and turn the
dining-room over to a succession of bland buffets: food and
drink quickly become the chief preoccupations of the underem-
ployed television staff while New York decides whether or not
it wants to hear anything from the people it is so expensively
accommodating.

Right now it was quiet, or as one of the idle technicians put
it, 'There ain't shit happening.' And that was the consensus
view. It was untrue, for there was plenty happening. But the
fact was that the press and television were here for a war in

which New York had lost interest. There was a restlessness in
the air.

'We got some great combat footage not long ago. And we
had another crew out with the g's for a couple of weeks, and
we put it all together into a three-minute package for a discussion show last Sunday,' said a producer from NBC. 'That's
the only thing we've had for weeks. An introduction to some
half-assed discussion. Show's got such a small audience, it
doesn't even make it into the ratings.'

Wars come and go, and right now the war in El Salvador was
out of fashion, relegated to a daily phone call or telex from
New York asking for events to be covered. Deep down they all
knew the material they transmitted would in all likelihood never
be broadcast.

The truth about the war in El Salvador, of course, was that it
didn't matter. Not really. What mattered was what Washington
thought was happening in the war. The conflict would scarcely
have been reported on American television if the White House
had not once decided that it was in El Salvador that the decisive
confrontation with international communism would take place.
And one day, Washington would probably decide that the
confrontation was more likely to occur somewhere else, and
then all the camera crews would pack up and set off there,
leaving the war in El Salvador to continue its bitter course.

I walked across the lobby of the hotel to a shop in the foyer.
A pianist was playing, very badly, 'My Way'. I had a headache
and wanted to buy some aspirin, but the shop didn't have any.
There were a number of T-shirts hanging from a rail in front of
the window. They carried crudely drawn cartoons and legends
— THANKS USA FOR HELPING US FIGHT COMMUNISM and PEACE
THROUGH SUPERIOR FIREPOWER. Who on earth would buy
these crass macho slogans? I guessed that they had been designed
after some elementary market research, in which case the people
who kept complaining about the press corps being communists
had got it seriously wrong. On the counter there was a tray of
painted crucifixes, bookends and drink-mats in 'naïve' style.
Among them was a clay model pistol, its barrel covered with a
piece of tissue paper, and I picked it up. As I did so, the paper

fell away and I realized I was holding a great flesh-coloured clay penis in my hand. I looked at the woman behind the counter. She sneered and said, 'It's Salvadorean art.'

In the early days of Washington's interest in the war, a small corps of dedicated reporters had done the best they could in a society which rightly recognized the liberal press as a threat to the worst traditions of Salvadorean history. As soon as President Reagan entered the White House, and El Salvador became the battleground on which 'Marxist Totalitarianism' would be confronted, the journalists began to arrive by the executive jet-load. A number of news organizations chose to despatch their State Department correspondents – an indication of the way in which they shared the idea of the war as an appendix to American foreign policy.

The war, not surprisingly, was dangerous. To some of the correspondents this was such an overwhelming drawback that they did everything they could to avoid going near it. One television reporter sent to cover the crisis got off the aircraft at the airport, delivered a statement to camera on the tarmac, and then flew out of the country again. One British tabloid news-paper sent its Hollywood correspondent, the only journalist available at the time. He was to be seen, tanned and soigné, stalking the pool at the Camino Real with an air of anxious bewilderment, wondering how long it would be before his office realized he had written nothing.

In those early days, few of the visiting reporters spoke Spanish, and fewer still had any knowledge of the area. They had come for a good war. As often as not the camera crews spoke better Spanish than the correspondents.

There were few distractions for the visiting press corps. Company could be found at 'Gloria's', a lacklustre bar where the journalists competed with visiting businessmen and marine guards from the American Embassy for the attentions of twenty or thirty pudgy girls with fifty words of English between them. Curfew began at nine every night and the hotel felt under siege.

Since then the war had changed, and so had the nature of the media coverage. The American Embassy had taught the police and army how to stage the sort of events which the reporters could write about, and the press corps had also become more professional. Most of the visiting journalists spoke Spanish now, and few were making their first trip to the area. Among the seasoned correspondents, there was the camaraderie of shared hardship. The work still wasn't without its hazards, though. Just recently a *Newsweek* photographer had died. John Hoagland, a tough, good-looking American with a heavy moustache and a slow, infectious smile, had been caught in dozens of gunfights between the army and the guerillas. In early 1981, when I first met him, he was recovering after his car had run over a landmine. His companion, a cameraman for ITN, had been killed in the explosion. Hoagland took shrapnel injuries in his head and arm, and had lost part of a finger. After that he had settled down a little, was living with a Salvadorean girl, and was somewhat more circumspect about the risks he took. Then, a couple of months before I arrived in El Salvador, he was caught in yet another firefight, hit by a heavy machine-gun bullet and died.

There were plenty of other journalists who had been killed. The most inexcusable deaths were those of a Dutch television crew shot down in a field by the Salvadorean army on their way to a rendezvous with the guerillas. But the dangers were worst for the photographers, always competing for the most elusive pictures, dangerously close to the action. And for each photographer who was killed or thought better of it, there was always another freelance, young, hungry, anxious to make his name or fortune. The best of them were generous and humane, and the worst callous, unthinking war junkies. And then there was the other category – those whom the war 'screwed up'.

It was noon, and I was sitting at the bar waiting for the arrival of the driver I had heard recommended. A tall, shambling fair-haired figure in his mid twenties came round the corner.

'Thank Christ there's someone else here. Can't have people saying I'm a dipso.'

He told me his name in a druggy drawl, originally English but overlaid with American. He sounded like a public school dropout who had run away to America ten years ago, for reasons he couldn't now remember. He was a photographer, he said, but was here at the moment writing a book.

'Anything happening in town?'

'No, just a labour rally. I missed the fucking thing. Wouldn't have made anything, of course, but there were a couple of guys there D'Aubisson had put on his death list. So it might have been the last chance to get piccies of them before they turn up decapitato. Hey Carlos, give me a beer.'

He sounded smashed, but there was something strange about the way he held himself, too. He turned to reach for the beer and I saw what it was. On his upper arm, a row of suture marks stood out in white lumps across his skin. As he put down the glass of beer, I could see that along the inside of his left forearm, from elbow to wrist, there was a trench gouged deep into the flesh. It looked as if someone had taken a sharp trowel and scooped the inside out. He could scarcely move the arm and the fingers on his hand stood out with unnatural stiffness.

'That's better. I usually find lunchtime is a good time to drop ten mills or so of valium and have a few beers.'

He caught me looking at his scars.

'I'm here on sick leave.' It was an explanation of sorts, but hardly adequate. 'Company think I'm up in the States, taking it easy, but I couldn't hack it.'

'What happened?'

'Ah, shit.' There was false annoyance in his voice – actually he was glad to talk about his wounds. 'I was out with an army patrol, and we got caught in the middle of an ambush. Fucking awful.' He paused, a little theatrically I thought, but perhaps it was just that he couldn't remember the details, or was caught somewhere between vainglory and self-pity.

'I was lucky,' he went on. 'Most of the poor bastards who get wounded here end up dying, because no one knows anything about field medicine. But there was an army doctor at San Vicente who'd been trained by the Americans, and he stitched me up pretty well. And then after that, they choppered me to the airport and the company sent an air ambulance to pick me up. I spent three months in hospital in Miami.'

The pianist had begun to play 'My Way' again. The photographer's foot slipped from the footrail, but he seemed not to notice.

'What are you doing here?'

'I told you, I'm writing a book.'

'What kind of book?'

'Oh, uh, how I see this place, what the fuck's going on here, that kind of thing.'

I wondered whether the book would ever be written. I guessed it was not the only reason he had been drawn away from safety back to the place which had disfigured him.

'This place is awful. You think you're safe, then, next thing you know, someone blows you away.'

'Why did you come back, then?'

'I don't know,' he drawled, 'I suppose I must like it. Want a valium?'

He lifted the glass to his lips. His wounded arm hung limply at his side, a cigarette burning between the first and second fingers. The arm looked so lifeless that if the cigarette had burned his fingers he wouldn't have felt any pain.

The pianist struggled into the reprise of 'My Way' for the twentieth time.

The driver arrived half an hour later.

'I am Billy de driver,' he said. Much of his conversation consisted of a naming of parts, and his description of himself was characteristically blunt.

'I got 1967 Toyotacar. Where you wanna go?'

There was three or four days' growth of stubble on his chin, and his accent was as sharp as the edge of a tin can. He wore leather boots, a pair of jeans with the bottom twelve inches of hem turned up around his calves, and a T-shirt covered in purple flowers which looked as if it had escaped from Haight-Ashbury in 1969. The flowers danced every time Billy laughed and shook his paunch. There was a pair of heavy horn-rimmed sunglasses perched on his head, nestling in a mass of uncombed curly hair. Over the next two days I never saw him at any hour of the day or night without them.

'You wanna see de bandits? Is OK for me. You wanna go?'
Billy never called the guerillas anything other than 'bandits', not
that the term implied any political judgement. Sometimes, when
he was excitedly recounting the mines, robberies and hijackings
which had befallen him on the road, it became difficult to tell
whether he was talking about guerilla bandits or army bandits.

'No, I just want to go to Honduras. I thought you could take
me to the border. Are the roads open?'

'Maybe the army don' let us through, so we go back roads. Is
leetle danger maybe, but I OK. Ha. Ha.' He snorted his
enthusiasm with a grin. When Billy gave a proper laugh it was a
different noise, a deep, rasping sound that began somewhere in
his bowels and fought its way up to the daylight where sometimes it so stunned him that he would stop in mid-guffaw and
look embarrassed.

We went outside to look at his car. It was, as he had said, a
1967 Toyota or, more probably, parts of several 1967 Toyotas,
resprayed a livid yellow. The doors could be opened only with
a screwdriver, and two of the tyres were completely bald. The
other two were almost as bad. Having driven journalists in his
taxi before, he asked for one hundred dollars a day. I told him
that I was paying my expenses myself and we agreed on fifty
dollars for two days.

'I sink is better we start early when we go. Dat way if de
army is on de road, we will be dere before dey wakes up. Is very
layzy army. Dey don't give us no problems if we go early.'

For purposes of public relations and protocol the pretence was
being maintained that power in El Salvador was exercised from
the little icing sugar presidential palace on the south side of
town. In fact – as everyone knew – the real centre of influence
in the country was the great grey fortress of the American
Embassy. Unlike the presidential palace, which was almost out
in the suburbs, the American Embassy was in the centre of
town. Every afternoon there were long lines of middle-class
men and women standing at the turnstiles in the walls, waiting
for their visas to enter America. The impression that some sort
of promised land lay behind the great grey fortifications was

reinforced by the abundance of armed guards detailed to keep people out. There were armed Salvadorean police on the street outside, armed Salvadorean soldiers on the turrets at the corners of the walls, armed plain-clothes security men who stuck a pump-action shotgun in your ribs when you tried to pass through the turnstile, armed American marine guards inside the bullet-proof doors of the main building. Even inside the offices, desk officers with the pallor of too many years spent inside government buildings walked around with pistols on their hips. With an afternoon to spare before leaving with Billy, I decided to call at the embassy.

I would have tried to visit the British Embassy, had any existed. The original building had been closed down after a series of kidnappings of British businessmen, a decision which ensured that at the very time that El Salvador was becoming a major foreign policy issue, London had no source of independent information. Now, years later, a British diplomat had arrived to reopen an embassy – but he had only been in the country for four days and was working out of his hotel room. In the meantime an elderly, skeletal honorary consul had represented the British government from an office where the air-conditioning was wedged into the window-frame as if the nose of a sixteen-wheel truck had crashed through the building.

By contrast, the American Embassy, and in particular the commander of the military advisers, or Milgroup, showered briefings on the press corps, although it was a condition of the conversations that the reporters did not name the officer who had talked to them. The correspondents collaborated because without the weekly access they would find themselves cut off from one of the few sources of information about what was happening in the war. Not that they necessarily believed everything they were told.

The briefings took place in the subterranean office of the official in charge of information policy. The journalists perched on the arms of chairs or sat on the floor while the colonel, a burly advertisement for the bodybuilding powers of prime beef, sat in a chair in the middle of the room. He and the public relations men were well aware that they had a 'problem' with the press: in Vietnam, the military briefings in Saigon had often borne no relation to what was happening out in the battlefields, and they were still trying to live down the aftertaste. The other problem was that much of the press, if they conceded that a revolution was taking place in El Salvador, believed the only thing wrong with it was that it had been too long in coming.

So the colonel would cram his bulky frame into a chair and josh with the journalists about why they kept on misunderstanding what was happening. His handicap was that although America was paying for the war, it wasn't fighting it. The Salvadorean army they had come in to 'assist' was made up largely of the unwilling and led by the more or less incompetent. The American military advisers spent their days helicoptering about the country, going near — but never into — combat, or trying to train almost illiterate conscripts to understand the calculations necessary to sight and fire a mortar. Meanwhile dozens of other Americans, whose presence was not acknowledged, skulked about the country running land-reform programmes, doling out money or spying.

The nameless colonel and his colleagues believed that the war in El Salvador was winnable. Where others recognized the similarities with Vietnam, they saw the differences. Notably, they saw that El Salvador was a small country near to home, where American boys weren't being killed. They became very angry if asked when they thought American troops might have to be committed, because they said it wasn't necessary.

Their biggest obstacle was that the Salvadorean army wasn't designed to fight wars. Its time-honoured role was to keep the Salvadorean people in line, a task summed up earlier by Roque Dalton, a young poet who joined the guerillas and was later murdered in a factional dispute:

> The President of my country
> is today called Colonel Fidel Sanchez Hernandez.
> But General Somoza, President of Nicaragua,
> is also President of my country.
> And General Stroessner, President of Paraguay,
> is also a little the President of my country,
> although less

than the President of Honduras, who is
General Lopez Arellano, and more than the
President of Haiti, Monsieur Duvalier.
And the President of the United States is more
the President of my country
than the President of my country
who, as I said, is today
called Colonel Fidel Sanchez Hernandez.

The political and social conditions of El Salvador – the military dictators, the tiny fraction of the population owning most of the wealth, the 'magic ballot box' the army deployed at every election – were perfect for the development of a guerilla cause. When the war began, the army and the police provided the men who would do the bidding of the organizers of the death squads, butchering those who dissented. The greatest domestic problem for the American administration was in persuading people that an army with as deplorable a record as the Salvadorean was worthy of support. There were people in the United States who balked at giving money to men for whom torture and assassination were merely the continuation of politics by different means.

The first time I visited the country, the bodies had been dumped on the streets, on rubbish dumps, on the hillsides around town, in the lake. The sight of the faces of the dead is something I can never forget and almost as disturbing was the way in which people had learned to deal with the fact of arbitrary murder. On one occasion I watched from a distance for an hour or more as bodies lay on a street corner in the early morning. Men and women walked by to work. Children carried their books to school. Each would glance down surreptitiously to check whether the hideous grey faces were those of people they knew, but no one stopped: to acknowledge an association with the dead was to invite death oneself. A hearse drew up. I thought perhaps it had been summoned to take the corpses away, but the driver merely got out of the cab, walked across to the bodies, and dropped his visiting card on their chests.

There were still thousands of people in El Salvador who had little idea of how or why their loved one had died. Each Friday the mothers and widows of some of those who had been abducted held a vigil on the steps of the cathedral, wearing white headscarves and dark glasses to conceal their identity. If you stopped to talk to them, they would pour out stories of how they had searched through the rubbish tips for the bodies of their children, met a wall of protested innocence from the police and army, and returned to an endless agony of bereavement and ignorance. But there were plenty of cynics who said they were a front for the guerillas, and when you could persuade them to talk politics, it was hardly surprising to find that whatever views they might have held previously, the experience had turned them into radicals.

At the American Embassy, I realized that the behaviour of the army was not, strictly, the province of the colonel: he was more concerned with the latest 'sweeps' and the shopping lists for new equipment. Later in the bunker another nameless official, a civilian, told me how the security forces were 'cleaning up their act'. The totals of those summarily murdered by the death squads were in rapid decline, he claimed. The death squads were now 'virtually non-existent', the Hacienda police disappearances unit had been wound up, and President Duarte had sacked the most notorious army officers. The official handed me copies of the most recent 'body counts' prepared by the embassy. I scanned one of them at random. In a two-week period 'only' twenty-two 'political deaths', with another ten 'found dead' (4 gunshot wounds, 1 knifed, 1 strangled, 1 poisoned, 1 drowned, 4 tortured). By the standards of El Salvador it was progress.

The official was enthusiastic. Not only was there progress as far as human rights were concerned, there were all sorts of other pieces of good news too. The country had had its first free elections for fifty years. Although previously the army had deposed and tortured him, this time President Duarte looked as if he was in control. His former opponent in the elections, the cashiered army officer and widely suspected organizer of the death squads, Major Roberto D'Aubisson, was keeping his mouth shut. And just last week, they'd finally managed to get hold of some videotape taken from a low-flying intelligence aircraft, showing arms 'being smuggled into El Salvador aboard shrimp boats from Nicaragua', thus supporting the American contention that the civil war was being kept going by foreign troublemakers. All in all, things were going well.

There was thunder and lightning all night, but by dawn it had stopped. By the time we had bought oil, gasoline and a new tyre for the car, it was around eight. We drove eastwards out of town towards the old national airport, now a military airbase encircled by barbed wire and concrete walls. If the country had a national architectural style, it was fortified concrete. The message 'Buen Viaje' which the tourist board had daubed up years before was still faintly legible above the road, fading in the sun.

Billy treacherously wove the car between the belching trucks running up and down the hills. We overtook on every blind corner he could find and as we drove he would let drop little pieces of information. There was a sign to Tenancingo.

'Dat's a ghost town. De bandits capture it, den de army bomb it, so all de people split. Just some kinda dogs dere now.'

The refugee camps to which the people had fled were miserable places built of cardboard, where a family of eight or ten would sleep in one little room. Every few months, if they were lucky, someone might come round to poison the rats. The rooms were filled with stinging wood smoke from the open fires on which they cooked tortillas, and the young children were naked but for surplus T-shirts proclaiming THE POPE IS COMING. If they were lucky, the men might find work for two or three dollars a day on the coffee plantations. No one knew exactly how many people had been driven from their homes by the war, but it could easily be one tenth of the population.

We continued to climb towards the east. At each bridge there were young soldiers stamping about in the morning damp, restoring the circulation after a cold wet night of guard duty. As Billy had predicted, they could not be bothered to stop us. In the streams, women used the rocks as scrubbing-boards for their brightly coloured clothes, then hung them to dry on the barbed wire at the roadside. Down in the valley, the hillsides were green after the heavy rains of the summer. Three men in thin cotton shirts walked along the roadside carrying machetes, the long flat-bladed swords that served as every tool from spade to screwdriver.

'You ever see machete fight?' asked Billy. 'I give you advice. One time I down at de beach, sleeping. I had a real bad hangover. Den I hear dese guys shouting. Was a fight, two guys wid machetes, against de one guy. He doing okay till he go like dis.' He stretched his arm. 'Den dey got him. Bam! Dey cut his head off.' Billy sniggered.

'If you get in machete fight, you keep de machete like dis.' He made a series of whirling movements close to his chest. 'You stick outta your arm, pretty soon you got no arm.'

The Pan-American Highway was a dirt road here, rutted by the downpours before the hard surface had been laid, and we pulled down into the town of San Vicente for a cold drink before continuing. Until the war began San Vicente had been a relatively prosperous provincial capital, but since then there had been fighting all around and in 1980 the guerillas had fought their way right into the town centre. Now it was under government control and thousands of American dollars were being spent on a 'hearts and minds' campaign in the area. The town had a garrison feel to it. The central square with its pink town hall and grey church was overshadowed by a new green castellated fort which spread three blocks in each direction. Architecturally it belonged out in the middle of a hostile desert, like something out of *Beau Geste*, but perhaps that was how the army regarded their position in the town. Half a dozen girls were hanging around outside the entrance. A cripple sat in the shade at the side of the barracks wall, his legs impossibly bent behind him, the stump of one arm swaddled in gaudy pink cloth. Someone had tied a plastic bag around his backside.

We sat on a verandah overlooking the square and drank a bottle of warm Coca-Cola. A group of soldiers walked past us into the café, tired and dirty after a patrol on the volcano. Billy looked at them.

'Here is quiet now, but Los Muchachos, de boys, is all around. All de rich split from here. Is no security for dem.'

A young woman left the group of soldiers and came across to us.

'Where are you going?' She wore an ingratiating smile.

'San Miguel,' said Billy. Whenever anyone asked where we were going he named the next or the last big town. To mention a particular village might imply a political affiliation. On the roadside we had seen the tatters of election posters – green for the Christian Democrats and red, white and blue for Arena, Major D'Aubisson's party. Political allegiances would change from town to town. One might be Christian Democrat, or even be taken over by the guerillas, and the next could be Arena territory, full of hard, humourless men who never returned a smile. Often there seemed no visible difference between the towns – the same dusty central square, adobe church and meagre market stalls. It mystified me as to why the poor in these villages should voluntarily support a party and a man so demonstrably the creature of the privileged. The Major had – to say the least – a somewhat ambivalent attitude to democratic politics: soon after I left he was implicated in a plot to assassinate the American ambassador, whom he suspected of communist loyalties. The closest I came to an explanation of why poor people should support him was delivered one night by an ashamed Christian Democrat. The poor fell for all that simplistic law and order stuff as easily as the rich, he said and added, 'Even if you beat a dog every day, it still comes home at night.'

The girl was still standing there, only half believing the story of our destination. She was pretty and lively, but when she asked again where we were going, and we gave the same reply, she sniffed.

'I wouldn't go there. Not today. You might get shot,' she said spitefully, returning to her soldier friends.

The soldiers glanced across, obviously talking about us. I smiled once when two of them looked over, but they ignored the gesture.

'Let's go,' said Billy, suddenly restless.

We walked quickly down the steps of the bar. Later, I felt we had overreacted. Perhaps the soldiers had merely been holding the sort of conversation anybody might have in a small town when a couple of strangers arrive unexpectedly. It was a measure of the sinister effect of El Salvador that I now thought such benign suppositions more unlikely than the most malevolent.

As we drove on, Billy changed the subject, talking about his family.

'My father, he Palestinian, from Bethlehem. He come here before de war. I am donkey of my family,' he said with a grin. 'I got one broder engineer, anoder broder play violin and my sister she psychologist.'

'Seems quite a small family by Salvadorean standards,' I suggested.

'I got two oder broders. One die in Mexico, he gotta kidney trouble. And my oder broder he in pacific demonstration at university, and de army shoot him.'

He said it without a trace of bitterness, as if it were as natural as dying of a kidney complaint. Deference to men with guns was something you learned in places plagued by military governments. It had been a few years ago now, and doubtless the wound had healed, but I wondered how many families could have remained untouched by the war. Not many.

Behind San Vicente the volcano rose in double peaks. The Indians called it 'the two bruises', others, 'the sleeping woman'. There was a violent grandeur to the countryside: death and fecundity seemed inseparably mingled.

Lake Ilopango was black and grey and suddenly silver, catching and rekindling the changing light. Until well into the last century the Indians had tried to avert earthquakes, which they took to be a sign of the lake god's hunger and displeasure, by throwing animals to drown in the water. Then if animal gifts proved inadequate to the case, they sacrificed adolescent girls. Before leaving her to drown, the priest would tell the child how fortunate she was to have been chosen for the honour of appeasing the gods of the lake. It somehow seemed an appropriate national custom.

To the west was the Izalco volcano, which breathed so much fire and smoke for so long that local people called it 'The Lighthouse of the Pacific'. Some entrepreneur had had the idea of building a hotel up there, whence tourists might gaze down into the seething crater in comfort. As soon as the building was finished, the fires in the volcano had gone out, but the hotel still sat there, caught between vision and redundancy, another of the country's lavish memorials to misfortune and bad judgement.

The volcanoes loped away to where the horizon and the border met. San Vicente volcano, Usulután volcano, San Miguel volcano, and beyond — lost in the grey and green haze — the hills of Honduras. On each of the volcanoes' precipitous slopes the guerillas had set up camps, and the army seemed incapable of dislodging them.

As the road wound around the hillsides, its surface improved. We came upon a bus, crammed like the rest of them, with passengers hanging out of the open back door. There were soldiers riding on the roof.

'Ah ha, dat's bad for de passengers. If de bandits see dat dey shoot de bus,' said Billy, nodding at the soldiers.

'But what choice did the driver have?'

'He don' have no choice. Dey wanna go, he gotta take dem.'

I was glad to be sitting in the little yellow car and not on the bus, and I was relieved when Billy found a suitable blind bend on which to pull past. We began to drop into the valley of the river Lempa, swollen a rich brown by the heavy rain. We crossed over the tributaries of the river on makeshift Bailey bridges paved with slabs of wood, which rattled like falling dominoes under the wheels. Every single one of the original bridges had been dynamited by the guerillas.

On the valley floor we were flagged to a halt by a group of National Guard, standing beneath yet another hoarding proclaiming I AM WITH MY COUNTRY, AND WOULD OFFER MY LIFE FOR YOU. They were teenagers, spotty-faced, nervous and assertive. They checked our papers. Where were we going? San Miguel. Why? To have a look around. Billy said I was a journalist and they asked for my papers, more friendly now that they had a foreigner to deal with. I offered the one by the window cigarettes, and suddenly there were a dozen of them clambering down from the rocks on the roadside. All wore the Nazi-like helmets which El Salvador had copied from the

Spanish National Guard during the Franco regime, even down
to the absurd duplication of the Spanish colours on the side.
They rummaged around in my bag and finally waved us through.
Around the corner I saw why they had been nervous.

The huge suspension bridge spanning the river had been
blown. The twin columns were still standing and the main
cables looped down in arcs above the water. But the causeway
was a mangled wreck trailing down twisted and useless. The
supporting cables dropped like steel lianas into the brown flood.

'De bandits make a pretty good job of de bridge, don' you
sink?' Billy gave one of his guffaws.

It had happened on New Year's Eve, he said. The army guard
had been celebrating, the guerillas had massed on the sides of
the valley, rushed the causeway and blown the biggest bridge in
the country to pieces. There had been other similarly spectacular
operations, as when they had stormed a barracks in the north
of the country, or driven seven hundred fighters into the
country's main hydro-electric plant in buses. Over one hundred
soldiers had been killed when they walked into ambushes trying
to recapture the plant.

The flooded river had washed away the temporary causeway
upstream of the shattered bridge, and we finally crossed over a
dam which European engineers were building a few hundred
yards up river. On the other side, we manoeuvred around
screeds of mud washed across the asphalt by the floods, then
past a cow sleeping in the middle of the road. A child stood
with a trussed iguana on one side, hoping for a passing
customer. Billy anticipated the question I was about to ask.

'Is aphrodisiac. Dat lady iguana. I like to eat man iguana.
Make you strong to make love.'

A few miles more and we were in San Miguel, the biggest
town in the east of the country. There was a modern motel in
the centre of town – a hoarding outside proclaimed it the
'Tropico Inn' – but the paint was fading and tropical weeds
were growing where the investors had once planned tropical
gardens.

'Was good hotel, like Camino Real,' said Billy, 'but now is

closed. No tourists. People don' wanna pay money and die.' He began one of his laughs, then stopped himself.

I was hungry, so we stopped at what Billy said was the best functioning restaurant in San Miguel. It was a simple place with plastic chairs and formica-topped tables, empty but for one other customer. As we sat down a very old Chinaman shuffled slowly out from the kitchen with a bowl of soup. His entire upper body seemed to have slipped down to his waist, where it was held together by the strength of his shiny Terylene trousers. After years of commerce and cooking, his face was the colour of a dumpling.

It would have been hard to find a more eccentric reckoning of the charms of El Salvador than that given by the old Chinaman. Jaime Quan liked El Salvador because, he said, 'In America or Hong Kong, everyone is always rushing everywhere. El Salvador is so peaceful.' He had plenty of experience upon which to base a judgement: born in Mexico and educated in Canton, he had been a film censor in Saigon, a trader in Hong Kong, a businessman and finally a restaurateur in El Salvador. He sucked his soup noisily through his few remaining teeth and called a woman to take our order.

She was many months pregnant, and as she turned away to the kitchens, the Chinaman winked.

'She likes foreigners. She has one baby already from an engineer who came to work on the dam. Who knows whose this latest is?'

The soup, when it came, was good and hot and rich. Jaime had begun a plate of chicken: he managed to suck the meat off the bone without the use of knife or teeth.

'Other people like to smoke or drink. I don't – I like to travel. I have made one big journey,' he said, letting a chicken bone tumble out of his mouth on to the plate. He recited the places he had been. New York, Amsterdam, Copenhagen, Milan, Rome, New Delhi. And yes, Peking.

'Bring me the photo album,' he called to the pregnant woman.

She came waddling out carrying a book covered in grease-proof paper, bound like a family Bible. There was something about the relationship between the old Chinaman and the woman which made me suspect that perhaps he was the father of her child.

He had opened the album, was turning the pages, showing Jaime Quan in a succession of European capitals. The pictures were indifferent little snapshots showing the old Chinaman at a variety of tourist sites, but the cardboard pages were soft with the thumbings of numerous witnesses to the old man's odyssey. The waitress came over with a handful of colones from the other customer to pay for his meal. The Chinaman took the money and shuffled slowly over to the counter. I turned the pages of the album. Here he was in China, the apogee of his journey.

At the counter the beads on his abacus clacked across as he computed the cost of the meal. The pictures in the album showed him standing stiff and unsmiling by the Great Wall, in fur hat and leather coat in front of the Gate of Heavenly Peace, po-faced, foot on a bench, in a Peking park. Now, at the counter he had bent down and fished a key from around his neck to open the till. He handled the key surreptitiously, almost as if he had stolen it. In the photographs he was another man – stolid, upstanding, hands on hips, an expressionless representative of capitalist success. In San Miguel he was round-shouldered, slow, alternately smiling and suspicious. Returning to China had been a statement of his achievement: now he was content to live out his days in the unhurried peace he had found in El Salvador. As we left his restaurant I noticed something else. He had the first cat I had seen since leaving England. Like him it was old and fat and sleepy.

No one in San Miguel seemed to think there was any chance of catching a bus from the border to the Honduran capital in what would be left of the afternoon. There was, however, a group of Irish priests in the town of San Francisco Gotera who might, perhaps, put us up for the night, so we could reach the border in good time the following morning.

'Shall we go on de back roads? Maybe see de bandits on de way to San Francisco?' Billy grinned.

'Why not?'

About twenty kilometres out of town, we pulled off the main

road, on to a track heading towards a town called Sociedad. Three soldiers stepped out from the roadside and flagged us down.

'Where are you going?'

'To Sociedad,' said Billy, and added, before they could ask, 'and we've come from San Miguel.' Always the same response – don't tell them more than you need. Who can guess what might make them suspicious?

'It's a bad town. Why are you going there?'

Billy gestured at me. 'He's a tourist, I'm taking him to see the market.' The soldiers were too stupid or indolent to recognize the absurdity of the notion of a tourist in El Salvador travelling to a market in the guerillas' main theatre of operations. Or perhaps they knew and didn't care. One of them said, 'Be careful down this road. There are guerillas about,' as if he was talking about a motoring hazard like flooding or defective traffic signals.

'Guerillas?' I asked in feigned innocence.

'Yes, perhaps they will kidnap you, perhaps they will kill you. Who can say? It's better you don't go.' Then he stood back from the car.

'Bullsheet,' Billy muttered as he restarted the engine and we drove off down the road. 'If anyone goin' to kidnap us or kill us is dose bastards.' For a moment I wanted to turn around to see if the soldiers were aiming their rifles at our ridiculous yellow taxi bumping down the unmetalled road, but I dared not for fear I might be right. It would be easy enough to claim that a strange taxi had been caught in crossfire, if the need for explanations ever arose.

The road was utterly empty as we drove towards Sociedad. Billy was still mildly ruffled by the soldiers' remarks.

'You know, dis a crazy country. De army know where de bandits are, but dey don' wanna fight. Dey like have quiet life, make money.' He steered around a layer of maize left to dry on the asphalt – the first sign of habitation since we had left the main road. 'Yeah, dey like make money. We have one major, he leave de army and set up security business – bodyguards, dat

kinda stuff. Next sing he start kidnap de people he bodyguard-
ing. Ha! Is good business. Dis crazy country.'

We came on Sociedad through a field tall with maize. It was a
scrubby little town like dozens of others, but something about it
proclaimed its independence from the rest of the country. The
few people walking or sitting about in the square stopped
whatever they were doing when we drove into town – it was
obvious that motorized visitors were a rare event. There was no
sign of a soldier or policeman, and not a trace of the left-over
tatters of election flags which we had seen in every other little
town. But the guerillas had scrawled their messages in big red
aerosol letters across the adobe walls of the square. THE POPU-
LAR REVOLUTIONARY ARMY WILL WIN, A PEOPLE UNITED WILL
NEVER BE DEFEATED, and their cynically defiant reply to the
elections of a few months earlier: YOUR VOTE IS WORTHLESS. A
couple of men in straw sombreros rode down the main street
into the square. In most respects this was a normal, poor
Salvadorean town, except that the government of El Salvador
seemed to have nothing much to do with it. I tried to speak to a
woman sitting with her child on the kerb.

'*Buenas tardes.*'

There was no reply. Just a nod, a cautious acknowledgement
of a pleasantry, but nothing more. We were not welcome. We
drove on, and at the edge of town I realized why they had been
taciturn.

The hillside was black with the smoking stubble of maize
fields. Everywhere smelt of burning vegetation, and here and
there a tree stump was still aflame. Billy said nothing, just
pointed one hundred yards ahead up the road where the trees
began again. A figure was standing on the roadside pointing a
rifle at us.

We drove slowly towards him and now saw three or four
other figures half hidden in the trees.

'Is de bandits,' said Billy quietly.

'Hello, comrades,' the lad with the rifle said as he approached
the car. 'Where are you going?'

'To San Francisco Gotera.'

'Where from?'

'From Sociedad, of course.' The response was the same. Don't tell them more than you need. Hope they don't get suspicious about why you're using such a circuitous route and take you for a CIA spy.

'What's been happening here?'

'The army have been bombing for a couple of days,' said the boy. 'They didn't do much damage to us, just wrecked some of the houses.' He was no more than sixteen, with the scrawny lopsided build of those who have never eaten a balanced diet. I handed him a cigarette, and soon his suspicion gave way to teenage self-consciousness as he rocked on his ankles, smiling at a joke Billy had made about the holes in his sneakers. Slowly the others emerged from behind the trees. There were four of them, all carrying modern American rifles which had once been issued to the Salvadorean army. I gave them all cigarettes, and we pulled the taxi off the road under the trees, out of sight of army aircraft.

They were country boys, speaking in a heavy accent, little different really to the boys in army uniform who had stopped us earlier, except that they seemed less bored and apprehensive. One of them, with a floppy jungle hat and a hand-sewn canvas patch over one eye, was regarding me with open-mouthed curiosity. There was a deep red scar down his face and across where his eye should have been.

'Did you get that in battle?' I asked.

'Yes.' He spoke in the flattest of mumbles, almost like a simpleton. He said nothing more, just continued to stare with his one eye, as if trying to place me in some half-remembered story. Finally he spoke.

'Are you American?'

'No.'

'We had an American here. He was killed on the road up there.'

'An American fighting alongside you?'

'Yes. He was a good comrade. The army killed him when they were bombing us one time. He was in a jeep, and they blew it up. Direct hit. Boom!' He gave a little laugh, daring me not to laugh with him. I smiled. He continued in his soft, flat voice.

'We had some hard fighting last week near Corinto. I killed a sergeant – three stripes. He was as close as you are to me now. Just like this. I was behind him, he didn't see me, then he turned round and I shot him in the chest. Boom! Three stripes! As close as I am to you now!'

He smiled again, the same look. Daring me not to be impressed.

'Give me another cigarette.' I handed him the open packet. He took the whole thing. 'You do understand? I killed him. Three stripes! As near as I am to you now!' He was unhinged by the experience, drunk on the exhilaration of combat and – doubtless – the praise which his comrades had given him. It was horrible.

But the other guerillas were friendly enough. They asked for 'war tax', the protection money they collect from lorries and buses, and I went through the motions of asking one of them why he had joined the FMLN. 'To fight for freedom and justice,' he said, which seemed a predictable answer. Finally, with a smile, they beckoned us through. I turned around after we had driven by and one of them waved goodbye.

A few kilometres further on we joined a bigger road. The soldiers at the junction asked us whether we had seen any guerillas. We lied. They went through the usual questions about where we had come from and were going to, and we gave the usual answers. From the checkpoint to the priests' house at San Francisco Gotera was only a short journey, through the most beautiful scenery in El Salvador, the nearer hills rich and green, and the more distant mountains a watery blue.

We entered the town of San Francisco under an image of Saint Francis, but after that all we saw was army. The town had been swamped. The old cuartel was inadequate to hold the numbers sent in to fight the guerillas, and they were billeted in shops, private homes, even the town hall. A new fort was under construction next to the church, built with American aid that, according to one estimate, was currently pouring into the country at the rate of thirty thousand dollars per guerilla. The only buildings not already occupied by the army were the cinema and the church – the rumour was that the army was now planning to demolish both of them to build more barracks. They could easily have put them on the edge of town, but they knew that if they were in the centre the guerillas would never attack for fear of the number of civilians they would kill. The townspeople were their insurance against violence.

In the church I found the priest saying evening prayers. His text was from Jeremiah:

> See what reproaches I endure for thy sake.
> I have to suffer those who despise thy words.

Outside the open church door three soldiers sat on an armoured car cleaning their rifles.

The housekeeper answered my knock at the door in the long wall running around the missionaries' home. A few minutes later the priest arrived from church, pulling off his heavy brown Franciscan robes and sitting down to talk in a pair of trousers and singlet. He had a soft, friendly Irish voice, and he smiled when he described things he could not comprehend or countenance, as if trying hard to forgive. He introduced himself as Alfie Loughran. There was something immediately comforting about his lively, bucolic face and strong yet gentle manner. Normally there were two other priests and two nuns based with him in San Francisco, but now they were all away, on holiday in Ireland or working out of town. Father Alfie had been in this little town for fourteen years: when he first arrived from Ireland the total population had been five thousand. Now there were fourteen thousand refugees alone. The priests had been transformed by their experience of the war and the conditions which had caused it. By a ludicrous coincidence their bishop was Chaplain General to the army.

'He thinks we're communists, of course,' said Father Alfie, smiling, 'but I remember the Bishop of Recife in Brazil. He said, "If I give bread to the poor, they call me a saint. If I ask why the poor have no bread, they call me a communist." So many people here can't see that wanting justice isn't necessarily the same as wanting to murder the rich.' He gave a wry grin. 'Something to drink? I'm afraid we don't have any beer, but what about a lemonade?'

A helicopter came clattering down to land in the camp. The priests' house was next door to the old barracks, and as the army had taken over the buildings around, they had become surrounded. There was a constant rumble of trucks and marching boots and shouted orders. The last commander had renamed his unit 'The Ronald Reagan Battalion', a christening which cannot have delighted the troops, since it made them an even more sought-after target for the guerillas. Still, it wasn't the colonel's problem any more. He had been posted to the Washington embassy and was doubtless sipping a buckshee Martini somewhere around Capitol Hill.

'The new commander is an improvement,' said Father Alfie, returning with a Coca-Cola and a couple of glasses of home-made lemonade. 'The last fellow used to set up mortars around the town, and then fire them off all night long. He never seemed to kill any guerillas, but the next day we'd get word about two or three peasants who'd been blown up in the night. At least they've stopped that – for the time being anyway.'

Another helicopter came down, waited a moment or two, and lifted off again. A man who worked for the church came in. He had been to San Miguel to collect his teenage sons, so they would not have to travel to San Francisco alone.

'Are you afraid of the guerillas?' I asked.

'The guerillas? Ha! No! The guerillas kidnap people for a while – maybe they need porters during an operation, or they want to do some indoctrinating, but they usually let them go. But if the army caught my sons, they'd take them off to do military service. Just like that. Kidnap them, and make them join the army.' It sounded plausible enough – some of the soldiers at the roadblocks were so young that their voices had hardly broken. Equally, the government was always putting about stories claiming that the guerillas had kidnapped so many hundred young men and forced them to go off and fight with them. The sooner the man could get his sons into seminary, the safer they would be.

Father Alfie showed Billy and me into the room we would share for the night, and said he would see us for dinner after he had finished some parish business. I wrote up my notebook. Billy ignored his bed, stretched out on the stone floor and fell into a loud snoring sleep.

The dark fell quickly and with it came the rain, a gentle persistent patter on the tiled roof around the courtyard. It should have been a peaceful evening, the only sound coming from the rain and the clicking of the cicadas. But still the noise of the soldiers continued, the incessant tramp of boots, the bravado of the chanted regimental war cries, and later on, the noise from the soldiers' radios and the sounds of a novice trumpeter.

'I heard some poor soldier was ordered to do a thousand press-ups yesterday as a punishment,' Father Alfie began after saying Grace. 'He shot himself last night.'

'What do you feel when you hear something like that?' I asked.

'It's terrible, isn't it?' He sounded genuinely moved. The housekeeper, old and stocky, passed the food through from the kitchen.

'Sometimes you just don't know what you can do. Anna there,' – he nodded at the old woman – 'she's lost seven of her family, all assassinated. Seven. You'd think it would be unsupportable. But when they lose someone they seem to take it all inside them and keep it there. They don't let it show.

'There's been so much killing here, you know, and some of it so brutal. You wonder what's happening to people inside.' His voice was sad and reflective. 'In one six-month period, we lost one hundred and sixty people, just from this parish. One hundred and sixty people murdered. Only one of them was mentioned in the papers – he was a teacher.' (This was important, because if killings were not mentioned in the newspapers, they did not figure in the American Embassy 'body count' which was held to be an index of the scale of the human rights problem.) 'Most of them were just buried where we found them. Every day we'd drive out and there'd be new corpses. And – what's worse – these people brutalize death. They'd cut up the bodies and arrange the heads in a row on one side of the road, the bodies on the other. After you've seen things like that, you wonder whether the army is ever capable of being reformed.'

On the other side of the dining-room wall, two soldiers were arguing above the noise from their radio. A jeep started up and rattled down the street.

'One time we had a new National Guard commander here. He took a lad out in his jeep to shoot him; they don't like to do it right here in town. But as he was driving back to his barracks afterwards, the jeep turned over and killed him. After that people started to say, "Well sometimes God does the right thing."' He stopped, perhaps guessing what I was thinking, that here was a priest endorsing violent death.

'You see what it does to you?'

Out on the verandah after dinner, we sat watching the warm rain fall on the plants in the courtyard. I asked whether the guerillas had said anything about attacking transport the next day. Alfie brought out his radio and connected it to a series of wires running across the roofbeams. There was crackling interference from distant thunderstorms and then, a few minutes past the hour, martial music.

'This is Radio Venceremos broadcasting to the people of El Salvador. The voice of the FMLN fighting against the oligarchy and imperialism.' It was a woman's voice, followed by a revolutionary folk song, 'How sad is the rain on the roofs of the cardboard houses'. The song had a lilting melody, played on a stretched tape from a transmitter somewhere out in the hills. No one knew exactly where the radio station was, although the government liked to maintain it was really in Nicaragua. Then a man's voice.

'The FMLN announce that it has *not* put a ban on traffic in the east of the country. This is a lie put about by the infantry brigade in San Miguel. I repeat, the FMLN has *not* put a ban on traffic . . . ' The radio faded, wavered back, then began again with brassy music, not unlike an old cinema newsreel.

'The FMLN announce that fifty soldiers have died in another useless operation mounted against the forces of revolution.'

In the street outside, the heavy footfalls of the soldiers

continued. Somewhere out on the wet hillside, a man and a woman were huddled over a microphone.

'The FMLN warns that it will eradicate the cotton plantations ... The FMLN warns people not to believe the lies put about by the Third Infantry Brigade and their colonel, Domingo Monterosa ... There is no ban on road traffic in the east of the country.' After twenty minutes, the station faded from the air with the announcement that it would be back again in the morning, and four times each day. The final words were 'We will triumph.' Outside, the soldiers were singing military songs.

'Well,' said the priest, 'at least you shouldn't have any trouble from the guerillas tomorrow. I'm off to bed.'

And then, as if it were as natural as any other good night wish, 'Sleep well. I hope there isn't too much shooting.'

We were woken by the sound of reveille, inexpertly blown on an army bugle. In San Francisco the army even determined when people went to sleep and woke up. Last night everyone had slept comparatively soundly, which was to say that we had been woken only twice by the bursts of distant gunfire. Billy had been as much of a disturbance as the war, lying on the floor snoring in great deep growls all night. In the early morning light he lay on his back, arms akimbo, exploding in grunts.

The room was cold and austere, crudely painted and furnished with a couple of thrillers and a handful of devotional works. There was a washbasin, lavatory and shower in one corner, a couple of faded photographs on the wooden desk at the wall. Normally it was occupied by one of the priests and represented the closest place he had to a home. Outside, the tramp of army boots resumed as platoon after platoon began to form up in the main square. I noticed that the priests' windows faced the central courtyard; none looked out on to the army-infested streets. Was it too tempting for a soldier to loose off his rifle into the house, or had the army tried to blot out the infection of the monks' liberal views? In the square the soldiers were starting to sing the National Anthem in a deep rumble, while Father Alfie said Grace before breakfast. As we drove away Billy articulated what I had been thinking.

'You know,' he said simply, 'dese are good men.'

The early morning was fresh and clear, and the green hillsides of Morazán as rich as spring in County Wicklow. The road was empty but for our rattling little yellow taxi. Here and there we came upon groups of soldiers setting out on patrol or returning from night expeditions, tired and grimy, their rifles slung across their shoulders. Occasionally three or four would be asleep on the roadside. Three times soldiers stopped the car and searched my bags – we were after all the only travellers on the road – but they were glad enough of a cigarette and soon let us pass.

Once we came upon a huddle of goats at the roadside. They had been left with yokes about their necks, like inverted wishbones. In silhouette they looked like little unicorns.

Finally, at El Amatillo we reached the border, marked by a swollen coffee-coloured river. The span of the bridge running out from the Salvadorean side had been blown by the guerillas, and a temporary metal and wood frame had taken its place. Everything in El Salvador – the bridges, the cathedral, the highway, the funeral homes, the shanty towns – was unfinished, waiting for the war to be resolved.

At the Salvadorean customs post, swarms of money-changers gathered around. I changed a few notes into Honduran lempiras and handed Billy the fifty dollars I owed him. One of the money-changers muttered something, and to my astonishment Billy suddenly thrust the money back at me. As we walked towards the bridge, he told me what the money-changer had said.

'He say, "Give me some dat money when he gone." But if I don' give him de money, he try robbery me when I leave here.' A soldier told us Billy could come no further. We shook hands at the edge of the bridge and I palmed him the notes, hoping the thugs back at the customs post would not see. I was sorry to say goodbye to him, because I had come to like his honesty, straightforwardness and good humour.

'Hey, you be carefully in Honduras,' he said, shaking my hand, 'is full of robbers.'

I smiled. 'More dangerous than El Salvador?'

'Oh yeah. Yeah, many more dangerous. Here we just got de bandits and de army. Dey got real robberies. You be carefully.'

It was true that the journey through the east of El Salvador had been safe enough, and I felt embarrassed at the nervousness which had made me duck out of my commitment to use only public transport. As it happened, the worst violence during those two days had been on the other side of the country, where sixty-six people had been killed when the guerillas attacked a land reform project, and in a suburb of San Salvador, where gunmen dressed like the Lone Ranger had killed a bank guard and held seventy-three customers hostage. In his weekly homily on Sunday, the Archbishop reported that one hundred and eighty-five people had died violently that week. That was what they called relative peace.

4

Whispers of Vietnam

I carried my bag across the bridge, paid a tax to leave El Salvador and another to enter Honduras. In the fresh warm morning I was the only traveller among two dozen officials and forty or fifty soldiers. The two countries lived in uneasy juxtaposition.

In essence the distinction between the two nations was that where Salvador was industrious and overpopulated, Honduras was sleepy and underpopulated. In the late 1960s hundreds of thousands of Salvadoreans poured into Honduras in search of work and land, provoking a serious challenge to the indolent conspiracy between the government, the rich and the plantation owners. Eventually, after a football match between the two countries ended in a riot, in the summer of 1969 the Honduran government ordered the Salvadorean peasants out of the country. It was a good enough cause for war, but the Honduran army was incapable of fighting much of a campaign and soon the Salvadoreans were well into Honduras. Hostilities ceased when, deep inside Honduras, the El Salvador army ran out of bullets. Since then the two governments have agreed to coexist in sullen alliance against what they see as the 'communist threat' which might destroy both of them. The Hondurans call the Salvadoreans 'gumps', and the Salvadoreans call the Hondurans the laziest people in Central America, a judgement which seems to be endorsed by a good number of Hondurans themselves.

A dilapidated Japanese minibus was standing a hundred yards or so from the border station, and I asked the driver whether there were any buses to Tegucigalpa, the capital. He assured me there were none, so I accepted his offer of a ride to Nacaome, where he said there were plenty of other buses. The journey would take twenty minutes, he claimed.

We had been travelling for almost an hour and had stopped to collect a mother and five children, all of whom were crying, when a shiny express bus emblazoned with 'Tegucigalpa' and 'Frontera' roared past.

'No buses from the border to the capital, eh?' I said to the driver.

'No buses of mine.' He laughed.

Nacaome, when eventually we reached it, was all mud and plastic bags and a pervasive smell of pigshit. It was steamily hot, and the perspiration stung my cheeks where I had shaved too closely in the cold water at the priests' house. Little boys ran up through the mud to the bus doors, clutching plastic bags filled with water. They held them against the passengers' bodies to let them feel the coolness. I guessed it wouldn't be too clean and bought a slice of water melon instead. There seemed to be an excessive number of pips until the vendor waved her hand and they all became flies and swarmed off to another piece of fruit.

Over the next four hours, waiting for a bus which was always 'just coming', I began to understand why they said Hondurans were lazy. If I had been waiting for the bus to work, the day would be half over by now. I drank a fizzy drink in a cantina where the bartender got up every two minutes to shoo a pig out of the doorway, then wandered back to stand in the shade again.

Then from nowhere, in a town where half the population had no shoes, and the other half were sleeping off the damage of the night before, there appeared a woman in a shocking pink jumpsuit, picking her way through the mud and pigmuck on high heels. When she arrived beside me, she pulled a lavatory roll from a little blue hold-all, unwound a dozen sheets, and laid them in a square on the step. Then she pulled her bag into her lap, smoothed her trousers across her backside, and sat down. Composed, she looked at me.

'You American?' she asked with a smile.

'No, I'm English.' It meant nothing to her. She smiled. It was a soft, friendly smile.

'England is near America, isn't it?'

'No, not really. It's a long way away.' I tried to think of a way of communicating the concept of distance. 'It takes seven hours to get from England to America.'

'Oh, that's not so far. It takes nine hours for me to get from here to home,' she said knowledgeably, smiling again and tossing her head.

'No, I mean seven hours in a plane,' I said, aware that I had begun to speak at the speed of those who believe they are addressing the simple-minded.

'Seven hours in a plane!' She whistled slowly through her teeth. 'Yes, that's a long way.'

Her name was Maria and she lived on the north coast. She'd been in Nacaome visiting her grandmother.

'I hate this town,' she said. 'There's nothing to do here, except watch the people. They drink a lot. And they all have pigs.'

'You're very smartly dressed for a town like this.'

'It's my best outfit. Do you like it?' She sat up a little straighter on her paper cushion, spat on her finger and wiped a dirty mark off her bosom. She looked preposterous.

'It's very pretty,' I lied.

'Only the suit?' she asked.

'What?'

'Only the suit is pretty?'

'Oh, no,' I said, 'you're very pretty too.' She was, if a little plump. An old man who had been watching us from the doorway across the street caught my eye, smiled, made his fingers into a circle and hit them with his other hand. Maria offered me a plum and dipped it into a screw of salt from her bag.

At last the bus arrived. We climbed aboard and my bag was thrown into a luggage compartment at the back. An angry chicken scuttled out from beneath it. The conductor came around the bus and we all shouted out our names so he could write them down on a slip of paper. Five miles further on we stopped at a police roadblock and a plain-clothes officer in dark glasses walked down the bus with the list. I showed him my passport, he compared the photograph with my present appearance and handed it back to me, a routine check on someone who was identifiably different. I guessed that probably the police were looking for guerillas from El Salvador. There had already been a handful of incidents in Honduras in which hostages had been taken in order to demand the release of imprisoned 'subversives'.

At the back of the bus, the officer demanded the papers of a youth, about twenty, wearing jeans and a soiled shirt. Although his age must have been given on the identity card, the policeman asked nonetheless.

'Nineteen,' muttered the boy, his passivity giving way to hostility for just an instant. The policeman and he looked at each other, each daring the other to say something which would turn a routine check into an incident. The moment passed, the policeman handed back the tatty card and walked slowly down the bus. I looked at the young man and knew from his conspiratorial glance that the policeman had been right to be suspicious. Perhaps he really was a guerilla over from El Salvador for a few days of rest and recuperation, or perhaps he was on some mission. Maybe he was only a common criminal, a petty thief or an army deserter. At any event, when he got off the bus a few miles further on, the atmosphere changed at once, as if he had been the carrier of some infectious disease.

The bus climbed slowly through the green and empty mountains, while across the valley the rain came down like a dirty net curtain. Here and there we passed an adobe house with a red tiled roof, but for the most part this was an empty backward country, the Appalachia of Central America, underdeveloped and, until very recently, remote even from itself. The road between the capital and San Pedro Sula, the country's commercial centre, had not been paved until 1971. Before then the journey had been possible only by mule over rough mountain trails: it was like having no link between London and Birmingham or Washington and New York.

The reasons for the nation's backwardness date from the years of the Spanish colonists. Physically remote from the seat of the administration in Guatemala, Honduras was used as a dumping ground for wayward priests, inefficient servants of the state and cashiered army officers. Since independence it had remained underdeveloped, exploited first by European fraudsters and then by American banana growers who used the country as if they owned it, which, in a sense, they did.

The banana boys, and particularly Sam 'the banana man' Zemurray, a Russian American with eyes like saddle-bags, turned Honduras into the original banana republic. Zemurray, who became so involved with Honduras that his favourite food was iguana stew, bought his first plantation there in the early years of this century. Soon he was treating the internal affairs of the country with the contempt he felt they deserved, even – despite official United States disapproval – organizing a revolution to place in the presidency a political figure who could be expected to grant the banana companies freedom to do as they liked. The incident demonstrated an early aspect of American relations with Honduras – the banana companies came first, the American government deferred to them, and the government of Honduras came as an afterthought. By 1914, the banana companies held nearly one million acres of fertile land in the north of the country and the poor people of Honduras were relegated to the barren hillsides. There were a number of consequences.

Since the banana plantations were in the north of the country, the companies became virtual lords of all they surveyed: while a banana boat took two days to reach New Orleans, a journey to the capital required four days' travel by mule. Central government was an irrelevance. Since the overriding preoccupation of the banana growers was to produce fruit at the lowest possible cost and to transport it to the United States in the shortest possible time, critical decisions about the development of the country were made on the basis of what was good for bananas, not what was good for Hondurans. Thus, although the country possesses a railway system, not a single line goes to the capital.

The men who presided over what was left of national sovereignty became parodies of what a president might have been. Hardly overburdened with affairs of state, many of them took to pursuits of the flesh. Local history has it that as recently as the 1970s, members of the cabinet had to take drastic steps after hearing that the president had spent the last week in an orgy of sex and alcohol. When the pile of documents awaiting his signature had grown to unmanageable proportions, they grabbed him, prised the whisky bottle from his hand, stripped him and locked him in the presidential bedroom. When the president awoke from his drunken slumber he clambered out of the bedroom window and slid down a rope of knotted sheets to the ground. He was then to be seen standing in his underwear, hailing a taxi to take him to his favourite brothel.

Maria personified one of the cultural legacies of the years of American dominance. She had been asleep on the seat next to me for the last twenty minutes. Now she woke up.

'Do you like me?' she asked.

'You're very nice.'

'I like Americans,' she said, seeming not to have absorbed the difference between Britain and the United States.

'Do you know many?'

'Yes, I have an American boyfriend, Mike. He's from California. He was working near my home in La Ceiba.'

'What was he doing there?'

'It was something for the army, but he wouldn't tell me what. He said it was secret.'

La Ceiba was one of ten military installations in Honduras on which the Americans were spending scores of millions of dollars. In the north, the banana industry continued to prosper under a semblance of Honduran control, but the main importance of the country to the Americans now was as a sort of terrestrial aircraft carrier from which spy flights could be flown over El Salvador, supplies ferried to the counter-revolutionaries in Nicaragua, and where American and local troops could train to fight the guerillas. La Ceiba was also the base from which, I later discovered, intelligence missions were flown by the CIA and NSA.

'Is he in La Ceiba now?' I asked.

'No, he went back to California. He's coming back to take me there. Have you been to California?'

'Yes.' I guessed Maria's story was the story of dozens of Honduran women now, as it had been the story of thousands of Vietnamese women during the Vietnam War, predictable but no less sad because of its inevitability. Mike probably had a wife and family back in America, and the chances that he would ever return to carry Maria away were slim. The bus ground slowly up the hill.

'Everyone has a car and a refrigerator and a swimming pool, don't they?' The American Dream.

'Can you swim?' I asked.

'No.'

'Then you don't need a swimming pool, do you?' She laughed. A few minutes later we were both asleep.

The bus was still crawling uphill when I awoke – the seat was hard and my knees were knocking against the back of the row in front. Maria's head was resting on my shoulder.

Somewhere in the middle of nowhere a gaunt man in a dark suit boarded the bus and sat across the aisle on the only free seat.

'Do you believe in the word of God?' It was a blunt, intrusive opening, and it made me brutal in my response.

'No.'

Then I felt embarrassed.

'I'm sorry,' I said, 'but I already have a religion.' He was undaunted.

'Those who reject the Lord are destined to eternal damnation.'

I closed my eyes again. When I opened one of them a couple of minutes later he was still gazing at me reproachfully.

On the edge of Tegucigalpa, the bus was stopped at another police checkpoint. The policeman who came on board no more than glanced at the manifest of passenger names. Perhaps he couldn't read. He was more interested in the contents of our bags, pulling everything out – fruit, vegetables, items of clothing, Maria's lavatory roll.

'What are you looking for?' Maria asked him, but there was no reply. As the policeman moved on, the man in the seat in front turned around and said 'guns'. But he found none and waved us through the checkpoint, down the hill into the capital.

As we honked our way through the narrow streets, Maria put her hand on my thigh.

'There is no bus to La Ceiba until tomorrow. Shall I come to see you in your hotel?' she said, moving her hand to the inside of my thigh.

'I don't know where I'm staying yet.'

'But would you like me to come?'

'I'm afraid I have work to do,' I said, casting around for an excuse.

'You know, I don't want any money. I just like you. I like gringos. Look, here is my address,' and she wrote in single, laborious capital letters the directions to her house. 'Come and see me, we can have a good time. It's the green house opposite the baker's shop.'

'OK. If I come, I will find you.'

She smiled. 'You must,' she said, and kissed me.

'I hope you get to California,' I said as we left the bus.

'Oh, I shall,' she grinned.

As a place, Tegucigalpa joined Ouagadougou and Nouakchott in the league of capital cities whose unimportance was matched only by the unlikeliness of their names. Resident foreigners called it 'Tegoose' for short, not so much in affection as out of a sense that so insignificant a place had no right to trouble them with such a cumbersome name. The only flat ground in the area had been used for the airport, so the houses of the city scrambled away over the hills round about. Their red-tiled roofs gave the city an attractive, Tuscan appearance from a distance. Through the town centre flowed a mucky little river named, preposterously, the Rio Grande. Another place in this condition might have been described as 'down at heel', but Tegoose had never seen better times. I found a cheap hotel where the sheets on the bed had worn through in the middle and went out to explore.

The central square appeared to be covered with a thousand white butterfly wings, where sixty or seventy lottery ticket salesmen had laid their tickets out on the ground and were holding them down in the breeze with round stones. Occasionally a superstitious gambler would point to a ticket in the middle of a sheet of several hundred, and the crippled vendor would struggle to pull the ticket free without letting the rest blow away in the breeze. An evangelist in a badly fitting black suit was haranguing the lottery ticket sellers through a megaphone, deafeningly close, but no one paid any attention. 'You know not the time or the hour when judgement will come,' his voice was thin and tinny through the loudspeaker. Behind him was an empty concrete fountain and a statue of the national hero, Francisco Morazan, who had died by firing squad in 1842. At least, it was reputed to be Morazan. The emissaries sent to Europe to commission the work had decided it was cheaper to buy instead a surplus statue of Marshal Ney, so now the hero of Borodino was also the hero of Honduras. No one seemed either to mind or notice.

The fountain in the square was empty of water and silted up with rubbish. A legless man on a trolley held out his hand as I passed. A lunatic walked by, his zip undone and his penis hanging out of his trousers. The preacher screamed, 'The communists are everywhere, but Christ can save us.' Further down the street, a vendor had laid out his wares. A dozen plastic Wonder Woman dolls.

Before leaving London I had called at the Honduran Embassy with the thought of asking for some sort of *laissez passer*. A young First Secretary in a shiny black suit had told me, with evident pride, that 'there are no guerillas in Honduras', before going on in the next breath to advise me not to travel anywhere near the borders with El Salvador and Nicaragua. I did not have the heart to tell him that I was only passing through Honduras because of its borders. After fifteen minutes we had run out of things to discuss and he rose to his feet.

'Since you are going to visit our country, we should like to make a small presentation to you,' he said, formal yet friendly.

For a delirious moment, I imagined he was about to invest me with some oversized cross or star. The man bent forward.

'These', he said, holding out a fat paperback, 'are the collected speeches of our president from 1979 to 1983.' Six hundred and four pages of the collected thoughts of one of the most insignificant political figures in the world. I thanked him.

'And these', he bent forward again, 'are the speeches from 1983 to date.' Another volume sagging under the weight of its grandiloquence. On the front cover, President Suazo Cordova smiled uncomfortably from behind a thin moustache and rolling fat cheeks. Across his chest he wore a sky-blue sash so broad it spread from throat to paunch.

The books were still in London, lying in my study unread. But since I knew no one else in Honduras, the thought of calling on the official spokesman for the president appealed to me. I waited for him at the palace, where toy soldiers in white, blue and yellow uniforms and plumed shakoes guarded the entrance. They were hung about with more tassels than the curtains of a Victorian theatre. One of them showed me into a waiting-room where plastic foam extruded from the arms of the armchairs, an old banana skin lay on the table, and dust blew in from the street through the broken windowpanes. After an hour, a soldier collected me to take me to the office.

The Official Spokesman had just returned from a visit to Washington. On his desk was a gaudy gold-plated paperweight embossed with the words 'The Washington Times', a newspaper owned by the 'Reverend' Sun Myung Moon, founder of the so-called Unification Church.

'They gave me that last week when I visited their offices,' he said. 'It's a very good newspaper. Do you read it? Or maybe you like the communist papers?' He gave a short laugh. I assumed he must have meant the *New York Times*, but before I could begin to answer, he was asking whether I would like a cup of coffee. The Voice of Honduras had a light in his eyes, the conviction of the zealot. In his bright green check jacket, chocolate shirt and chocolate tie, his hair slicked back with lashings of oil, he would have been at home at any insurance salesmen's convention.

'Isn't the *Washington Times* a Moonie newspaper?' I asked. It was a disingenuous question, as I knew the newspaper had been set up to give an outlet to Moon's extraordinary views on life, the universe and the battle against the forces of darkness. The Unification Church saw the struggle between Christ and Satan as identical to the battle between 'democracy' and 'communism'. With its primitive political message, mass ceremonies and creed of total obedience to Moon, it claimed to have three million members. I wondered whether The Spokesman was one of them.

'Are you a Moonie yourself?' I tried to sound only mildly curious.

'No, sir, I am not. I am sympathetic to the Reverend Moon's ideas. In fact, sir, I am only in favour of the family, freedom and justice.' The disclaimer had a well-practised fluency. I subsequently discovered that there were many thousands of Hondurans who claimed to be 'sympathetic' to the views of the fat little South Korean. Honduras seemed such an unlikely place in which to discover a following for the sect, backward and wretched as it was, but the Moonies preached the sort of fundamentalist, anti-communist sermons which the Honduran military liked to hear. The message had particularly appealed to the recent head of the army, General Gustavo Alvarez, who formed an 'Association for Progress', a right-wing pressure group known as 'the political wing of the armed forces', which was granted a substantial cheque from the Unification Church coffers. Unluckily for the general, the Catholic bishops, sensing an erosion of the church's position in the country, made such a vociferous complaint that he was obliged to return the money. Now, it appeared, the Moonies were more discreet in their behaviour in Honduras.

'I have seen the work of the Unification Church in Taiwan and Japan,' said The Voice. 'The Victory Over Communism Foundation. You know, in Japan, they have three million young people in their organization? Three million young people ready to recognize and denounce communist ideas when they see them. It's the only way to stop the Marxists in the universities.'

'But are there many communists in Honduras?'

'Ah,' The Spokesman paused to make sure I was paying attention. 'We are in the front line here. The revolutionaries say "Yesterday Nicaragua, today El Salvador, tomorrow Honduras." They say there can be no peace in the world until capitalism disappears. In my humble opinion, sir, this is the peace of the Gulag. Or the cemetery.'

On the wall, the president smiled down from behind his blue sash. The Spokesman rambled on through his Moonie-speech, with the single-minded conviction of the impotent. After half an hour he recollected himself. I got up to leave.

'Before you go,' he said, 'there is something you should read.' He scanned the desk, but didn't see what he was looking for. 'I will have the collected speeches of the president delivered to your hotel so you can read them in comfort.'

Pursued by the thoughts of the president, I decided to change hotels. I chose the Hotel Maya, an unimaginative concrete building in the embassy district. In the lobby American service-men mingled with American mercenaries, Nicaraguan counter-revolutionaries drank with their CIA paymasters and, in the basement, the Dale Carnegie Institute organized courses on how to win friends and influence people. In a country where the official voice of the government spoke as much on behalf of a sinister South Korean priest as he spoke for the president, the Hotel Maya was as authentically Honduran as anywhere.

The perplexing question about Honduras was one which had been relatively easy to answer elsewhere: who ran the country? The place was miserably impoverished: El Salvador had an oligarchy, but in Honduras even the rich were poor. The distinctions between the political parties were less significant than the differences inside them. Manifestoes, elections and political bluster were merely a ragged irrelevant folk-dance the country went through occasionally: president today, exile tomorrow, the underlying features changed hardly at all. The only organization which mattered was the army. It was certainly a path to riches.

A few months before I arrived, the head of the army, General Gustavo Alvarez, had been 'replaced'. After dinner with a gathering of right-wing businessmen, a group of junior officers had handed him a typed letter announcing his own resignation, clapped a pair of handcuffs on his wrists and put him on a plane heading out of the country. As one of them explained later, 'Other places, they would have put him in front of a firing squad. We prefer to send people into exile. We think it's more – how shall I put it? – sophisticated.'

The reasons for the general's unceremonious departure into exile were instructive. When he took over the armed forces he had been a colonel; soon he had promoted himself to five-star general. Like many of the senior officers in the army he had contrived to avoid the country's one recent experience of warfare, with El Salvador in 1969, by being abroad at the time. This in itself was no offence: fighting was the last thing a Honduran army officer expected to do. Nor was it even the suggestion of corruption: the opportunity to build up a tax-free cushion for their old age was the reason many of them had entered the service of their country in the first place. No, the general's offence was that he had lost his sense of proportion. The unwritten convention laid down that the officers shared the proceeds of their peccadillos. Adequately distributed, there was enough to provide everyone with an exceptionally comfortable lifestyle.

But the general was considered greedy. He had sat on the board of several firms. His own company had a monopoly on the import of dynamite, which meant a tidy commission on civil engineering projects. On a salary of less than thirty thousand dollars a year he somehow managed to run two homes worth half a million dollars each. Even money-making on this scale might have proved acceptable, had it not been for the fact that he had begun to ignore his fellow officers. The general was an autocrat. He had to go. And so, after a modicum of discussion, he was bundled on to the aircraft and sent to serve the remainder of his military career in a Miami condominium.

But while the army represented the traditional source of power in the country, the new element was the Americans. In a poverty-stricken backward nation, their influence was pervasive. Around the pool at the Hotel Maya they sat in little groups, towels wrapped around walkie-talkie radios, lean short-haired men of unmistakably military bearing talking about Beirut and Grenada and Korea. Flabbier men in civilian dress – mercenaries, arms dealers and others from the shadows of the war business – could be found at all hours in the bar, drinking and talking about the power of different types of firearm. They were sometimes still in the smelly little room which called itself a casino when it closed at three-thirty in the morning. Across the street outside the hotel, prostitutes patrolled the pavement, pausing to call out when one of the Americans appeared. And as soon as darkness fell, the taxi drivers would hiss, 'Something special? I know a nice place.' Downtown, the girls gathered in bars with names like The Crazy Horse, where they sat at plastic tables in mini-skirts, the beer was served in bottles smelling of dirty water and military police patrols came around every couple of hours. It struck me how much the whole scene – the hotel, the girls, the military police, even the mini-skirts – was reminiscent of images of Vietnam.

The comparison with Vietnam was one which the American Embassy did their best to avoid for obvious reasons. Yet the echoes were there. Even some of the personnel were identical. The American ambassador, John Negroponte, had been a rising political officer in Saigon, and dozens of other officials had similar experience. In applying the new domino theory, the experience of the banana companies and the importance of the army made Honduras the best place in which to establish a forward base.

But the American presence was almost certainly responsible for the fact that Honduras retained a notional civilian government: in public relations terms it was essential, even if the ambassador did act more like a proconsul than a diplomat. But I wondered whether in moving into Honduras, Washington might not be sowing the seeds of future revolution. The occasional wall daubing proclaimed YANKEE SOLDIERS = YANKEE IMPERIALISM. And in the newspaper that morning was an advertisement which recalled other Latin American nations in turmoil, placed by the relatives of one hundred and twelve people who had 'disappeared'. I wondered how closely the list followed the one drawn up by the army when a senior officer said that in order to ensure peace and stability it was necessary only to 'remove a couple of hundred people'.

The one blessing conferred by poverty upon the country was that it had been able to avoid the turbulence which had overtaken its neighbours: like everything else in Honduras, the revolution was underdeveloped. The Hondurans seemed to have an astonishingly low opinion of themselves. '*Somos Haraganes*,' a lottery ticket salesman had said with a smile and a shrug. 'We're good for nothings,' as if their past condemned them to an unalterably hopeless future. The country had slumbered in threadbare isolation for decades, with few illusions about its importance in the world. Doubtless, most of its citizens would have preferred to remain in obscurity, but there seemed little chance of their wishes being granted.

Near the sleepy fishing village of Trujillo on the Caribbean coast, tens of millions of dollars had been spent on developing a training centre at which Green Berets instructed Honduran and Salvadorean troops in the techniques of counter-insurgency. But because Americans were still sensitive about the commitment of their troops overseas, the fiction was maintained that there were scarcely any American soldiers in Honduras. Official figures showed that the permanent military presence in the country amounted to no more than a dozen personnel at the office of the military attaché and as a 'Military Assistance Group'. However, a constant series of exercises ensured that for the previous two years there had been thousands of American troops in Honduras. The exercises they conducted – amphibious assaults, parachute drops, rapid construction of new airstrips and bases, Special Forces 'behind enemy lines' raids – demonstrated that the sort of mission for which they were training was a direct military intervention.

A one-hour bus ride from the capital, in the middle of a plain encircled by steep green hills, I came to the main American military base in Honduras. A column of heavy bulldozers was passing through the gate and as the barrier went up, a little crowd of fifty men and women scattered to let them pass. A cloud of choking red dust settled over them. They were poor, ragged people, and I asked one man why they were there. 'We're looking for work. There's so much going on in there,' he pointed at the American base, 'there must be work for people like us. I'm not afraid of hard labour.' Inside two large concrete sewer pipes at the side of the entrance, a family was sleeping. A girl in a white dress and high, shiny shoes arrived and stood a little apart. A very dark woman with a shockingly blond child approached the black military policeman on the gate, asking to see the commander. The guard told her she couldn't and turned away to increase the volume on his radio. If the father of her child was an American serviceman, he had left long ago: by the simple expedient of sending personnel home every six months, the Pentagon was able to maintain it had no permanent presence in Honduras.

The camp was still under theoretical Honduran control and there were two Honduran military policemen on duty with the Americans. They both wore Ray Ban sunglasses and affected swaggers. The black policeman was teaching them English.

'Cocksucker,' said the American with a grin.

'Cohsock,' the Hondurans repeated, and grinned proudly.

'You're listening to Armed Forces Radio, Honduras,' a soft female voice announced, and one of the Hondurans smiled, touched his dark glasses and turned the volume up further. 'Mr Tambourine Man' began to jangle through the heat and dust.

Inside the gates, the earthmoving equipment was being used to extend the runway, to accommodate everything in the American inventory short of the Space Shuttle. In the centre of the camp, behind a barbed wire and sandbag entanglement, there was a cluster of radio antennae and satellite dishes. At the field hospital a medic said the commonest illness was homesickness and on the wall of the camp radio station someone had written, 'This *isn't* the end of the world, but you *can* see it from here.'

It wasn't a popular posting, stuck out in the middle of nowhere with only mosquitoes and diarrhoea for company, but the rows of wooden huts with their tin roofs testified to the increasing permanence of the base. A few months earlier, the troops had been living in tents. I asked about the function of the base.

'We're training, and planning for future exercises,' said the officer.

'But officially, what are you doing here?'

'The official function of the base is classified,' the officer said, ignoring the absurdity of the pretence.

As I left, a Chinook helicopter was putting down on a landing pad, its twin rotors throwing up a swirling cloud of red dust. The dark-skinned woman with the fair-haired child was still waiting at the gate. And the military policeman's radio had begun to play 'Get Off My Cloud'. It could so easily have been Vietnam twenty years ago.

By the time I got back to Tegucigalpa, it was dark and a soft rain was falling. I walked back to the Hotel Maya through the crowd of soliciting prostitutes. Two of them left the main group, sidling up and murmuring, 'Like some company? It's not so expensive.' I looked past them at the group of women standing in the shop doorway. One of them, a short, plump figure under an umbrella, seemed familiar.

'Maria?'

She turned around and I caught her eye. But she looked embarrassed and pulled the umbrella down across her face.

Of all the borders in this troubled area, the one between Nicaragua and Honduras was almost the only one where the frontier itself was the seat of fighting. The Hondurans allowed rebels trying to overthrow the Nicaraguan government to base themselves at camps along the border, whence they mounted attacks into Nicaragua. Since the rebels had been financed, trained and armed by the CIA, the Honduran government would probably have had little choice in the matter, had they wanted to resist. But the consequence was that much of the mountainous border was now the setting for a continuous series of ambushes in which untold numbers of people had already died.

Before continuing my journey across the border to Nicaragua, I arranged to meet one of the leaders of the 'Contras', as the counter-revolutionaries were called, in Tegucigalpa. To maintain the ridiculous pretence that the Contras were in the country illicitly, he arrived at our meeting place in a Toyota with darkened windows, then overthrottled the engine and we screeched off, leaving rubber on the quiet street. Another man – a bodyguard, I assumed – sat in the back seat. Curiously for a bodyguard, he was half the size of the man he was supposed to be protecting. As we careered around the streets, absurdly obvious in the only blacked-out car in town, he told me his name, Frank Arana, and explained that before the revolution in Nicaragua he had been a bank manager there. At a restaurant decked out like a film-set ranch, he got out of the car – a great blubbery man with a goatee beard and flushed, flaking skin. He was an odd sort of guerilla, but then, as he explained, he didn't do any of the killing himself; that was left to the professionals. Frank's job was to eat lunch with anyone who'd lend an ear.

Frank strode into the restaurant, clapped the proprietor on the shoulder and ordered beers. It did not occur to him that this was curious behaviour for a man, as he put it, 'living in a very clandestine way'. Every time a woman walked by on the street outside, his eyes would follow her and he'd drift off in obscene reverie. I brought him back to the present.

'Who are your enemies, Frank?'

'Fidel Castro, Colonel Gaddafi,' he rattled off, and added without pausing, 'and Tip O'Neill, he's a communist too.' Odd, I thought, that he did not mention the Sandinista government in Nicaragua. But soon I realized why. To Frank, the Contras were heroes of world democracy. We talked for a while about how the war was going, how many men they had inside Nicaragua, how it wasn't true that but for the CIA they'd fall apart, and how they'd be in Managua within the year. I'd been warned not to trust Frank and I began to understand why. But there were really only two questions I wanted to ask him: why they were fighting and why they kept killing civilians.

'What are you fighting to achieve?'

'To get rid of the Marxists in Nicaragua and to restore democracy.' Frank had been asked the question a thousand times before and the answer came out pat. But it had contained a critical admission, because the counter-revolutionaries had only been forged into a cohesive force by the CIA. The plan, which flew in the face both of declared policy and American law, had later been justified by the Reagan administration on the grounds that the rebels were fighting to intercept supplies of arms said to be going from Nicaragua to the guerillas in El Salvador. By Frank's own admission, it had been a bogus argument.

He ordered another beer, and we talked about this and that. Sir Alfred Sherman, Mrs Thatcher's confidant, was a personal friend – they had met when he visited Honduras. The Nicaraguan vice-president was a queer. And I shouldn't believe the Nicaraguan atrocity stories about the Contras. It gave me the opportunity to put my second question: why did they keep killing civilians?

'We are only attacking military targets,' he said, taking a swig of beer and draining the glass. 'If they militarize the country and put everyone in the army, then everything is a military target.' He smiled, smug as a child who had remembered his homework. 'Another beer?'

Frank was an effective public relations man. An hour in his company and you were incapable of associating his good humour and talk of 'democracy' with stories of wedding parties being machine-gunned by his comrades-in-arms. By the time he had driven off, I almost believed him.

The constant raids by the counter-revolutionaries had turned the border area into one of the most hazardous in Central America. The Contras would infiltrate into Nicaragua, attack a coffee plantation, a village or an army post, and slip back into Honduras. The Nicaraguans had, in consequence, turned the whole border area into a military zone and conscripted local people into militias. There were constant incidents along the frontier, where Nicaraguan soldiers would shoot into Honduras. On one occasion, they had fired a rocket-propelled grenade into a car carrying two American journalists along a border road and blown it and them apart. Another time they had shot down an American helicopter.

Although the Nicaraguans maintained that there would be no border problem but for the activities of the Americans and what they called their 'mercenary army', it was important to the American case that Nicaragua be seen as the cause of the violence. American diplomats in Honduras (who would only talk to visitors on condition that they remained anonymous 'observers') liked to cite the case of one invasion from Nicaragua into Honduras. The version I heard went like this:

A few score of Honduran revolutionaries, led by Jose Reyes Mata, a doctor who had once fought with Che Guevara, had slipped into the country the previous summer after receiving arms and training in Nicaragua. They were accompanied by a Catholic priest, Father James Carney, known as Padre Guadalupe, an American missionary who had spent most of his ministry among the very poor in Honduras. True to form, the Honduran government had expelled Padre Guadalupe from the country in 1979, on the grounds that his work with the poor was 'subversive', whereupon the priest had indeed become subversive and joined the revolutionaries. Each of the little column of insurgents carried two rifles, one for his own use, and one to be given to the person he would recruit, for they were to be the spearhead of the revolution in Honduras. Padre Guadalupe carried a Bible, a chalice and his robes – the accoutrements of a military chaplain. The insurrection was to begin in Olancho, a sprawling underdeveloped province of mountains and jungle, where the small population felt ignored and hard-done-by.

But the great empty topography of Olancho condemned the revolution to failure. As a site for an uprising, it was disastrously ill-judged. Within days of their entering the green wilderness, a handful of the revolutionaries deserted and were captured by a police patrol. Now the remoteness of the place, which might have been the guerillas' ally, became their executioner. Since there were so few roads, they used the river as a means of communication. Yet once the army had captured the deserters, they needed only to lay ambushes along its banks. Crisis became catastrophe when they discovered and dug up the guerillas' food dump. Faced with the possibility of starvation, the guerillas began to throw grenades into the river to catch fish, but in the vast uninhabited stillness of the mountains, the sound of the explosions echoed for miles, revealing their position to the army. It was only a question of time before the hungry rebels were tracked down and meanwhile, American psychological warfare experts had arranged for selected deserters to tape-record appeals to their former comrades, asking them to give themselves up; the messages would then be broadcast from aircraft flying low over the jungle.

The predictable result was that the insurgency failed before it had even begun. Of the two best-known figures in the group, the army announced that Padre Guadalupe had 'died of starvation' in the jungles, yet were unable to provide proof. And Jose Reyes Mata was said to have been 'killed in action', in a position from which the army had been unable to recover his body. Curiously, a photograph of his corpse appeared soon afterwards in a Honduran newspaper. The word among those who knew the country was that both the priest and the guerilla commander had been taken alive and died under torture or by summary execution.

The last of the gamblers were straggling out of the casino at three-thirty on the morning I left Honduras. The air was rank with stale cigarette smoke, and the girls had finally abandoned their beat outside the hotel. The night was wavering between darkness and dawn. As I walked down the hill from the hotel, I thought how untypical of the rest of the country was its island of decadence. I remembered Blake's comment:

> The whore and gambler by the State
> Licensed, build that Nation's fate.

In the little streets around the bus station dogs barked as I passed. A rat scuttled along the gutter. Within half an hour, the sky was beginning to lighten and – surprisingly for a capital city – dozens of cocks had begun to crow. In the space of one hundred yards I had walked into the backstreets of a little country town. I took a seat on the bus and glanced at the newspaper someone had left behind.

Millions were being spent in Olancho on roadbuilding and water supplies: presumably the hope was to buy off potential support for the next invasion. A 'war without quarter' had been declared on cantinas and brothels. A reader had written to the editor to praise, for no apparent reason, Tom Mix, Hopalong Cassidy and Ronald Reagan for the 'marvellous thrills of cowboy movies'.

This early in the day the police were too sleepy to leave their little huts at the roadside checkpoints and the conductor jumped down from the bus and ran through the darkness to hand them a copy of the passenger list. They never came aboard to check it, and anyway it soon bore little or no relation to those on board the bus. A misty light had broken over the mountains and we began picking up and depositing travellers with increasing frequency. They all came aboard with a friendly 'Buenas Dias' to the other dozy passengers, travelled a few miles to work, and alighted with similar courtesy. We crossed a plain which looked, unexpectedly, like a Scottish moor, and began to climb through the hills along the frontier. The road was now more like a winding country lane, although it still called itself the Inter-American Highway. We passed a group of children walking to school, faces flattened by the wind, and then deposited their teacher at a building in a field miles from anywhere.

Just outside San Marcos the bus stopped and almost all the passengers got up to leave. Only one woman remained sitting at the back. Three slightly better dressed men came aboard. I thought for a moment that they might be plain-clothes policemen, border guards or customs officials, but then they offered to sell Nicaraguan currency. The official rate of exchange for the Nicaraguan cordoba to the dollar was either ten or twenty-eight to one, depending upon the reason for which the currency was to be used in Nicaragua. The money-changers offered two hundred cordobas to one dollar. For a foreign visitor prepared to use the black market, Nicaragua would clearly be staggeringly cheap. But any Nicaraguan wanting to travel had to buy *dinero verde* (green money) at a rate ten times its official value: it was therefore impossible for most people to leave the country. I changed fifty dollars, wondering how long it would last.

The Honduran border-post, high in the hills, was the first crossing-point where there was not a single other traveller. A dozen soldiers stood around on the roadside, well-wrapped against the damp mountain air. Before the war, the bus would have continued south towards Managua. Now the company wasn't prepared to take the risk: the bus turned around slowly and went back into Honduras. I picked up my bag and walked over to customs.

The Honduran border official stamped my passport and waved me through without once looking up. Perhaps I should have found his indifference reassuring, but for some reason I was uneasy. Outside, I looked around for the Nicaraguan border-post, but could see nothing. I approached a soldier in a camouflage hat with two belts of machine-gun bullets crisscrossing his chest.

'Is it down the road here?'

The soldier laughed. 'Yes, five kilometres.'

'Five kilometres? Why so far?'

'Ha! You'll see. Those bastards have got some problems!' He said it matter-of-factly, a soldier's professional observation. He smirked. 'Have a nice walk.'

I slung my bag over my shoulder and started off down the road. It was a crisp morning and pleasant enough for a walk, if only it were not through a battlefield. I had taken only a couple of paces when I felt a touch on my arm. I had forgotten about the other passenger: she was short and fat, over-made-up and about forty-five I guessed, although it was hard to be sure.

'Please,' she said, still holding my arm with one hand, with the other palming a ball of paper into my hand. 'Take this through for me. It's dollars. Twenty-seven dollars.' She had the look of someone asking for change for the telephone, as if carrying money illegally into Nicaragua was a conventional civic obligation. 'It's all I have, but I'm Nicaraguan and if they find it they'll confiscate it. You take it through for me – you're a foreigner, they won't take it away from you.' She paused, sensing I was hesitant, then changed her tone and added plaintively, 'Please.'

I started to refuse, to say that I never took anything through any border for anyone, but I weakened. The expression on her face suggested that she had simply never doubted that I would help her. I shoved the money into my pocket and was about to ask if she wanted me to carry her bag across No Man's Land, but she interrupted me.

'I'll see you on the other side.' She patted my arm, and hurried back to the Honduran customs station.

5
Freedom, But No Toothpaste

The Nicaraguan border-post was a squat little building looking like a 1930s bus station. It had been built in the days of the Somoza dictatorship, when such symbols of national significance had mattered a great deal. Now there were bushes spreading across the forecourt, grass sprouting on the roof and the windows were smashed. After the revolution the Sandinistas had taken it over, but once the CIA funds had started pouring into the Contra bases in Honduras it had become too vulnerable. There was a mound of spent cartridge cases inside the shattered immigration hall, testament to some particularly fierce battle. Before abandoning the border station, someone had daubed revolutionary slogans across it in black capital letters: DEATH TO IMPERIALISM. DEATH TO THE SUPPORTERS OF SOMOZA. It looked forlorn, ridiculous, alone in the middle of nowhere.

I had walked a little further down the road when a group of teenagers in military clothing carrying Russian assault rifles stepped out in front of me. I was feeling exposed and alone, but whereas the Honduran soldiers had been hard-faced and truculent, these were scruffy, straggle-haired and friendly.

'*Buenas Dias*,' I said.

'*Buenas Dias*, comrade,' one of them replied. That word, comrade (*companero*), was the commonest form of greeting in Nicaragua.

Perhaps the Nicaraguans had given up the idea of a static border station altogether. I expected the boys to search my bags, or at least to check my passport. But to my surprise they clustered round in an inquisitive group and asked if I had any cigarettes.

I had a couple of packets of Marlboros which I had bought at the American PX in Honduras.

'Here, have one of these.'

'American cigarettes! Wonderful!' They helped themselves to two or three each. I wondered whether to tell them exactly where the wonderful cigarettes had come from, but decided against it. 'Go ahead, comrade. You'll find the new control post down the road.'

'Is there anything happening?' I asked, trying to sound vague and nonchalant.

'Nothing much today. But you never know with those bastards. Maybe something will happen later. But it's a nice morning – enjoy your walk.'

As the militiamen had said, it was a beautiful morning: crisp, though still slightly damp from the overnight mist, and utterly quiet but for the occasional bird-song. After a while it was impossible to reconcile the peaceful green hillsides with the war which had driven the Nicaraguan frontier several miles back into the country. Yet every day, all around here, there were skirmishes, sieges and surprise attacks. (The following day I heard that after I had passed through, the militia had encountered a Contra patrol and three of them had been killed in the shooting which followed.)

Down in a little valley ahead, I could see the new border-post: four weather-beaten wooden shacks at the side of the road, a couple with improvised oil-drum ovens baking tortillas, one selling soft drinks. The last of the four was the Nicaraguan customs office. More slogans: NICARAGUA IS THE HOPE OF CENTRAL AMERICA. YANKEE IMPERIALISM IS OUR ENEMY. Another youth in military uniform gave me a form to fill in – nationality, age, where coming from, where going to. The border officials, like almost every other official in Nicaragua, were approximately half the age of those I had met in the other countries. Partly, I guessed, it was a result of the fact that the older functionaries had fled or been replaced after the revolution in 1979; partly it was evidence of Nicaragua's birthrate: three-quarters of the country's population were said to be under thirty-five.

I had to fill in the same form three times because there was no carbon paper – a result of the shortage of dollars in the National Bank. It demanded an exact record of the currency I was carrying: I declared all I had, including the illicit twenty-seven dollars, but the customs official didn't bother with any-thing more than a very superficial flip through my money-belt and bag. I sat in the shade to await the arrival of the Nicaraguan woman.

An hour later she waddled into sight, sweating heavily, weighed down by two enormous hold-alls. When she reached the customs hut, she breathed out heavily and dropped her bags in the dust. She dabbed at her forehead and armpits with a paper tissue. I glanced at her but she pretended not to see me, anxiously repairing the damage in the mirror of her powder compact. Clearly I could not return her money to her here, yet equally, if I were to leave now, there was no guarantee we would meet again.

I strolled over to a truck standing on the other side of the road. Another uniformed youth – sixteen, he said he was – was poking around in the engine.

'Something wrong?'

'Not that I know of.' He glanced up long enough to see who he was talking to. I tried again.

'Do you need a hand?'

'You good at looking for things?' asked the boy.

'Not bad,' I said. 'What are we looking for?'

'Bombs.' The boy pulled his head out of the engine and grinned.

'How do I know what to look for?' I asked.

'Oh, it's very difficult, comrade. I've no idea what a bomb looks like. A rifle, or a grenade, those I understand, but a bomb? Just a bit of wire, a battery and some gelignite. In an old truck like this?' He pointed at the battered bonnet. 'It's imposs-ible. What can we do?' He shrugged and wiped his hand on his trousers. 'We had one come through here last week. I looked inside it, but I couldn't see anything. Then after it had gone through the checkpoint, it just blew up. What can you do?' And he stuck his head back into the engine.

I walked back to the customs hut, where the boy in the green uniform was systematically taking the woman's luggage to pieces. He took out two tubes of make-up and a lipstick.

'Where did you get these?' The demand implied some sort of ideological purity, as if possession of cosmetics might be enough in itself to make the woman an enemy of the revolution.

'I bought them a long time ago,' she said, lying awkwardly. I guessed that if she were not already so flushed, she would be blushing.

The guard pulled out a pair of white knickers, still in their cellophane wrapping, then two more, then one soiled pair, stained at the crutch.

'What are you going to do with these?' he asked, pointing at the three new packets.

'They're mine,' said the woman.

'No, these are yours,' said the young man, holding up the dirty pair. 'What are you going to do with the others?'

The woman was confused, although whether from embarrassment or because she really was a lingerie smuggler, I neither knew nor cared. The way border guards treat foreigners indicates nothing very much — except perhaps how keen they are to encourage tourism, or how desperate for hard currency — but you can tell a great deal from the way in which they treat their own citizens.

In the back of the hut the argument over the underwear continued, the woman maintaining it was for her own use, the youth disbelieving her. He noticed I was watching and turned towards me.

'Comrade. We checked you a long time ago. You can go.' It was an order.

I was reluctant to leave the customs post in case it meant losing contact with the woman. But now I was glad I had agreed to carry the money, if only to spite a system which demeaned people by pulling out and exhibiting their dirty underwear. I walked across to where a dilapidated Japanese minibus was waiting. Although there had been no other travellers crossing the border, the bus was already full with about twenty peasants and soldiers. Two militiamen sat on the roof and reached down for my bag. I stood outside, waiting for the woman to come across from the customs hut. Another five minutes went by. Suddenly the bus began to roll downhill. One of the soldiers shouted 'Come on!' I had to choose to lose either the woman whose money I was holding, or the bag containing my own clothes, camera and notebooks. I jumped on the bus just as it picked up enough speed to cough into life. I looked back at the border-post, but there was no sign of the woman.

I crammed in next to three soldiers holding well-worn AK47 rifles between their knees. The black paint had rubbed off the barrels and the magazine clips and the metal shone silver. The soldiers were tired and their eyes kept closing as we rattled along. When their heads jerked up, their eyes immediately darted around at the hillsides with a nervous scan, looking for signs of an ambush. The bus was stopping every few hundred yards to pick up more passengers – local farmers mainly – and somehow they all packed in. Every conceivable millimetre of space was occupied by human flesh contorted into some unlikely position. There would, I thought feebly, have been no possibility of escape if the bus had been attacked. Bumping against the green and brown shirts of the militiamen, I kept remembering the conversation I had had in Tegucigalpa. 'They have militarized the whole country,' Frank had said, 'so everything is a military target.' It was the sort of remark which was spoken and heard without much thought in a comfortable restaurant a hundred miles away.

I was ashamed of my nervousness when I thought that the people who were travelling on the bus had to live with the danger every day of their lives: I, after all, was only passing through once. They were poor, no poorer than I had seen in El Salvador or Honduras, but no richer either. The valley outside looked luxuriant and green and the cattle in the pastures well fed. But I noticed that the only new buildings in the fields were military bases.

Half an hour or so later, the bus stopped at Somoto, a dusty town in the hills. For a bus station there was a surprising absence of buses. I paid an old man one cordoba to unlock the padlock on the lavatory at the end of the verandah and discovered a porcelain bowl clogged with scraps of revolutionary newsprint screaming YANKEES PLAN INVASION OF NICARAGUA.

In the back of the waiting-room, the manager of the bus

station was asleep on a pile of sacks. When he opened his eyes, I asked about buses going south. He explained that there used to be an express service running late every morning, but he didn't think it would be coming today: there just weren't enough buses. No one could get the dollars to buy new ones and you couldn't get the spare parts to repair the old ones. However, there'd be a bus to Managua sometime that afternoon. I took out my map to think about an alternative route. It had been difficult to find a good map covering the whole region, but I had finally found the ideal document – covering the whole area from Belize to the Canal – at the US Government Printing Office in Washington. I spread it out on the counter and saw that buses going to Condega or Estelí would take me a reasonable part of the distance to Managua. I asked if any were expected.

'I shouldn't take one if I were you. There are no more buses from there to Managua and anyway, you're a foreigner, you need a permit to be in the north.' He was looking at me with an odd expression, either resentment or suspicion. I assumed he was annoyed that I had disturbed his sleep, then with a crumbling sense of foolishness I looked at the foot of the map in my hand: 'Prepared by Central Intelligence Agency, Copyright US Government', it said. I grinned, mumbled something about waiting to take the express to Managua, and stuffed the map back into my bag, cursing myself for not having removed its border before arriving in the one country in Central America where the CIA was waging a clandestine war. But as the day went on, I decided that the manager couldn't have noticed – he seemed irritated rather than suspicious. It wasn't easy trying to run a bus service without buses.

An hour or so later the bus returned from the border-post and disgorged another load of farmworkers and soldiers. Last out came the fat little woman. Three hours ago she had looked a solid, middle-class housewife. Now, as a consequence of the nervousness, the trudge across the border, the embarrassment at the customs post and, doubtless, the fear that I had run off with her money, she was a wreck. The last of the morning make-up had run in long rivulets down her face and her sky-blue blouse had turned navy in big patches below the armpits. She hauled her bags off the bus. I went to help her.

'I thought you'd gone with my money,' she hissed. 'I was so upset. It's all I've got.'

I passed her the dollars in a little ball, as inconspicuously as I could. Perhaps the border guards had been right to be suspicious of her. Perhaps she was guilty of attempting to smuggle luxuries into the country. But now, flustered, sweaty and relieved at getting back her twenty-seven dollars, she seemed pathetic.

'Look,' I said, 'I'm going to find a drink. Would you like something?'

She nodded, and we walked out of the little dustbowl where the buses were parked. There was nothing much in Somoto, as far as I could see – no bar, no café. I found a shop with a Pepsi sign outside and a stack of empty bottles against the wall, awaiting collection. A little woman came blinking into the light, obviously astonished to have a customer.

'Two Pepsis please.'

'We don't have any.'

'But there's a sign outside.'

'They're not delivering any more.'

'Do you have anything else to drink?'

'No.' The shopkeeper sighed with tired resignation and went back into the darkness.

'You see,' my companion muttered once we were outside, 'this country doesn't work any more.'

'What do you need the dollars for?' I asked her as we walked back up the empty street.

'You can buy anything with dollars here. My husband earns his living driving a pick-up, but he cannot get spare parts for it unless he has dollars. You see, the Sandinistas, they don't know anything about running a country, so everything is in short supply. Sometimes you can't even get milk for the baby. Imagine! No milk even!'

She tutted, absurd in her puffy smudged face and stained clothes. Many of the very rich had fled Nicaragua when the Sandinistas overthrew the Somoza dictatorship, but for small businessmen like her husband, escape had never been a possibility: even had they wanted to flee, countries like America or Costa Rica only found room for the wealthy. Doubtless, like most of the population, she and her husband had supported the uprising. Now, with her currency-smuggling and rumour-mongering, she was well on the way to being declared an Enemy Of The Revolution.

By the time we had walked back to the bus station, she was wheezing and perspiring again. I continued on up the street to try to buy something to eat. I found the town baker sitting reading a newspaper, his oven blackened by smoke, but cold and empty.

'Could I have some bread please?'

'I haven't got any.' There was no hostility in his tone — it was merely a statement of bald, indifferent fact.

'But this is a bakery.'

'There's no flour.' He looked back to his paper. The headline announced 'NEW CIA OFFENSIVE AGAINST NICARAGUA'.

'Why not?'

'Haven't you heard? It's rationed. I get an allowance to last me a month, but it's only enough for three weeks. So I only bake a little bread every day, just to keep going.'

'How long has it been rationed?'

'For a year or so now. It used to be that we exported food from Nicaragua. Now we can't even feed ourselves.'

'Who do you blame?' I asked.

'The Americans,' he said, without a moment's hesitation. 'They're making war on us. They won't give us any help. They even try to stop other countries helping us. Do you know what Somoza left in the National Bank when we finally got rid of him? Nothing. Just a lot of bills for his mistresses and a billion dollars of National Debt. This country's so poor. And what do the Americans do? Nothing. At least the Russians help us a little bit.' He paused, looked at his paper, then added, 'I used to be baking all day every day. Now I spend most of my time reading the paper.'

'Were things better before the revolution then?' I ventured. It was a mistake.

'At least we have our freedom,' he said firmly. It struck me later that those words might be said to be the cry of the Sandinistas: things are difficult, but at least we're free. I walked back to the bus station to tell the fat woman that I had failed to find anything to eat. I doubted that she would share the baker's assessment of either the reasons or justification for the shortages.

As I arrived she was wrestling her bag into the back of a taxi. Two other women were already sitting inside looking impatient.

'We're taking a taxi,' she said. 'I can't wait any longer.'

'There's no bread,' I told her.

'You see.' She scarcely looked up from her struggle. 'Nothing works any more.' She forced her fat backside between the bag and the back of the seat and slammed the door.

Three, four, then five more hours went by. By late afternoon, there were signs that the bus was imminent and the manager began to sell tickets. At the black market rate of exchange, the fare to Managua – half the length of the country – was the equivalent of eighteen cents. We had been arranged into an orderly line, but when the bus finally appeared, discipline broke. In a melee of elbows, knees and flying packages, we scrambled to get through the door. I was fortunate, being near the head of the line, and got a seat. Sixty bodies later, we embarked upon the journey.

By comparison with the Nicaraguan buses, the rehabilitated old school vehicles of Guatemala and El Salvador seemed the height of luxury. They had been painted up in lurid colours, with intricate whirling designs and plastic streamers hanging from the wing mirrors, and names like 'The Sunshine Express', 'Love Child' or 'The Sheikh's Girlfriend', and mottoes across the windscreen – 'God is my Guide', for example. There was always a cassette recorder with at least four speakers blasting out a muffled, distorted tape, or a badly-received radio station. But the Nicaraguan bus was unadorned dark green, with neither streamers nor music, and grated on every gear change. It seemed to reflect a mood of national seriousness.

From the look of the northern towns we passed through, there was every reason for a serious mood; nowhere was untouched by the war. In some of the villages the flags flew at half mast for local militiamen killed by the Contras, and everywhere the walls were plastered with slogans: FIFTY YEARS ON, SANDINO LIVES, above a silhouette stencil of a figure looking like Tom Mix, in broad-brimmed stetson and leather knee-boots. Beyond each village, the mountains and volcanoes rose from the cattle pastures and scattered homesteads.

At Estelí there was a line of forty people waiting to board the bus, although to all appearances it was packed to capacity already. The conductor jumped down and began to shove people inside. 'Hey, hombre, move up there! There's another twenty trying to get on! Come on, this is the only bus to Managua, bunch up inside!' Somehow we jammed in most of them and moved off at last, doors at front and back open, people hanging on by their fingertips, others perched on the roof. An old woman standing behind me prodded me with her elbow.

'Señor, you have a seat, can you take this please?' She lifted an old rice sack and swung it over my head. As it came across it smelt bad, but only when it landed on my lap did I realize it was moving. There was a sound of clucking and then the head of a chicken appeared through a hole.

'It's OK,' said the old woman, 'he can't get out. Just push his head back if he annoys you.' She laughed toothlessly.

I tried, but with one arm trapped behind the man sitting next to me, it was impossible. Five minutes later another head was sticking out of another hole, jerking around inquisitively. And then a third protruded. More clucking noises.

And so we travelled on towards Managua, now and again passing convoys of East European army trucks heading north to the war with the Contras. Occasionally, in defiance of the laws of volume, we would stop and collect even more passengers. The conductor, hanging by one hand from the wing mirror, shouted out, 'Going to see your family? Why bother? By the time we get there you'll know the other passengers better than your own father and mother!' If anyone coughed or sneezed or spat, everyone received the benefit. When we stopped, people would somehow disentangle themselves from the human concertina and leave the bus, but always there were new passengers, slinging the old white rice sacks which were their luggage up on to the roof, and managing to hang on from an open door or window. Then the sellers of tortillas, corn-heads, onions and beetroot would surge around the bus, and the occasional customer with one arm free might manage to buy something through the window in the thirty seconds before the vehicle lurched off again.

Darkness fell and an hour or so later – eighteen hours after leaving Tegucigalpa – we saw the lights of Managua across the edge of the lake.

The Inter-Continental Hotel, even though it was built of concrete and glass, had apparently been designed to resemble an Aztec temple, and since it was almost the only building of any height left standing in the city, it looked preposterous. Inside, everything about the place suggested it had seen better days, from the threadbare carpets to the scum floating on the surface of the swimming pool. The revolutionary government had hung an illuminated profile of one of the Sandinista heroes, Carlos Fonseca, down the front of the building, so when they could afford to switch on the lights his face gazed over the remnants of the city. Otherwise, nothing seemed to have been done to the place since the overthrow of Somoza: doubtless there were better things on which to spend what little hard currency was left in the country. It could take as much as an hour to order a sandwich in the restaurant, and at any time you were likely to find your room had been taken over by a visiting delegation of Libyan students whose main interests in life seemed to be exploring the effects of cane spirit on their bodies and their own effect on the bodies of the pretty Nicaraguan women assigned as their guides. Like the rest of the country, the hotel oscillated between neurotic seriousness and joyful shambles.

I bought a packet of cigarettes at the newsstand selling three-month-old copies of *Newsweek* in the hotel lobby and discovered that what I had taken to be a filter tip was merely a differently coloured piece of paper. There obviously weren't any supplies of whatever it was they needed for making filters. (Later I realized that I had made the wrong choice altogether –

the Cubans had taught Nicaragua how to make good cigars.) Each wax match I struck refused to light, until the head on the ninth one suddenly exploded, flew on to my shirt and burned a hole.

Managua was quite unlike any other city I had ever seen. Apart from the hotel and one government building, the centre of town was no more than a collection of one-storey shacks and ruins: it was like a Monopoly board on which one player had managed to erect two hotels, but no one else had built anything at all.

The appearance of the city was a perfect reflection of the intrinsic realities of the country. If it was a Monopoly board, for over forty years the Somoza family had been the only successful players in the country. By the time of the revolution in 1979, their interests included the national airline, national shipping line, vast plantations, the country's best hotel, television stations, newspapers, mills, refineries, breweries, distilleries, factories and construction companies. Theirs was one of the few dynasties of whom it could literally be said that they 'owned the country' – or at least, all its assets.

Managua's dereliction was the result of an act of God: soon after midnight on 23 December 1972 it had been shaken to the ground by an earthquake. At least ten thousand people were killed or injured and three hundred thousand made homeless, a perverse act of judgement which punished the exploited and left the Somoza dynasty unscathed.

Now it was a city without maps. The random nature of the rebuilding which had taken place after the earthquake made it hard to detect any logical planning and even Nicaraguans gave directions on the basis of a capital which no longer existed. In Honduras and El Salvador they had located places not by the number of the house or the junction at which they were sited but by their relation to landmarks – 'opposite the butcher's' or 'near the cinema'. In Managua they used buildings which were no longer to be seen as points of reference. 'Just above where the Panamanian Embassy used to be' or even, once, 'on the corner where the big black dog used to bark'.

There had been a group of Russians in the lobby of the hotel, waiting for a bus to take them off on a tour of the achievements of the revolution. There was always some tour or other in progress: if it wasn't visiting Eastern European trades unionists, it was well-meaning church organizations from America or itinerant ideologues from Western Europe. The tours often amounted to a conspiracy to see only those aspects of the revolution which would reflect favourably on the Sandinistas. On one occasion the visitors had been taken to see a group of reformed prostitutes who were now employed by the state filling sausages, an activity for which they were said to show a great natural facility. The problem for those who were not part of the official tours was that in order to travel independently, it was necessary to have authorization from the government.

So that morning I walked up the hill behind the hotel to a villa near the military hospital which served as the government press office. The Sandinista government recognized that the Western press was largely sympathetic to the revolution and did their best to help and guide visiting journalists.

Two Frenchmen were arguing with a large-eyed woman of about twenty-two sitting behind the reception desk. A collection of people in beards and sandals sat around the edge of the room, filling out forms.

'But this is ridiculous!' one of them shouted, the shorter, squatter of the two. He was wearing a waistcoat covered in pockets and buckles which he no doubt thought gave him the appearance of the ultimate French war photographer. Instead he looked like a bulging suitcase.

'We asked to see captured counter-revolutionaries!' The suitcase shrieked at the girl behind the desk.

'I know,' she said blandly, and turned the page of a dog-eared American fashion magazine.

'We have been waiting for two weeks to find something to do, and what do you do? Send us to interview Somoza's National Guardsmen who've been in gaol for the last five years.'

'But you said you wanted to see captured counter-revolutionaries,' said the girl, not comprehending his anger and apparently convinced she had done what he asked.

'Yes, but captured recently, not five years ago!'

'Oh,' she said, turning another page.

'Fucking hell,' the Frenchman muttered to his colleague, an epicene figure who clearly spoke neither Spanish nor English. 'These people are impossible.' He turned back to the girl.

'Look,' he said, making a theatrical attempt at self-control, 'we're in the news business. News. That means we're interested in what's happening now. Not what happened five years ago.' He paused, then articulated slowly and with histrionic superciliousness, 'Do . . . you . . . understand?'

'Tell her we're not waiting for permission for anything from now on,' said the other. 'This place is as bad as Russia.'

The two men flounced out. The remaining reporters sitting around the edge of the room looked up briefly, nodded agreement that the Frenchmen had behaved outrageously, and continued to fill out their forms.

They were a strange-looking group, unlike any collection of foreign correspondents I had come across anywhere else. A number of them looked as if they had come straight to Managua from a 1960s rock festival, all Indian cotton trousers with drawstrings on the ankles and hand-dyed T-shirts. They smelt of commitment and cheap lodgings.

It had occurred to me that I might try to make the next part of the journey by boat down the Atlantic coast of Nicaragua, thence up the San Juan river to Costa Rica and afterwards on towards Panama and the Canal.

'You need special permission to go to the Atlantic Coast,' the receptionist informed me, pulling out a form from her drawer. 'The whole of that side of the country is a "special region" and you need permission from the army. It'll take about a week to get an answer.'

I told her I didn't want to wait for a week and she offered me another couple of forms to complete, similar to the ones the others were filling in. They were solicitations for interviews with members of the government: apparently, any request to talk to anyone in any official capacity had to be made on one of these forms. The system, which had doubtless seemed reasonably sensible when first devised, had the disadvantage that it did not differentiate between the correspondent of the *New York Times* and the teacher on holiday who was planning to write an article for the *Skibereen Eagle* when he returned home. In consequence, the forms accumulated in dusty mounds all over the press centre. Little expecting anything to come of it, I filed a request to interview Father Miguel d'Escoto, the priest who served as foreign minister for the Sandinistas. The receptionist promised a response within 'a day or so'.

I walked slowly back to my room in the intense heat of the late morning. On a wall below the hotel someone had painted a mural depicting the history of Nicaragua. The early panels showed the Indian civilization, then came the Spanish conquistadores riding down defenceless women and children, a Grim Reaper swathed in the Stars and Stripes and a panel showing the beginnings of the Sandinista revolution. The final sections showed workers labouring to construct the new society. Appropriately, although whether by design or because they had run out of paint (both equally plausible), the mural was unfinished. I retreated to the cool of my room at the hotel to remind myself of the history of American involvement in Nicaragua.

In 1845, the editor of the *Democratic Review* had coined a phrase which soon became an article of faith for all patriotic Americans. It was, he wrote, 'our manifest destiny to overspread the continent allotted by God for the free development of our yearly multiplying millions'. He had been referring specifically to the debate over the decision to annex the state of Texas, but the phrase 'manifest destiny' soon came to be used to justify American expansion throughout the hemisphere, a signal of the innate superiority of the American Way. Among the small collection of books I was carrying – an anthology of poetry, an unread Trollope and *The Diary Of A Nobody* – was the autobiography of William Walker, an adventurer in whom Manifest Destiny had been made manifest.

It was a battered old volume I had found in a bookshop in Oregon, published in New York in 1860, and written entirely in the third person. Walker had dedicated it to his former comrades in arms, in the hope that 'we may soon meet again on the soil for which we have suffered more than the pangs of death – the reproaches of a people for whose welfare we stood ready to die.' The book was hard going but the story which emerged was that of a man who, although still in his twenties, recognized the fact that while America was vigorous and expanding, her neighbours to the south were weak and declining. There seemed no reason why the benefits of American democracy and freedom under the law should not be conferred upon these unimportant little states – by force of arms if necessary. Rejoicing in the epithet 'the grey-eyed man of destiny', in 1853 Walker set out from San Francisco to capture Lower California, a province of Mexico, where he planned to establish a utopian republic of which he would be president. The venture ended in humiliation eight months later when the remnants of his force, under constant debilitating attack by Mexican and American bandits, limped home across the border. Like all truly obsessed people he concluded from his experience simply that the circumstances had not been right.

In 1855, during one of Central America's innumerable civil wars, another opportunity arose when the Liberal army in Nicaragua appealed to American private enterprise for military support. A deal was negotiated whereby the Liberals would give land to American soldiers willing to fight for their cause and in June, Walker and an advance party of fifty-five men arrived in Nicaragua, lured by the promise of land grants should they turn the tide of the war. Within four months, Walker had captured Granada, the Conservative capital, and under the terms of the truce agreement he emerged as head of a unified army, a position he consolidated by arranging for his opponents to be executed by firing squad. In the best frontier tradition he then began to 'develop' the country, blazing trails through the jungle, reopening abandoned mines and importing American settlers with the promise of Nicaraguan land. Large factions of American public opinion supported Walker in his venture – after all, the policy enunciated by President James Monroe in 1823 had stated that the Europeans should stop meddling in the Americas – and it was the shortest of steps thereafter to conclude that if there was going to be meddling in the area anyway, it ought to be Americans who were involved. Walker finally failed in his venture, however: not because of Nicaraguan opposition to him, but because of developments with the United States.

In 1849 gold had been discovered in California and the Gold Rush began. Tens of thousands of desperate opportunists sold everything they had to start a new life prospecting on the West Coast. The single greatest problem for prospective forty-niners was reaching California in time to discover their own seams of gold before the supply was exhausted. Their greed to be on the West Coast first meant they would pay substantial amounts of money to anyone who could guarantee them a fast journey. The available choices were daunting – either to travel three thousand miles overland, through uncharted Indian territory, or to sail eight thousand miles around Cape Horn. But the hour produced the man: Cornelius Vanderbilt, the shipping and railroad millionaire, who immediately saw the potential profits of a quicker transit. He began to run steamers from New York to the Caribbean coast of Nicaragua and from there his passengers travelled in shallow-bottomed boats up the San Juan river and across Lake Nicaragua, the huge inland lake in the middle of the isthmus, which the Spanish had at first taken for the Pacific. From the western shore of the lake it was just a short stagecoach journey to the Pacific coast, where another Vanderbilt steamer collected the prospectors and took them on to San Francisco. The route quickly became immensely profitable.

William Walker's success was a potential disaster for Vanderbilt. Much of the money to pay for Walker's army had been raised by Vanderbilt's opponents, who were assiduously promoting an alternative route across Central America. When the war ended, Vanderbilt's business was confiscated, an action which was to ensure the formation of an insuperable alliance against Walker. But oblivious to the imminent danger he blathered on, issuing decrees, recruiting more American settlers and attempting to turn Nicaragua into an effective adjunct of the United States.

When he realized how attractive it could make the country to new settlers, Walker abandoned his opposition to slavery. By a series of decrees which his obsequious Spanish translator described as a combination of the best of Cicero and Doctor

Johnson, he legalized slavery, offered huge tracts of land to settlers and, irritated by his constant need for a translator, declared English the official language. There was talk he planned to seek Nicaragua's admission to the American Union as a slave state.

By now his plans had created enemies everywhere. The other Central American nations felt first outraged and then threatened by Walker's schemes, and Vanderbilt was sufficiently provoked to supply European officers for the force they raised to oppose him. Britain, the most powerful maritime nation in the world, provided guns and financial support for Walker's enemies, and then mounted a blockade to ensure that reinforcements could not get through to him.

In the war which followed, Walker's forces were insistently driven back, until finally they were offered the promise of a safe passage back to the United States in a government warship. Of Walker's original band of colonists, a mere two hundred men were left: the rest had deserted, died of tropical fevers or succumbed to their wounds. His second foray into Central America had lasted no more than two years.

Walker, who might have been expected to return home in humiliation, was received like a conquering hero. On arrival in New Orleans he was besieged in his hotel, mobbed in the street and then toured the country giving a series of passionate speeches in which he claimed he was the victim of an indecent alliance of enemies of the American Way. Yet his adventure had cost the lives of perhaps one thousand Americans, several thousand Latin Americans, ravaged the country and, as it turned out, put an end to the Nicaraguan transit route – by now there was a railway across Panama.

The end came soon after his autobiography was published. He tried once more to return to Nicaragua, but this time his force was intercepted by the American navy. Then a group of English-speaking residents of the Bay Islands, furious at a decision by the British colonial government to hand jurisdiction over to Honduras, approached Walker for help in declaring themselves an independent republic. He was unable to resist the opportunity, raised a rag-tag army and landed on the Honduran coast, where he was quickly captured by a detachment of British Marines. Walker might have thought that the British would offer him some form of protection, but instead they delivered him to the Honduran government. At eight in the morning on 12 September 1860, they marched him out to an old fortress and executed him by firing squad.

The bare facts of Walker's life, with the precedent they set for Nicaraguan neurosis about invasion, were more interesting than the autobiography itself, which was full of screeds of self-justification. I finished the book in a couple of hours, walked down to the unnecessarily dark bar and ordered a rum and Coca-Cola. They called it a 'Nica Libre', or 'Free Nicaragua', the way Cubans called the same drink a 'Cuba Libre'. It was a national drink – Nicaraguan spirit and American fizz – of which William Walker would have approved.

By late afternoon the sun had softened and a wind was gusting in off the grey surface of Lake Managua. It lifted the top layer of dust from the open spaces where the city had been before the earthquake and deposited it in a film over everything. On the scuffed patch of ground in front of the hotel, Sandinista soldiers in green and brown fatigues were batting a baseball around. Two teenage boys were sitting in the shade trying to puzzle out something in a schoolbook. There was hardly any traffic on the road, because petrol had been rationed for as many months as anyone could remember.

I walked downhill towards the centre of town. The cinema was showing *The White Desert*, a Russian film about heroic Soviet soldiers battling against the elements. It didn't seem the sort of film the average Nicaraguan would go to by choice – popular previous screenings at the cinema had included films like *Scum* and *The Transsexual*. I walked on towards the lakeside, past the remaining shells of one-time buildings: in many of them lines of washing hanging from twisted arms of reinforced concrete provided shabby testimony to the fact that families were still living among the ruins.

In the central square, on the edge of Lake Managua, the clock on the big grey cathedral showed the time at which the city had ceased to be. The roof had disappeared; the walls were cracked from top to bottom. On the twin turrets at the front of the building, one cross stood upright, one lay horizontal. Once the square had been the heart of the capital city. Now, three boys were playing a form of *boules* with old bottle-tops, but otherwise the place was utterly still.

I went into the cathedral and listened to the metal rafters clanging in the breeze. Grass was growing in the aisle. Someone had scratched a giant penis and vagina on one of the columns, and the sacristy floor was being used as a lavatory. Across where the main altar had been, an optimist had scratched in charcoal CHRIST IS COMING.

At the time of the earthquake, money to rebuild the city had poured in from around the world, notably from the American government. But the National Guard had stolen and then sold the food, blankets and generators, while much of the reconstruction work had been parcelled out to companies owned by the Somoza family, with the consequence that only a quarter of the results had been achieved for ten times the price – if the work had been done at all.

With his face like an overripe fruit and an aura of almost tangible seediness, Anastasio Somoza had seemed a parody of the archetypal Latin American dictator and, because a carica-ture, somehow less dangerous. Since he had spent much of his time inside his air-conditioned and custom-built bunker, he was able to wear the dark business suits and ties which his time in the United States had taught him were the antidote to accusations he was a 'spic'. Outside, in the tropical heat, the clothes would have been unbearable, but amid all the vulgar chrome and leather and mahogany in the bunker, he looked much like a suburban bank manager. And at rallies for what passed for elections, haranguing the barefoot crowds about 'freedom and prosperity' from a booth of bullet-proof glass, the illusion was complete. His appetite for liquor and sex was more gourmand than gourmet and the assignations with his mistress, Dinorah, a teenage telephone operator when he first seduced her, were such common knowledge in Managua that the dictator's wife eventually abandoned her humiliation and the country and went to live abroad.

The dynasty had been created in 1936 when Somoza's father, then commander of the National Guard, had seized the presidency from the elected incumbent. During parties at the palace his soldiers were dressed in togas, sandals and helmets, in imitation of the great days of the Roman empire. But however much he seemed a comic-opera dictator, the elder Somoza was a calculating, cynically shrewd individual who recognized that American presidents would guarantee his position as long as he could offer the one thing they valued above everything else in the area – 'stability'. This formed the basis for a thoughtless, ill-conceived alliance which in the end allowed a tinpot general to tie the hands of a superpower. Once or twice dissenting voices were raised, but most American policymakers were content to acquiesce in the judgement attributed to Roosevelt that 'He may be a son-of-a-bitch, but he's *our* son-of-a-bitch.'

Originally Somoza had seemed to offer the Americans an escape from an unwanted and squalid war which in some ways prefigured Vietnam. On the one side was the American government, several thousand marines sent by Coolidge to 'pacify' Nicaragua and the American-trained Nicaraguan National Guard under the command of Colonel Somoza. Against them was gathered a force of irregular guerillas led by Augusto Cesar Sandino, fighting, they proclaimed, for national independence.

In July 1927, five de Havilland biplanes staged one of the first dive-bombing raids in history – ten years before the Nazis destroyed Guernica during the Spanish Civil War. Plummeting down upon the town of Ocotal from a height of fifteen hundred feet, they released their bombs at three hundred feet and, as the plane pulled upwards away from the blast, the tail gunner mowed down any survivors. It was a radical and murderous new technique of warfare, to which Sandino responded by transforming his force into a proper guerilla army, constantly on the move, seeking shelter among the people, and always using the weapon of surprise. 'In Nicaragua,' it was said, 'the mouse eats the cat.' The fact that Sandino, the guerilla who loved books and music, could survive the assault of the Yankee war machine gave him the status of a romantic hero. Cecil B. De Mille even contemplated making a movie about him, until the State Department scotched the idea.

If a serious effort had been made to reach a settlement acceptable to Sandino, there would probably never have been a revolution in Nicaragua. Sandino was no Marxist, but since he insisted upon making the National Guard accountable to the people, he represented a threat to Somoza. When he went to Managua in February 1934 for a peace meeting, National Guardsmen surrounded his car and shot him dead. Somoza seized the opportunity to transform the country into his private fiefdom.

Walking around the centre of Managua it was hard to imagine what the city must have been like in the days of the family dictatorship. I walked up what had been known as Roosevelt Avenue, the main street in the city, now overgrown and empty, past the ruins of the Grand Hotel, where once white-coated waiters had served cold drinks to the bored and pampered wives of the cotton barons. There were plans now to turn it into an art gallery. A little further on was the skeleton of the department store which had boasted the only escalator in the city. Every tropical December, a white-bearded and red-robed Santa Claus had handed out presents to the children of the rich, while other children, who never went to school and rarely got enough to eat, played in the drains outside. The store had been owned by the father of two brothers who had become Jesuit priests, then joined the revolution and were now serving as government ministers. A tattered cotton curtain hung across the front entrance, an attempt at privacy. Two broken plastic chairs indicated that a family was living in the rubble of the rich man's dream palace.

Further up the street two teams were playing basketball in a park where once there had been shops and offices. A supporter of one of the teams, a black youth from the Atlantic coast, told me the park had been designed by the Minister of the Interior, Tomas Borge, a squat, pug-faced man who had been one of those to breathe new life into the ideals of Sandino during the days in the 1960s when it must have seemed that the revolution would never succeed.

'You know,' the boy said, 'he designed this place while he was being tortured. Somoza had him in prison for being revolutionary, and the National Guard used to beat him up every day. They say they cut off one of his balls.'

The boy was short, probably about fourteen. He was waiting for the opportunity to run on to the court and practise with the enormous players from the Puerto Cabezas team. He spoke in a mixture of Caribbean English and Spanish, picking the difficult words from whichever language came more easily to hand. The stories of torture came incongruously from his lips.

'He planned everything – the basketball courts, the trees, the floodlighting. It was a way of taking his mind off what they were doing to him. He was planning for what would happen after the revolution, you see, how Managua would be changed into a city not just for the rich but for everyone.'

The boy was too young to have understood much about what had happened under the dictatorship at the time it was happening. He had learned it at school or from conversations in the street. His attitudes were slightly unusual in that much of the Atlantic Coast, dominated as it was by English-speaking former slaves and Misquito, Suma and Rama Indians, was at best lukewarm about the Sandinista regime. Probably he had had the benefit of the national literacy campaign, whose textbooks began by teaching people how to write 'Revolution is action. The nation is in motion.'

'There's only one thing missing from the park. He wanted to build a swimming pool, too, but there isn't enough money.' Then the whistle blew for the end of the game, and he got up and ran excitedly on to the emptying court, grabbing the ball and throwing it through one of the hoops.

It was hard to understand how Somoza had managed to fool both himself and several American presidents that the Sandinista threat could be contained indefinitely. He had bled the country dry, and maintained his grip only by the tyranny of the National Guard, yet presidents like Nixon had supported him in almost everything he did. The dictator's friends had been a weird combination of the bad and the mad. Howard Hughes had been to stay, locking himself away in the suite of a Managua hotel. Nixon had appointed as ambassador a crony of Bebe Rebozo who spoke not a word of Spanish.

An eight-year-old boy walked by, bowed by an impossible pile of newspapers.

'*La Prensa*! *La Prensa*!' He bawled the name of the newspaper. A few streets away was the memorial the Sandinistas had erected to the previous editor of the paper, Pedro Joaquin Chamorro, the most prominent figure in the opposition to Somoza and a hero of the revolution. The monument was an uninspired concrete amphitheatre, but it commemorated an event which had precipitated the final, decisive stage of the struggle to overthrow the Somoza dictatorship. As editor of *La Prensa*, Chamorro once ran a feature previewing the elections with the headline CANDIDATES WHO WILL WIN TOMORROW'S ELECTIONS. The newspaper had campaigned against human rights abuses, given space to the activities of the opposition, and exposed a group of seedy Cuban exiles who ran a centre exporting the blood of Nicaraguan down-and-outs for sale to American drug companies. In January 1978 Chamorro was driving to work when he was shot in the face and chest by gunmen in a green pick-up truck. The extent of the riots against the National Guard which followed his murder, the fact that so many people from the poorer areas of town had the courage to take on the regime, gave the Sandinistas fresh cause for hope and marked the beginning of the end for Somoza.

I walked back down towards Lake Managua. At the water's edge, a gang of labourers was working on a massive mound overlooking a newly cleared square of grey dust and grit, surmounted by a row of flagpoles. It was called the Square of Heroes and Martyrs, I later discovered, and was situated near the spot where the National Guard had dumped the bodies of Somoza's torture victims. At the top of the tumulus was a grey concrete podium. I could imagine the Sandinista leadership in their austere olive uniforms, standing there to take the salute as the army marched past below, as if they were in Red Square.

WE ARE THE HOPE OF AMERICA, it said proudly on a giant billboard opposite the podium.

Opposite the lake, its pink paint faded, and two huge portraits of Sandinista heroes hanging from the central columns, was the National Palace, Nicaragua's imitation of European gentility, pseudo-Baroque and tatty at the same time. During the Somoza dictatorship it had been the seat of the Congress, where trusted political geldings had met for the formal debates which enabled the dictator to claim that his country was a democracy. On the occasions when Somoza had bothered to visit the place, sweeping through in a slipstream of obsequiousness, his guards had cleared a path before him, shouting '*Viene El Hombre*' – 'Here comes The Man'.

At lunchtime on 22 August 1978, a Tuesday, following the familiar announcement of the dictator's arrival, twenty-six soldiers jumped out of two army trucks. They pushed their way through the crowds of people waiting to pay their taxes, shouting 'Here Comes The Man'. The guards inside the palace, accustomed to the dictator's neurotic obsession with the danger of assassination, surrendered their weapons to the presidential guard. When the soldiers reached the Blue Room, as the Chamber of Deputies was called, they stormed in screaming, 'This is the Guard! Everyone on the floor.' The astonished politicians dived under their desks, believing a military coup was under way.

But the soldiers soon revealed their affiliation, stringing a huge red and black flag across the podium. They were the colours of the Sandinistas – red for struggle and black for death. They had captured more than a thousand hostages, including forty-nine deputies, and managed an operation so spectacular that it would ensure them headlines across the world.

Somoza's immediate reaction was to launch an attack on the palace, regardless of the possibility of several hundred casualties. A helicopter flew overhead strafing the building and soldiers, led by an American mercenary, attempted to storm the entrances. For a while, furious at his humiliation, he considered bombing the building flat, with the guerillas, deputies and over

one thousand civilians inside, but the attack was called off
when Somoza realized that the hostages included members of
his own family.

The guerillas demanded the immediate release of several
dozen political prisoners, a ransom of one million dollars, the
broadcasting of Sandinista propaganda on the government radio
station, and safe conduct out of the country. The archbishop,
Monsignor Obando y Bravo, offered to act as intermediary,
and two other bishops and the ambassadors of Costa Rica and
Panama also volunteered their services. Somoza haggled with
the guerillas over the amount of money to be paid, but after
forty-five hours conceded the rest of the demands. The Sandinista statement, all one hundred and five minutes of it, was
broadcast on the radio and published in the newspapers. The
political prisoners were to be delivered to the Sandinistas and
they would all leave the country together on planes supplied by
Panama and Venezuela.

The impact of the seizure of the National Palace astonished
even the guerillas who had carried it out. The publication of
their statement had been an achievement in itself, but the
enthusiasm with which it was greeted was considerably more
significant. The distance from the palace to the airport was
twelve kilometres, and all along the route people stood and
cheered as the convoy of Red Cross representatives, Sandinista
guerillas, the remaining hostages and the bishops passed by.
Hundreds of others ran to try and keep pace with the motorcade
flying the Sandinista flag. At the airport, thousands more
crushed through the terminal to cheer the Sandinistas, who
responded by striking defiant poses, brandishing their rifles
above their heads and promising to return.

The seizure of the National Palace had been carried out by
twenty-six guerillas, their average age only twenty. The three
leaders of Operation Pigsty had given themselves the *noms de
guerre* of Commander Zero, Commander One and Commander
Two. Commander Zero, the inventor of the plot, was a former
medical student of forty-two, a handsome, broad-faced man
whose real name was Eden Pastora. For him the revolutionary
war had been addictively satisfying and now he led a rag-tag

band of guerillas from Costa Rica to overthrow his erstwhile
comrades in the Sandinistas. Commander One became a junior
minister of defence, and Commander Two, a twenty-two-year-
old woman, a senior party official.

As the Sandinistas' final offensive closed in on the capital in
the summer of 1979, the dictator began to drink more heavily –
vodka mainly, neat, with ice. His public statements began to
bear less and less relation to reality: in towns in the north the
fighting was so intense that they were burning bodies in the
streets because there wasn't the time to bury them, yet Somoza
maintained the guerillas were retreating. He claimed the cordoba
was secure, then devalued by forty per cent. An American
reporter was murdered in cold blood by the National Guard;
Somoza said he had been shot by the guerillas. As the war
began to threaten the bunker, Somoza – dressed in the uniform
of an army general – became increasingly manic. Finally, when
the Sandinistas were on the edge of the capital, he ordered the
airforce to bomb the poorer parts of town where the guerillas
were believed to be sheltering. His last gift to his people was to
drop bombs on to those who had paid for them.

Inside the bunker, in one of his last acts as president, Somoza
signed an order entitling both his wife and his mistress to
military pensions for life. Then in an armour-plated limousine
he headed for the airport. At five in the morning he boarded the
plane which would carry him into exile.

Fourteen months later, on 17 September 1980, he left his
home in Asuncion, Paraguay, to travel to a meeting. He kissed
Dinorah goodbye and stepped into a white Mercedes. As the
car moved off, it was blown to pieces by a rocket grenade. His
mistress ran screaming towards the wreckage but they shielded
her from the sight of what was left of the body of the general.

Next morning it sounded as though the long-awaited American
invasion of Nicaragua had begun. For some time the nation had
been living in a permanent state of nervous tension, every
pronouncement from the government suggesting that at any
moment squadrons of US paratroopers might drop from the
skies above the capital. Periodically, after particularly bellicose

rumblings from the White House, the population was issued with rifles and set to work digging trenches. Now, something was finally happening. It was late morning, judging by the stilettoes of light coming through the curtains, and the first moments of consciousness were a confusion of unintelligible impressions – thudding explosions, shouting, the low rumble of great numbers of people on the move. I lay in bed and wondered for a moment whether the whole impression was a feverish fantasy. The sickness I had picked up in Guatemala had returned the previous evening and I had passed out as I walked across the hotel lobby. One of the porters had helped me to bed. Much of the night had been spent running for the bathroom. By about three o'clock in the morning, when there was nothing left in my stomach, I felt considerably better and had fallen into a deep sleep.

I opened the curtains: just the usual collection of jeeps and soldiers on the worn-out patch of ground outside the hotel and a lot of scraps of paper; but also, extraordinarily, three horses. It looked as if one of the tribes of Israel had passed in the night.

I showered and shaved and went downstairs. In the coffee shop the two Frenchmen from the press office looked up from their newspapers and gave condescending nods of recognition. The headline announced REAGAN SENDS MORE PLANES TO KILL IN EL SALVADOR. I wondered whether they had been sent to Nicaragua, too, considered asking the Frenchmen, but decided such a question might seem excessively ingenuous.

Outside the day was already oppressively hot, promising thunderstorms and torrential rain later. There was no sign of either American marines or panic-stricken refugees. There was no doubt, however, that large numbers of people had passed by. The road was strewn with chewed corn cobs, and plastic bags, and liberally spattered with dollops of black grease. In twenty minutes I caught up with the tail of the crowd, a gaggle of old ladies, street vendors and children, walking slowly, talking and laughing and sharing out their food. Clearly it was some sort of festival procession, and many of the men already had the vacant, dumb animal look that they acquired when the cheap alcohol took control. Many of the adults and most of the children had their faces smeared with black paint or grease.

Further into the crowd, two boys dipped their hands into plastic bags filled with black gunge and ran at me. They smeared my face and ran off to the fringes of the side of the road, laughing. It was axle-grease. A man walking alongside looked at me and grinned. 'Now you don't look so much of a gringo,' he said. His own face was covered in the black grease and his shirt was dirty beyond redemption.

'It is the day of Santo Domingo, the patron saint of Managua. Ha! You gringos think Managua doesn't have much, but we do have a patron saint, and we know how to enjoy ourselves!'

A group of children pushed past, their bodies painted with a red ochre, bands of feathers on their heads. They were supposed to represent the indigenous Indians of Nicaragua, but their appearance as 'red' Indians had been copied from the Westerns on television.

The procession moved slowly on, making for a church in the hills seven or eight miles from the centre of town which, since the destruction of the cathedral, had served as the bishop's church. Somewhere at the front of the procession, a school-teacher said, a boat containing an effigy of the saint was being carried on the shoulders of a dozen men.

The sky had filled with heavy low clouds by the time we reached the little road which led up to the church of Las Sierras. Around the bottom of the track, roadside stalls sold corn cobs and stringy strips of roasting meat. The smoke and the cooking smells floated over the crowd. Ice-cream vendors who had pushed their wooden trolleys all the way from the capital tinkled little bells. I realized now what had caused the sounds of explosion I had heard earlier: teenage boys were setting off home-made rockets wrapped in brown paper and attached to bamboo canes. They jostled among the crowd, lighting and letting off the fireworks wherever anyone gave them a cordoba.

It was then that I saw the first of the crawlers. She was a poor woman of about fifty. Her shirt was stuck to her back with sweat, her hair glazed in strands across her shiny forehead. She was making pitifully slow progress, supported by the hand of a friend under each armpit, almost delirious with pain and exhaustion. A daughter walked backwards in front of her, fanning her face with a shirt. Three half-naked men had formed a chain and laid pieces of rag and cardboard on the ground to protect her bleeding knees, throwing them over her head when she had passed, to be laid in front of her once more.

The closer we came to the church, the more tightly packed was the crowd on the road. Twenty or thirty times, the people parted a little to allow one of the crawlers through. Sometimes they were blindfolded. Some carried babies. All would have collapsed had they not been held up by loyal friends or relatives.

Sometimes the slow tide of humanity up to the church would separate to avoid stepping on a man collapsed in the street from exhaustion or drink. No one even attempted to move the bodies to the side of the road.

By the time we came in sight of the church, the crowd was several thousand strong and jammed solid around the little concrete building. The effigy of Santo Domingo had already been accepted by the bishop and taken back into the church, and the black-faced pilgrims were forcing their way through the doors and up to the altar to give their offerings to the saint.

The afternoon was charged with the imminence of the thunderstorm, and inside the church there was scarcely air left to breathe. An aisle had been left free in the middle of the melee of pilgrims to allow those on their knees to crawl to the altar. Five nuns stood behind the altar-rail, saying Hail Marys in repetitive unison through a tinny loudspeaker. A sacristan threw white lilies into the crowd. The image of Santo Domingo himself, I noticed, was no more than six inches high, contained in a glass case beyond the reach of the overenthusiastic.

Slowly the crawlers made their painful way to the altar. Each was awash in his own sweat, and the dust and blood and axle-grease had turned to mud and given them a primordial appearance. Now they pulled out the offerings they had brought for the saint in gratitude or hope: coins, cheap medallions or necklaces, nothing worth more than a few cordobas. As they moved through the noise and prayers and heat towards the little effigy of Santo Domingo they wept with emotion, pain and gratitude. In a harsh unremitting world, they had made a deal with their saint, inflicted additional suffering upon themselves. And survived.

In the latter stages of the revolution, the Roman Catholic church had been in virtual alliance with the Sandinistas. Much of the clergy had reached the conclusion I had heard in El Salvador, that the proper role of the church was to support the poor. Priests had given shelter to Sandinista guerillas during the civil war, acted as intermediaries with the Somoza government and served in the rebel political organizations. But now, although many of them still supported the popular church and the revolution – and four even held senior government office – the hierarchy was abominated by the Sandinista government.

Archbishop Obando y Bravo, with his humble background and heavy peasant features, had become a figurehead for those who were dissatisfied at the course the revolution was taking. And there were plenty of reasons for frustration. A combination of inexperience, persistent pressure from the Americans, the war with the Contras and a shortage of hard currency meant that even basic foodstuffs were rationed. Rice, beans, cooking oil, sugar, milk, soap and toilet paper could only be obtained at the official price on presentation of a ration card, which in turn was only obtainable from the local Sandinista Defence Committee, a method of ensuring that only those prepared to pay court to the party would be able to eat. The remnants of the business class, like the woman I had met at the border, were in a state of perpetual ferment as they faced shortage after shortage. One month it might be toothpaste: very well then, toothpaste was a bourgeois luxury, and the ideologically pure cleaned their teeth with salt. But the following month it would be something else – none of the complaints amounted to anything approaching popular opposition to the government, but there was always cause for some grumble or other. The leadership of the church had become the focus for the discontent.

When the government introduced universal conscription, the

archbishop lambasted them, and when his criticisms were transmitted on the Catholic radio station, the government censored
the broadcasts. The Sandinistas began to call the church leadership counter-revolutionaries, and when the church suggested a
dialogue with the Contras, they were censored again.

Occasionally the hostility between the church hierarchy and
the government took violent or theatrical forms. The spokesman
for the archdiocese was caught by an irate husband one day
paying a 'pastoral visit' at the home of a female parishioner, and
thrown almost naked into the street. Government photographers
happened, conveniently, to be on hand to take pictures of his
embarrassment. When the Pope visited Managua to call for
unity within the church, Sandinista youths shouted down much
of the service. Most recently, the government had released
secretly recorded videotape showing a priest handling weapons
and explosives apparently smuggled in by the Contras. Ten
foreign missionaries in Nicaragua had demonstrated against
what they called an entrapment operation and were all expelled
from the country so quickly that one of them did not even have
time to collect his false teeth before being put aboard a plane
for Costa Rica.

On Sunday mornings the archbishop's church at Las Sierras
was packed. To the accompaniment of guitar, triangle and
tambourine, the congregation sang about redemption. When
the big, heavy-jowled archbishop Obando y Bravo came down
the aisle, they began a surging chant, 'O . . . ban . . . do, O . . .
ban . . . do'. Privately they called him 'the black mule', although
with his heavy jowls and broad shoulders he really looked more
like a bull, or a great ox who drew a cartload of the people's
frustrations behind him.

The government dismissed the archbishop as the mouthpiece
of the rich, but the people who made the pilgrimage to his
church that day were the poor. As they lay on the church steps
with their knees a mass of dirt and blood, and their shirts stuck
to their backs, I realized it would take more than a change of
political regime to shake their cruel, primitive faith.

Outside boys were lighting more home-made rockets which
exploded with a dull blast in the air above the crowd and then

fell back hot and spent on to the people below. A little way up the track they had improvised dance halls where, for one cordoba, men swayed on the dirt floor to scratched records, one hand holding their partner, the other clutching a bottle of beer. The dust hung in a cloud around their legs and usually the women seemed to be supporting them. Under one of the canvases, a farmer was sitting round-shouldered, grinning drunk, on the back of a cow, occasionally prodding at the animal's legs with a stick to make it dance. A drunk lay collapsed in the ditch outside the tent.

There was a makeshift bull-ring at the top of the hill, made of what looked like old railway sleepers. The gallery was full and so, for half a cordoba, or a quarter of a cent, I pushed into the tunnel beneath the stand where the beer and the sweat from the spectators above dripped down on to those of us in the steamy darkness below. Between the slats, if you pushed the ankles of those above out of the way, you could watch the volunteers from the audience try their luck with the bulls.

They had tied a big white bull to a stake in the middle of the arena. Two men pulled on the rope attached to its halter so that the animal's head banged against the pole. Two others jerked on its tail. The bull was exhaling hot angry plumes from its nostrils and pawing the ground. There was a girth around its waist and a little saddle with a single handle on its back.

Several men – boys, more accurately – had already tried to ride the bull when an older man jumped down into the arena. He wore a white sombrero, and his body had the wizened leanness of someone who has worked hard and eaten indifferently all his life. As he levered himself on to the back of the bull, a sousaphone and a drum struck up a fanfare from a pile of empty beer crates in the far corner of the ring. At the same time the two men holding the head of the bull tugged at the rope and drove its nose hard into the stake, the two men at the rear jerked on its tail and another kicked the beast deep in its stomach. Then simultaneously they slipped the halter, loosed the tail and ran for the edge of the arena. The enraged bull careered around the ring, the wiry little man in the sombrero clinging to the saddle. The audience cheered and then just as the animal seemed to calm down, boys began jumping down into the ring and running at the bull to provoke it. The animal would paw the ground for a few seconds and then it charged them, kicking up clouds of red dust as it went. The boys leapt for the safety of the sidewalls, moments before the bull slammed into them with a solid thud. The sousaphone continued its epileptic blast.

Amazingly, the little man stayed on the back of the bull. The audience began to rain down empty beer bottles, sticks and stones, but soon the animal seemed tired and resigned. Its fury had been induced by the torments of those who had tethered it; free of the stake, it was docile and passive. Sensing the safety of its exhaustion, one of the tormentors jumped down from the gallery, ran up to the bull with a heavy stick and swung at the animal's face. He missed by a fraction but the momentum of the blow carried him onwards. As he overbalanced, the boy put out a leg to steady himself. The bull dropped its head and, lifting it up again, caught the boy on his side. The boy bent himself with unnatural flexibility and fell back to earth. The bull pawed the ground and butted the unconscious body. Still the crowd cheered and the sousaphone belched on. Other youths ran into the ring not to help the injured boy but to taunt the bull again, as if it had suddenly demonstrated the game was worth the effort.

For another few minutes the boys tormented the bull, with the thin man still on its back. The crumpled body lay in the dust in the middle of the arena, but no one attempted to remove it. No one tried to stop the game, either, and periodically the broken shirtless body would shake from a kick of the bull or one of the boys. The crowd continued to cheer, and still the perspiration of those above dripped down into the fetid tunnel below.

Eventually the tough little rider slipped down from the bull, threw his sombrero into the air and sprinted for the edge of the ring. The bull stood panting and pawing the ground until three men roped him to the stake and pulled his legs from beneath him. Only then, as an inconvenient afterthought, did someone jump down into the ring and drag the boy's body by its feet towards the gate. A couple of his friends slapped at his face to try and bring him round. His colour was distinctly grey.

I pushed my way out of the tunnel and into the crowd outside as the rain began. Within minutes it had turned the dirt and chewed corn cobs into a glutinous mud mousse. I walked down the hill and hitched a ride back into town from a passing pick-up truck. The driver, a middle-aged man in an American sports shirt, looked at the black grease on my face and smiled.

'You're enjoying Santo Domingo, then?'

'More or less.'

'American?'

'English actually.'

'I thought you might be a gringo. You know what they call them? "The enemies of humanity".'

I wasn't sure whether he was being serious or not, and my expression must have revealed my uncertainty.

'Really. It's in the Sandinista anthem.' And he started to sing part of the party's catchy song in a strong baritone.

> The children of Sandino
> Won't be bought, nor surrender.
> We struggle 'gainst the Yankees,
> The enemies of humanity.

He laughed. 'The enemies of humanity! Where are you going?'

'Back to my hotel room to clean this stuff off and change my clothes.'

'Perfect. I'll show you a real party. It used to be that we – I mean the rich – rode in the procession for Santo Domingo. What horses! Beautiful pure-bred Spanish stallions!' I remembered the horses I had seen from my bedroom window. 'This is the first year we haven't taken part. A few people were going to ride from the football stadium to the centre of town, but no one was very enthusiastic about the idea. Didn't seem any point.'

'Why not?'

'Maybe you should ask some of the people at the party,' he said. 'I think you'll find that people like me don't think there's much of a place for us here any more.'

We arrived at the hotel and he gave me his name, saying all I had to do was to tell the doorman that I was his guest. I could tell from the noise of the band that the party was already in full swing behind the high walls by the swimming pool. I went to my room, took a shower, lay on the bed for a moment and fell asleep.

When I awoke again it was dusk. From the balcony at the end of the corridor I could look down on the party at the pool, where one hundred or so remnants of the middle class were dancing to a brass band in the rain. Embattled and withdrawn into themselves behind the high walls, they were an incongruous sight in a revolutionary state.

'A few years ago,' said a female voice at my shoulder, 'I would have known everyone down there.'

She was tall for a Nicaraguan — but then so were most of the middle class — with hair like polished mahogany and big dark eyes. There was no regret in her voice.

'You know, I only recognize three people there now.'

'What's happened to the rest?'

'Oh, gone to Miami, New Orleans, Costa Rica, Venezuela. Anywhere they could get their money out.'

Her name was Alicia.

'I'm going to the party,' I said. 'Would you like to come?'

'All right.'

We walked down the entrance to the pool, past the newsstand in the lobby of the hotel. I gave the doorman the name of the man who had picked me up on the road into town. I noticed that the music had stopped.

'You can't come in.'

'But I have an invitation.'

'It doesn't matter, the party is over.'

'But it goes on until midnight.'

'Not any more,' said the guard, shifting to stand four square in front of the entrance and grabbing the sides of the doorframe with each hand. 'There's been a fight. People got thrown in the swimming pool. The party's over.'

There was no point in arguing with him and we turned to

walk away, past two Sandinista soldiers lounging against the outside wall of the swimming pool.

'He's right, you know,' said Alicia, 'the party's over. For all of them.'

REAGAN GOES MAD! was the headline in the newspaper. 'What can one say', the article began, 'when the keeper of a lunatic asylum begins to go off his head himself?' It was the day after the president had taken to the radio to announce that he had outlawed the Soviet Union, and 'the bombing begins in five minutes'. Even if it had been a joke, as the paper had the grace to admit later, the spectacular ineptness of the remark sent shudders through a nation already besieged by a clandestine army created and financed by Washington. Reading other front-page reports of the latest Contra atrocities, which included decapitation, sexual mutilation and torture, I understood why Nicaragua seemed to be in the grip of a collective neurosis, part improbable convenience and part horrific fact.

At the international press centre there was the usual scene: the same scattering of beards, shoulderbags and sandals around the edge of the room, the same mounds of forms, slightly higher than the day before. And the same word from Paola – no word about any of my requests. The combination of muddle and East European bureaucracy was paralysing. Dealing with it was like trying to swim in treacle.

I started again to explain my plan to travel to the Atlantic coast, then down to the port at San Juan and on up the river which Vanderbilt's steamers had used. Paola giggled, seemed unsure about where exactly I meant and said that anyway there was nothing she could do about it, but perhaps permission would come through from the military sometime in the next week, if I was lucky. In the meantime, what about a visit to a collective farm? I thanked her and declined the offer.

The urge to travel on south along the Atlantic coast, which had begun as curiosity, grew stronger the longer the journey was delayed. My interest in the coastal area had been sparked by an old leatherbound book I had come across in a secondhand bookshop while on a walking holiday in Wales. Published in

1869, *Dottings On The Roadside In Panama, Nicaragua and Mosquitia* was an account of the Central American ramblings of Captain Bedford Pim, RN.

Not much had seemed to please the fastidious old naval engineer as he made his way grumpily across the isthmus. Managua had 'absolutely nothing we associate with the idea of a capital of a country – no public libraries, museums, theatres, places of amusement, etc'. Leon was 'extremely dull', and the Nicaraguans themselves were lazy, troublesome and filthy. There was, he claimed, no such thing as a bed anywhere in the country. 'Even the best families use no linen sheets. The upper classes lie down with most of their clothes on: and in the morning, get up, shake, but do not wash themselves, light a cigarette and drink a cup of coffee . . . All classes are dreadfully afraid of water, and whenever they see a European wash himself, especially early in the morning, they never fail to tell him of the danger which he is running . . . With very few exceptions their houses are very filthy and full of vermin . . . I strongly advise future travellers to provide themselves with a tent, and thus escape the necessity of seeking any shelter but their own.'

At a gold mine in the north of the country the appalled officer had come across 'some who practise the revolting habit of earth eating', in which for days on end they sustained themselves by licking the ground like cattle. Pim described the soil as having a slightly soapy taste and the colour of cream. The earth-eaters were thin, emaciated creatures, he found, easily recognizable by their livid, sickly colour. Taken habitually, he said, the earth killed its victims without mercy.

Finally Pim arrived on the Atlantic shore of Nicaragua, known variously as Mosquitia, Misquito, or the Mosquito Coast. Landing from a small boat on the jungle-covered shore, he was met by the King of the Mosquitoes. Having been travelling through the uncivilized wilderness of Spanish America for months, he was suddenly confronted with a man whose cultural aspirations were utterly different. Waiting to greet him at the end of a stone and coral jetty paved with cockle-shells, the king was about five feet seven inches tall and swarthy, with pure Indian features. He wore a felt hat and a jacket, waistcoat and trousers, all in white. His name, he announced in perfect, unaccented English, was King George Augustus Frederick. 'He said', wrote Pim, 'that he felt more like an Englishman than anything else, and in fact considered English his proper language.' He went on to recite passages from Shakespeare, Byron and Sir Walter Scott.

The thought of an Indian king quoting flawless Byron in this remote, inaccessible corner of Latin America intrigued me, and when I had finished Pim's description of his journeys, I set out to discover more about the Kingdom of Mosquitia. In A.O. Esquemeling's *The Buccaneers of America*, published in 1684, I found an account of the early relations between the Indians on the coast and the French, British and Dutch pirates who had sheltered in the Caribbean waiting to attack the Spanish treasure ships returning to Spain. The pirates found the Indians friendly and receptive allies.

. . . everyone has the liberty to buy for himself an Indian woman, at the price of a knife, or any old axe, wood-bill or hatchet. By this contract the woman is obliged to remain in the custody of the pirate all the time he stayeth there. She serves him in the meanwhile, and brings him victuals of all sorts that the country affords. The pirate moreover has the liberty to go where he pleases, either to hunt, or fish, or about any divertissements of his pleasure . . . Through the frequent converse and familiarity these Indians have with the pirates they sometimes go to sea with them, and remain among them for whole years without returning home. Whence it comes that many of them can speak English and French, and some of the pirates their Indian language.

As the freebooting of the buccaneers gave way to organized colonization, the friendly relationship with the Indians became more important and more formal. Since the Mosquito shore was cut off from the rest of the isthmus by impenetrable jungle, it was natural that it would fall under the influence of whoever dominated the Caribbean. And while the British nursed few ambitions to expand through the Spanish-dominated Central American isthmus, control of the Caribbean coastline would offer a measure of security for their valuable possessions in the West Indies. They chose to exercise influence through a monarchy: they selected one of the Indian chiefs and took him to the colony of Jamaica, where the governor arranged for him to be dressed in European clothes and designated him 'King of the Mosquitoes'. A coronation was arranged but shortly before the ceremony, the king disappeared and was later discovered hiding in the branches of a tree. When finally coaxed down, he was 'crowned' with a cocked hat.

The children of the Mosquito kings, all given English names like Charles, Frederick and Jeremy, were taken to Jamaica or England to be educated. Their subsequent coronations were conducted with all the pomp the colonial administration could muster, at the colonial church in Belize, when they received imposing titles and paste jewels from British clergymen acting on the instructions of the British government, while along the coast real power was exercised by a superintendent appointed from London. However, after the War of Jenkins' Ear the Mosquito Coast became a 'voluntary protectorate' from which the British could be asked to leave at any time, though it was unlikely that any king would ever choose to spurn the hand that had crowned him.

The kings of Mosquitia were a piquant collection. Many seem to have succumbed to the effects of drink and died prematurely; King George Frederick was even strangled by his own wife, who threw his body into the sea.

The British, for their part, did their best to maintain the pretence that the Mosquito Kingdom had as real a monarchy as the United Kingdom. In Dunn's *Guatemala*, published in 1828, I came across a description of the coronation of King Robert of Mosquitia written by a disapproving American. The king was delivered to Belize in a British warship and arrived at the church for his coronation on horseback, accompanied by two British colonial officials. His chiefs followed on foot in pairs, wearing cast-off scarlet jackets and surplus pairs of seamen's trousers.

His majesty seemed chiefly occupied in admiring his finery, and, after the anointing, expressed his gratification by repeatedly thrusting his hands through his thick bushy hair and applying fingers to his nose, in this expressive manner indicating his delight at this part of the service.

Before, however, the chiefs could swear allegiance to their Monarch, it was necessary they should profess Christianity and, accordingly, (with shame be it recorded), they were baptized 'in the name of the Father, Son and Holy Ghost'. They displayed the most total ignorance of the meaning of the ceremony, and when asked to give their names, took the titles of Lord Rodney, Lord Nelson, or some other celebrated officer, and seemed grievously disappointed when told they could only be baptized by simple Christian names.

After this solemn mockery had been concluded, the whole assembly adjourned to a large schoolroom to eat the coronation dinner, where the usual healths were drunk, and these poor creatures became all intoxicated with rum. A suitable conclusion to a farce as blasphemous and wicked as ever disgraced a Christian country.

The tinsel pageantry of the coronation ceremony aside, the Mosquito kingdom itself was a miserable place, consisting of a few wooden shacks and several hundred miles of jungle-covered coastline. Originally it had mattered to the British because it bordered the Spanish Main, then, as the power of Madrid declined and the British Empire strengthened, no one else had the means to mount an effective challenge to the British presence. Indeed, although the coast played little part in the imperial plan, the British were far and away the most important power throughout the region during most of the nineteenth century. It was British sea power which controlled the lanes of commerce through the Caribbean, British diplomats who forged and severed alliances between supposedly independent states, British banks which underwrote the budgets of local governments, British investors who financed their railways and British merchants who controlled the market for their coffee, indigo and cochineal.

Understandably, British confidence was boundless. The government representative for much of the time, Frederick Chatfield — a squat little man of remarkable ugliness — meddled wherever and whenever he chose in the promotion of Pax Britannica or, more precisely, Industria Britannica. Chatfield, puffy-eyed, bald but for two mutton-chop sideburns, and with pustules exploding across his cheeks, was the single most significant figure in the area. Central America can hardly have been a sought-after posting, but he applied himself rigorously to the making and unmaking of alliances as if the entire future of the Empire hung upon it. Ephraim Squier, his American counterpart, remarked, 'The whole history of British relations and diplomacy here has been characterized by an effrontery and unscrupulousness almost incredible and absolutely unprecedented.' But the spotty Chatfield had a confidence born of the power of the Empire. If, as happened in Honduras in the 1870s, a government threatened to default on a debt, British warships simply opened fire.

In the scanty archives at the Public Record Office dealing with Mosquitia and Central America, two entire volumes of correspondence are devoted to the problem of how the dignity of the British government was to be restored after an incident in May 1874. The vice-consul in the Guatemalan port of San José had made an apparently routine call upon the local commandant of the docks and found, to his astonishment, that the consul had been grabbed by soldiers, tied up, and then personally lashed by the officer two hundred and ten times. When the unfortunate vice-consul escaped and reported the incident to his superior, urgent despatches began to pass between London and the local legation. 'An almost unpardonable assault has been committed against the honour and dignity of His Majesty's Government,' it was said. The commandant responsible ('a drunken thieving rascal who belongs to a class that does not exist outside Spanish America', as the representative explained) had to be punished. Indeed, when they came to consider the case fully in London, only an 'ample apology' from the government would be adequate. The Guatemalans were to be made to salute the British flag and pay the thrashed consul £10,000 compensation.

Honour might have been satisfied had the matter not descended into farce when the aggrieved diplomat decided to abandon his claim for the £10,000 damages. With enormous speed he was transformed by the British government from an injured, insulted envoy of the Crown into a feckless oaf 'not of the class needed as consul in these countries', and fired. The British government insisted upon the reparation being made nonetheless, and finally the Guatemalans paid up. The last element of burlesque came after it had been agreed that the ceremony to honour the British flag should take the form of an artillery salute. When it was discovered that there were no guns in San José, the two governments agreed that a battery would be dragged all the way to the coast in order that the ceremony might be completed.

It was, of course, only a question of time before the high-handed British domination of the area was first questioned and then supplanted as a result of the aggressive expansion of the United States. It began in Mosquitia where American diplomats adopted, if anything, an even more condescending attitude towards the indigenous peoples. Ephraim Squier was particularly angry at the pretensions of Mosquito Coast 'sambos' towards the status of a protected kingdom, because he felt they simply did not deserve it. Clayton, the American Secretary of State, put it even more starkly: the United States did not accept that Mosquitia was a kingdom because to do so would be to recognize the rights of the Indians, which was 'a mere right of occupancy', acknowledgement of which 'would deny the title of the United States to our own territories'.

In fact, it was control of the route across the continent that was of greatest significance to both nations by the middle of the nineteenth century. In 1848 the British seized San Juan del Norte, a shabby collection of fifty or sixty thatched huts on the Costa Rican border, with a population mainly made up of former slaves from Jamaica. They promptly renamed it Greytown, in honour of the Governor of Jamaica, and proclaimed it part of the Mosquito territory. The United States was furious, partly because it violated the view expressed in the Monroe Doctrine that Europeans should be kept out of 'their' hemisphere, but more because of its position at the mouth of the San Juan river, up which Vanderbilt planned to carry the thousands of people heading from New York to California. The American press thundered at the perfidy of the British claim to protect 'the squalid nationality of some few hundred illegitimate savages, born of indiscriminate concubinage, and leprous from a commixture of every unique blood, to whom she alternately administers crowns, Christianity and Jamaica rum'. The anger spread through America so quickly that both Washington and London recognized the need for some sort of agreement to relieve the tension.

In 1850 Britain and the United States concluded the Clayton/ Bulwer Treaty under which they agreed to collaborate in the construction of any canal which might be built across the isthmus, and in the meantime not to expand their possessions in the area. The Americans, however, believed that the treaty committed the British to withdrawal from the Mosquito coast, which they showed no inclination to do. Matters quickly came to a head in Greytown.

In November 1851, Cornelius Vanderbilt arrived at the port aboard his steamer, the *Prometheus*. Despite the fact that the port itself consisted of no more than a few tatty huts, it was vital to the millionaire's business because it was the point at which passengers transferred from the vessel which had brought them from New York into the smaller boats which would carry them up the San Juan river and into Lake Nicaragua. The British officials in Greytown demanded port charges which the American millionaire refused to pay, ordering the captain of the *Prometheus* back to sea. As the boat began to leave the harbour, a British brig fired across her bows, forcing the furious millionaire – who saw the tax as naked extortion – to pay.

Relations deteriorated even further. Two years later, a local mob set out to tear down the Transit Company buildings. Then in 1854, an American government official was hit in the face by a bottle thrown by one of Greytown's regular rioters. An American man-of-war was despatched to the port to 'protect American citizens'. When complaints from travellers persisted and the inhabitants of the town showed no sign of apologizing, the captain trained his guns upon Greytown. At nine o'clock one July morning they began shelling, and in mid-afternoon a party was put ashore to burn to the ground those buildings left standing. By that evening there was nothing left of the place. It was the beginning of the end of British involvement on the Mosquito Coast – another example of the way in which American policy in the area was driven by the plans of entrepreneurs, and a recognition of the increasing power of the United States in its 'own hemisphere'.

The British abandoned the Mosquito Coast, leaving its control in the hands of the Nicaraguan government forty years later. They put King Robert Henry Clarence in a gunboat and deposited him in exile in Jamaica. A grateful colonial administration granted him a pension for life, but the last of the Mosquito kings did not enjoy it for long: he died in Jamaica at the age of thirty-five.

It was the same story at the press centre every day: Paola giggled and apologized that there was no response to my requests either to talk to the foreign minister or to travel to the coast. In the meantime, what about an interview with some of the Americans living in Nicaragua who thought their government were murderous fascists? The beards and sandals nodded that they thought this a good idea. I called Alicia and invited her to lunch.

We met at a restaurant where the menu came on elaborately decorated sheets of cardboard. I ordered roast pork, but the waiter said it wasn't available. Mixed grill was off too. Finally we settled on a steak. For several months, steak had been the only dish on the menu which the restaurant actually served. I asked the waiter why they bothered to hand out the menu at all, if they didn't have most of the things they advertised. 'It reminds us of how things used to be,' he said, fingering his bow tie.

'There used to be plenty of places like this in Managua before the revolution,' Alicia said, 'but now, with all the shortages and everything, they can't keep going. Anyway, half the people who used them have left the country.'

I noticed that all the other tables were occupied by foreigners: presumably they were the only ones who could afford to eat out. At the black market rate of exchange the meal, including a bottle of imported wine, cost five dollars for two, but anyone who had access only to Nicaraguan currency would have found it exorbitant.

I began to explain to Alicia the problems I was having getting permission to travel down the Atlantic Coast. She listened with a sympathetic ear, occasionally interjecting, 'Oh yes, it's like that if you want to do anything,' or 'You've got to understand, it takes time to learn how to run a government.' Finally she shook her head.

'Look,' she said, 'you can forget about going down to San Juan. You'll never make it. It's impossible.'

'Why?'

'It doesn't exist any more. The Contras hit it a couple of months ago. It's all gone.'

'But there must be something there.'

'*Nada*, nothing. The whole town was destroyed. The Contras came in from Costa Rica and killed all the Sandinistas in the town. Just smashed into the place and took it over. They say Commander Zero himself even took part in the attack. Then the government tried to recapture the town, but they dropped so many bombs on to the Contras that they wrecked the place. There wasn't much there before – just a few shacks really – but there's nothing at all left now.'

It was not, I reflected, the first time that the little town had been destroyed.

'Who controls the town now?' I asked.

'Right now, the government, but the rest of the river, once you get inland, it's all Contra territory, right the way along the border with Costa Rica. You don't want to try going up the river – the Contras would blow you out of the water. And don't think they'd make any exception because you're a foreigner – they don't understand things like the rules of war. You'd never find a boatman to take you anyway.'

'But why didn't anyone at the government press office mention it was impossible to travel up the river?'

'Probably they don't like to give the impression that the government doesn't have control of the whole country. The truth is that the Martians could control most of the land down there, and it wouldn't make the slightest difference to anyone – it's all just jungle and mountain. But it's important for the government's self-esteem. Anyway, you'd better abandon any thought of going down there. You'd never get anywhere.'

I thought for a moment about how soon I might move on to Costa Rica – by road it could not take more than a couple of days, I guessed. But having requested a meeting with someone in the government, I might at least see if it was going to be possible before I left the country, though if the government information office was so dilatory about responding to requests to which there were foregone answers, I had little confidence that anything would come of my request to talk to the foreign minister, Father d'Escoto.

'Do you know people in the government?' I asked Alicia.

'Of course, everyone knows people in the government. It's a small country. Daniel Ortega used to teach my brother, and my cousin was at college with two of the other commandantes.'

'Do you have the foreign minister's telephone number?'

'Sure. Let's go and call him,' she said, as if the inhabitants of Managua were used to telephoning the foreign minister whenever they felt like an afternoon chat.

We left the restaurant and drove back to the hotel. I dialled the number. A woman answered. I asked to speak to Father d'Escoto.

'He's very ill. He's just come out of hospital. He can't talk to you.'

Suddenly the priest himself came on the line. Within a couple of minutes we had arranged an appointment for the following morning.

Alicia grinned. 'You see how friendly Nicaraguans are? You can do anything here. This is a revolutionary country.'

The foreign minister's house was on a hill on the edge of town, a low villa surrounded by a high wall with a heavy steel gate. An old guard with a cracked grimy face and a shotgun in his hand opened the gate and let me in.

'The Father will be out shortly,' he said, and sat on a stool watching suspiciously. Two other armed guards emerged for a moment from a little cabin, glanced at me and went back inside. The house was separated from the courtyard by a wire-mesh fence behind which, I guessed, were guard dogs. It was hardly a conventional priest's home, but in the confusion of propaganda, paranoia and fearsome threat which dominated life in Nicaragua, the precautions were understandable enough. In the previous couple of years, the Sandinistas claimed to have discovered a dozen plots to murder members of the government, ranging from bombing attacks in light aircraft to schemes for poisoning a bottle of the foreign minister's favourite liqueur. There was rarely any supporting evidence, but then there was usually little to bolster Washington's claims that Nicaragua was planning to invade her neighbours. The point had been reached, anyway, where proof would be almost unrecognizable in the general maelstrom.

Within the revolutionary government, many ministries seemed to be teetering permanently on the brink of chaotic collapse, due to lack of experience. The foreign ministry was steadier than many, although its personnel was not noticeably better qualified than that of others. It included among its staff a number of heroes of the revolution including a young lawyer, Nora Astorga, who according to Sandinista legend had arranged the 'execution' of El Perro, The Dog, the second-in-command of Somoza's National Guard. The Dog had earned his title by his barbarous talents as a torturer. Nora Astorga had lured him to her home, sent his bodyguard to buy cigarettes and taken the general to the bedroom. As she held him in her arms, the story went, two guerillas crept out of a wardrobe and slit his throat from ear to ear. Miss Astorga had recently been proposed as ambassador to the United States, a suggestion to which the Americans had taken vociferous exception.

But it was Father d'Escoto who most annoyed Washington. Whenever they produced spy photographs, intercepted documents and other sensitive material in a splash of expensive propaganda designed to show that Nicaragua was a danger to the stability of the Americas, the fat little priest would appear on American television and – in flawlessly literate and outraged English – accuse Washington of lying and preparing to invade. At the very mention of his name, blood pressures would rise all over the State Department.

Now, Managua was alive with rumours that the Pope had had enough of priests serving in government and had ordered Father d'Escoto and three other clerics to choose between the duties of the priesthood and those of a government official. It would be a momentous decision for any of them to make, since their involvement with the revolutionary government was the natural consequence of their view that the role of the church was to support the poor. But the current view in Rome was that the liberation theologians needed to be brought under control, and the position of the Nicaraguan priests was one of the first issues to be tackled. I wondered how easy Father d'Escoto would find it to disentangle church and state.

He appeared a few minutes later, a fat, bespectacled man leaning slightly to one side as he walked and dressed in a loose sports shirt and corduroy jeans. He opened the gate, shook my hand in a fleshy grip, and led me down the side of the house to a palm-thatched arbour where a tasselled hammock was slung between two columns. We sat down in rocking chairs. There was a white radio telephone on the low central table, its antenna partially retracted. A servant brought drinks, a Coca-Cola for me and a glass of water for Father d'Escoto – he had just returned from Cuba where surgeons had operated on his gall bladder, which explained his slight stoop. He lit a long thin dark cigarette and began, in a voice unexpectedly thin for such a stocky body, to tell me of the roots of his involvement in the revolution.

'For me,' he said, 'it began in Chile. When I left seminary I was breaking out of a shell. I had been in training in New York and my order, the Maryknolls, sent me to work in Chile. At that stage I knew what was wrong in Nicaragua – you couldn't live there and not see it – but I still thought that Christian Democracy could bring about change and improve the lives of the people.

'But little by little I began to see,' he said, reflecting on what had obviously been a profound realization. 'This may sound scandalous to you. I saw that Catholic social doctrine was no more than an attempt to salvage Western capitalism by humanizing it somewhat, rather than any attempt to put the gospel imperatives into the context of the exploitation in which people lived. I decided we had to go deeper than things like papal encyclicals.'

The language he used, flawless, spattered with sociological

jargon, made it sound almost as if he were reciting the memorized answers to a catechism. I imagined he had rehearsed his reasoning a hundred times, in preparation perhaps for cross-examination by the inquisitors of the Vatican.

'Our century is characterized by an exodus of rural people to the towns in search of a better life. But they lose in the trade-off. In the rural areas, they have no possibility of bettering themselves, but at least they feel more human. I discovered in Chile that once they got into the towns, they ended up in ghettoes. I worked a lot with slum-dwellers, and one of the conclusions I arrived at was that a lot of the effort dedicated to uplifting people was counteracted by oppressive environmental conditions. If you treat people like scum, they don't respond, but if you treat them like humans, they act like humans. I began to reflect on habitat, and concluded that an inadequate physical environment almost inevitably had spiritual consequences.

'You know, nutritionists say that if a baby doesn't get adequate food in the first three years of life, its brain can be damaged irreparably: environmental deprivation does something similar. But to the spirit.

'After the earthquake here, I came straight back to Nicaragua, to try to put some of my ideas about a decent environment into action. There was this idea of "housing for the poor" – the principle was that housing shouldn't cost more than twenty per cent of average earnings. It was ridiculous. If people were getting less and less pay – as they were – eventually the Ministry of Housing would end up supplying people with umbrellas. The proper response was to realize that there are some basic needs which are the same whether you're rich or poor, and housing is one of them.'

An enormous black and brown Rottweiler dog sloped down the path from the villa and sidled across the terrace to sit at the priest's feet. He stroked the dog's broad head as he continued.

'Well, from what I could see, what we needed was a fundamental about-face, a revolution if you like, so that we'd have a system where every human being was important, instead of the majority being used for the advancement of the minority. It would be a society where we could all honestly say "Our Father" and mean it, because we'd all be brothers.'

He paused, drew reflectively on his cigarette, and took a sip of water. There was a disquieting touch of vanity about his performance, as if this eloquent yet softly stated public rehearsal of his political progress was as significant as the conclusions he had reached. Perhaps the vanity was the inevitable consequence of conflict with Rome. The dog slumped to lie on its side across his feet.

'So, we had to proclaim the universal fatherhood of God, and the bond of fraternity between us. And at the same time we had to denounce anything which divided us and stood in the way of achieving brotherhood. Then we'd suffer persecution – that's what happened to Christ. To accept Christ meant to do his father's will, to proclaim the brotherhood of man. So the church here had to denounce what was happening under the dictatorship. And we had to accept the consequences.

'I never really believed we could change things peacefully, but it was important to make an appeal first. To try to make the ruling classes aware. After all,' he smiled and prodded out his cigarette on an earthenware bowl, 'it's easier for a camel to pass through the eye of a needle than for a rich man to be saved. So I started talking to the archbishop, trying to get him to make the church take a stand against the status quo, to take the lead in creative non-violence. I was trying to persuade him that if we spoke out and took a lead, maybe the conflict would take on a Christian physiognomy.'

'It was a bit late, wasn't it?' I asked. 'There hasn't been any other revolution where the church has managed to hang on to its position in society, has there?'

'It hasn't happened anywhere else, because we haven't preached opposition. On the contrary, we've generally preached resignation in the face of evil, which is really nothing more than complicity in evil. Anyway, to go back to my point, I believed passionately in non-violent change. I had a picture of Martin Luther King which I kept on my desk – it's still there as a matter of fact. I went to the archbishop and told him it was time to flood the streets with people armed with prayers and rosaries. I told him that if there was a danger, it was a danger we should face. After all, we are celibates. I didn't want to be celibate all my life, but it means that we have no excuse not to go all the way. Besides which, there was the question of the position of the church – I told him, "If we in the church don't promote peaceful change, it will come violently, and we'll lose whatever influence we have." He told me, "Nothing will happen here. Our people are patient."

'Well, they are patient, but came a time when they realized they had to struggle with the only means available. By the time the church had begun to preach passive resistance, the people had already taken up arms. It was too late, you see. We couldn't expect to reap what we hadn't sown: we had a church which not only had not rebelled against the system, but which had collaborated with it, validated it. For me, now, there was only one course open. I had to accompany my people.'

If the process taking place within the priest's mind was similar to that in a nuclear reactor, we had reached the point of going critical, the point at which the fission chain would become self-sustaining. The priest, the preacher of 'Thou shalt not kill', would have to reassess his attitude to killing. The resolution of the problem would create a series of inevitable consequences which would change everything.

His voice strengthening, he explained that he had been asked by the Sandinista Front, the Frente, to join their political wing. It had happened, he recalled, in late 1975, after they had heard of a sermon he had preached on 'Creative Non-violence'. It was a curious basis for his revolutionary involvement, for in embracing the Frente he would be accepting their campaign of violence.

'I had to accept what St Thomas Aquinas accepted – the idea of The Just War.' He sat forward as he spoke, flinched from the discomfort of his operation scar, and gingerly straightened his back. 'You know, St Thomas even calls tyrannicide legitimate?'

It was, he could see from my reaction, not good enough as an explanation.

'When the Frente asked me to join them, I knew it would change the course of my life. I thought I might be expelled from

the Maryknolls. I felt almost a physical pain. But then I thought,
"They're not in my shoes, I must make the decision." I wondered
what Rome would say, but in all candour, knowing church
history – knowing how the church reacted when we were
seeking our independence from Spain – I thought, "Well, God
knows how they'll react. Let God sort it out."

'Then I saw myself before the Lord, and I wondered how to
explain that I had been going to Jericho and I hadn't got off to
help my countrymen bleeding by the roadside. How would I
explain that because I was afraid of reprisals from my own
church, I had passed by? Rome hadn't asked me to pass by, I
had no ultimatum from them, and I knew that Christ was
urging me to be with the people. I knew what I would choose,
because years earlier I had undergone a reflection which had
paved the way.

'It was Mardi Gras, the day before Lent, around 1974. I had
stayed alone in my room. The picture of Martin Luther King
was on my desk, staring at me. He seemed to be pointing at me,
saying, "You're a coward!" I sat there alone with the photograph for two and a half hours, reflecting on Christ's message,
trying to understand, and praying. Finally, I asked, "Lord, help
me to understand the mystery of the Cross, and give me the
guts to embrace it in whatever shape you send it." '

For some minutes I had been trying to determine whether the
priest was acting – albeit very plausibly – or genuinely expressing his beliefs. Was he putting on the sort of performance he
laid on when he knew that an American television network was
carrying him directly into the homes of the American electorate?
But now he had come to the moment which had been the
turning-point in his spiritual and political development, his
manner had altered. It seemed for a moment that the inner man
was speaking.

'From that moment,' he said, 'things were changed in my life.
It used to be that I was afraid of everything, even going to the
dentist. Now I had no fear, because my life wasn't my own – I
had given my life to God. Fear is the great enslaver, but life, to
live properly, means not being afraid. And when you lose fear
of death, you come alive. Once I had begun to lose my sense of

fear, my shame was replaced by satisfaction, I was liberated inside. After that it was inevitable that I would be with those who sought freedom.'

He suddenly, vividly, recalled the days of the revolution.

'The feeling when we were saying Mass in fields in the countryside during the war! That feeling was wonderful. It was the sense, the long awaited and deserved sense that the people were free!'

The memory had carried him back into the declamatory role of government propagandist. He knew he had not given a direct answer to the point at issue. I tried another approach in a direct question.

'What did you feel when you heard that Somoza had been murdered?'

He altered the question at once, confidently back in the public persona.

'What did I feel when Somoza was brought to justice?' he corrected me. 'Well, my reaction was one of sadness, the sadness I always feel in the face of tragedy or failure. I don't hate anyone – Somoza, Reagan, whoever. I may hate what they do. I may denounce it in the way the gospel denounces crime, but I always pray for the possibility that in the final moment people may repent. But there was no evidence that Somoza had changed. When I heard the news I just thought "Well, God help him." I had a sense of relief that he could do no more evil.'

His face had gone grey from the exertion of the conversation, his voice had faded. His physical weakness prompted me to think of the ox-like body of the archbishop. There was, it was well known, no love lost between the two men. Recently the archbishop had been to Rome to enlist the support of the Pope in his running battle with the government. When the Pope had visited Nicaragua, d'Escoto had suddenly found pressing business on the other side of the world. When the hierarchy had asked him to resign his job as foreign minister, he had, inevitably, refused. In d'Escoto's mind, the relics of his seminary training, his experiences in Chile, his political convictions were all interwoven. He had developed the certainty of the besieged. His answer to an archbishop who told him he could not serve both God and the young men in green Sandinista uniforms was to accuse him of playing politics himself.

'The church isn't motivated by principle so much as by political considerations,' he said. 'The hierarchy only turned against Somoza once they saw him no longer as the guarantor of their position in society, but as a menace to it. Now, I think the archbishop really believes that the Americans will overthrow our revolution, and he's getting on the bandwagon.

'You know what I pray? I pray that God will save the church from itself!'

A few minutes later he became too tired to continue and showed me to the steel security gate, carrying his radio telephone down the path with him. Once a priest, always a priest: they could not take that away, but they had stopped him saying Mass.

Inside the first security fence we shook hands – the same weak grip – and he wished God's blessing upon me. The guards opened the gates and showed me into the courtyard. I waved as I passed through the outer gate and he grinned back at me from behind the grille. I thought how like a prisoner he looked.

On the way back from d'Escoto's house I called in at the press office where, as usual, Paola giggled and apologized for having achieved nothing. I was beginning almost to feel sorry for her – it could not have been much fun spending her time making excuses. There was a bus to Costa Rica in the morning, anyway. But as it happened, the journey into Costa Rica began sooner than expected. In the afternoon Alicia called, saying she was going to Granada to deliver some books to a friend, and since Granada was on the way to the Costa Rican border, would I like a ride?

We passed through Masaya, a dirty little town where the walls were pockmarked by bullet holes: in the latter stages of the revolution, Somoza had ordered his airforce to bomb the marketplace. There were little crosses in the walls where families commemorated the death of their loved ones. For the first and only time in Nicaragua I saw a picture of Marx stencilled on a wall, and the inscription MARXISM IS THE HOPE OF THE WORLD.

Generally the slogans were written in a uniform style – both in terms of typeface and content – which indicated that they had official approval, such as SANDINO YESTERDAY, TODAY AND FOREVER, or FIFTY YEARS ON, SANDINO LIVES. Occasionally, however, there appeared a genuinely spontaneous message – BEWARE, A CONTRA LIVES HERE, for example. But in most cases, as with many other aspects of the revolution, enthusiasm had been replaced by orthodoxy.

Radio Sandino, 'the voice of the revolution', was playing Boy George as we approached Granada, a gracious town on the edge of Lake Nicaragua. Once it had been the national capital; now it had an air of down-at-heel gentility which was rather attractive, like Antigua without the preservation orders. Alicia dropped me off near the centre of town while she went to deliver her books. A row of horse-drawn taxis was standing along one side of the square. Before the revolution the rich had hired them for afternoon outings. These days, with oil products rationed throughout the country, the carriage owners were enjoying an improvement in business. In the centre of the square was a statue erected in memory of Francisco Cordoba. 'Unveiled by the President of the Republic of Nicaragua, His Excellency . . .', said the inscription, and then there was a blank where someone had scratched out the hated words 'Anastasio Somoza', as if exorcizing a ghost.

On the fourth side of the square, Lake Nicaragua stretched away grey and flat to the horizon: here and there pustular little islands poked out of the glassy water, improbably small in such a vast expanse. An old ferry was tied up at the end of the jetty. Beneath the iron supports, a little boy was standing up to his thighs in the water, dousing his dog and working a frothy white lather along its neck and back. To judge from its appearance, the pier might have been built by Vanderbilt's steamship company as a berth for the ferries which called in on transit to the Pacific shore.

In the distance rose the volcano of Momotombo, which featured on Nicaraguan matchboxes. Had it not been for the Nicaraguans' pride in the volcano, the country might well have become the site for the canal which was finally built in Panama.

Enormous vested interests had fought to persuade the American government of the benefits of one route against another. The monetary and political advantages accruing to whoever controlled the 'vital artery which would determine the future of the western hemisphere', as one lobbyist put it, would be of inestimable value. Initially, it had seemed that Nicaragua would provide the better route, not least because although the distance from the Atlantic to the Pacific was far greater than in Panama, the presence of Lake Nicaragua meant that the construction of the canal would cost considerably less. Vanderbilt himself had already chosen the Nicaraguan route and the Nicaraguan government argued as forcefully as they could in favour of a canal across their territory. But in the event, they provided the backers of the Panama plan with their greatest propaganda coup.

When the Americans took over the uncompleted French plans initiated by de Lesseps in Panama, they began a ferocious campaign to persuade United States public opinion to abandon the Nicaragua project. The most vociferous of the supporters of the Panama scheme, Philippe Bunau-Varilla, a diminutive French engineer who had worked with de Lesseps and now held a financial stake in the American project, produced a pamphlet seizing on one aspect above all others – the existence of volcanoes in Nicaragua. Suggesting that the Nicaraguan temperament was as unreliable as the inside of a volcano, and that a volcanic eruption there might at any time destroy the canal which was going to cost the Americans millions, he wrote:

Young nations like to put on their coats of arms what best symbolizes their moral domain or characterizes their native soil. What have the Nicaraguans chosen to characterize their country on their coat of arms, on their postage stamps? Volcanoes!

By the day on which the US Senate was to cast a final vote in favour of the Panama or Nicaragua route, Bunau-Varilla had visited every stamp dealer in Washington and bought ninety Nicaraguan one-centavo stamps, each depicting Lake Nicaragua and, behind it, the Momotombo volcano in spectacular eruption.

He stuck each one on to a sheet of paper and typed underneath 'an official witness to the volcanic activity on the isthmus of Nicaragua'. The precise impact of this final assault is unquantifiable, but the vote was carried by eight votes in favour of Panama. The Nicaraguan government, in glorifying one of their few national assets, had unwittingly collaborated with the most effective act of lobbying yet seen in Washington and irretrievably altered the course of their own history.

I was sitting watching the clouds piling up above the volcano like the nineteenth-century eruption when Alicia returned.

'Want to go for a swim? Let's take a boat out to one of the islands.'

A little way down the shore we found two men sitting in a café arguing over whose turn it was to pay for the latest of the several bottles of beer lined up on the grubby tabletop. One of the two, a filthy white singlet stretched across his flabby belly, owned a boat and offered to take us to one of the islands.

The boat was long and thin and low in the water. We sat on the hot tin canopy and the boatman steered us down the creeks towards the open lake. A family, mother at the front, three children in the middle, father at the rear, paddled by in a dug-out canoe.

We passed a fisherman, chest-deep, casting a circular net into the water. When he pulled it in, two flashing silver fish were trapped inside. Mango trees leaned out from the shore, trailing lianas. Small freshwater turtles were sunning themselves on black volcanic rocks at the water's edge.

'You know, there are sharks in Lake Nicaragua,' said Alicia. 'People think that once they were ordinary salt-water sharks, which swam up the San Juan river from the sea. There aren't as many of them as there were because Somoza used to encourage people to kill them, but my father remembers losing a school-friend. He vanished, eaten by a shark.'

The air was still, warm and heavy. The noise of the engine reverberated across the rich brown water. Beyond the end of the creek we passed the skeleton of an old steamer, beached high above the water, like a prehistoric creature which had crawled from the deep and expired.

The boatman steered us towards a little island out in the lake, where the branches of the trees hung in a bower over the water. We pushed through them to a place where someone had once made a jetty from the rocks, and clambered up the hill which dominated the island. The place was covered in mango trees and not a minute went by without a ripe mango crashing through the warm shade to splatter on the rocks. Underfoot the ground was covered in the sticky, feathery flesh of the fruit, and we slid as we walked.

At the top of the hill there were signs that someone had once planned to build a house but abandoned the scheme even before the foundations were complete. A couple of shallow trenches and a pile of stones were all that remained. We slithered down between the trees to the water's edge. Alicia moved behind a mango tree to take off her clothes. I undressed on a rock and dived into the water.

It felt warm and glutinous, so dark that your arms were invisible beneath the water's surface. We swam in fairly relaxed fashion for twenty minutes or so, then made for the shore again.

Alicia cut her leg on a rock climbing out and I bent down to offer her a hand out of the water. We had no towels and we stood close together on the rock, wet, naked and slightly embarrassed strangers.

'You see,' she said, 'you can do anything in Nicaragua.'

The nearer we came to the centre of Granada, the more clearly we heard the metallic tones of a loudspeaker. In one of the squares a dozen buses were standing empty. An old couple had pulled their armchairs out on the roadside to chat in the gathering darkness. We asked them what was happening.

'The boys are home!' said the old woman through a mouth in which a solitary tooth leaned like an ancient standing stone.

Closing through the darkening streets on the source of the sound we came upon some of the soldiers about whom the old woman had been talking. They were tough and dirty young men, the grime of several months in the mountains engrained in their skin and rubbed into their beards. Their boots were scuffed and worn down, their rucksacks battered and held together with bits of string. The silver crucifixes several of them wore around their necks had tarnished during their duty in the hills.

'We gave those sons-of-whores a beating!' one of them was saying to a teenage boy, perhaps his younger brother, who had stayed in Granada during the campaign. Behind him another soldier was quietly consoling a weeping pregnant woman. The dirt from his shirt had smudged across her face.

The walls along the length of the street were daubed with the slogans of opposition parties preparing for the elections in three months' time. It was noticeable that of all the elections taking place in Central America – Belize, Guatemala, El Salvador, Nicaragua and Panama – the Nicaraguan poll was the only one the Americans disregarded. Everywhere else the elections were 'a step in the right direction' or 'the beginning of true democracy'. In Nicaragua they were 'a device by the Sandinistas to legitimize themselves and persuade the Europeans to support them'. No one doubted the outcome of the Nicaraguan elections, of course: the Sandinistas would win comfortably. The Washington administration made great play of the fact that the biggest of the opposition parties was refusing to take part, yet there were great swathes of opinion unrepresented in Guatemala and El Salvador, and those elections were considered 'helpful', 'free and fair', and 'positive'.

The catalogue of Sandinista offences produced in Washington – the seizure of private property, expulsion of priests, censorship of the press, for example – suggested the country was totalitarian. Yet it was nothing of the kind. Not yet, anyway. Personally I didn't much care for the fact that the commandantes liked to dress up in army uniforms, but the country was freer than El Salvador or Honduras or Guatemala even in that respect: in Nicaragua people did not seem frightened of the army. And if there existed a tendency towards authoritarianism within the inexperienced young men in the government, it was only reinforced by the expenditure of millions of dollars sowing mines in the country's harbours and providing right-wing guerillas with the training and wherewithal to embark on a campaign of mayhem and murder.

At the end of the street we came to a dais above which the local party had strung Sandinista banners. On the platform, party officials were praising the soldiers for their feats of arms against the Contras. In revolutionary Nicaragua, neither the army nor the police (nor, for that matter, most of the organs of government) were separate from the party. The soldiers fought in a Sandinista army, laws were enforced by the Sandinista police, ration cards were issued by the Sandinista defence committees, and children were encouraged to join the Sandinista children's organization before graduating to the Sandinista Youth. It was all reminiscent of Eastern Europe, but understandable, perhaps, in the context of what had gone before.

The men in the square were young militiamen from the irregular battalions drafted into the hills to fight the Contras. The regular army was being kept mostly in reserve, which had the effect — doubtless intended — of making the war touch the entire community far more effectively than if the fighting had been left to the properly trained professionals. These men had been called up six months previously, and had learned much of the business of soldiering after the fighting had begun.

'The battalion was in combat thirty-four times!' shouted the party cheerleader on the platform. A cheer rose from the civilians in the crowd, but most of the soldiers looked tired and anxious to get home.

The speaker paused for a moment, and the crowd filled the silence.

'To the stupid animal reactionaries!' A woman's voice, high and wobbly, screamed from the back of the crowd.

'The Sandinista Front will clean you up!' came the roared response.

'*No pasaran*! They shall not pass!' The crowd began to chant in a surging roar which crescendoed on the sixth repetition and had died away again by the twelfth.

It was a ritual slogan, but in the arena of light in the middle of the darkened old city, the air hot and still and the town happy with the return of its missing combatants, it had resonance.

Alicia was talking to a soldier with a rolled-up hammock slung across his rucksack and a parrot on his shoulder. He was enjoying telling her horror stories of the Contras – how they beheaded people, how Contra women would bare their breasts at windows to lure them into ambushes, how there were Cubans and Argentinians, Canadians and Koreans fighting with the Contras, how they had even killed a Korean.

Alicia asked him why he had volunteered to fight. 'Volunteer?' he queried with a laugh. 'My union told me I had to go. I had no choice.'

'Would you go back?' I asked.

His bravado fell away. 'Not if you made me a commandante and gave me a car,' he said.

The conversation was cut short by the opening words of the Sandinista anthem. The crowd of dirty militiamen and townspeople stood in the street and sang, deep and unaccompanied, the ratatat refrain:

> We're struggling against the Yankee,
> Enemy of humanity.

I wondered how many of them thought it hyperbole.

We walked off down the street to a restaurant where they served plates of beans and bottles of warm beer, and found a table from where we could watch the militiamen celebrating their safe return. They were a happy group, so good-humoured that even when one of them noticed I was a foreigner and assumed I was American, instead of expressing hostility he just joked about my 'friends' against whom they had been fighting.

I took a room at a faded grey hotel in the centre of town, and late that night Alicia returned to Managua.

'Enjoy Costa Rica,' she said as she left. 'You should come back to Nicaragua soon. Before the American Marines arrive.'

6

The Leprechaun's Utopia

Nicaragua was the first country I had left without dire warnings. Belizeans had predicted the Guatemalans would mug me, Guatemalans that the Salvadoreans would murder me, Salvadoreans that the Hondurans would rob me, and Hondurans that the Nicaraguans would forcibly turn me into a communist. The only thing any Nicaraguan advised me about Costa Rica was to enjoy myself.

The name Costa Rica, 'Rich Coast', was coined by the Spanish, and the closer we came to the border, the more accurate the description seemed. The tops of the volcanoes were shrouded in mist, and all the way from Granada to the frontier we were crossing slow brown rivers snaking across the plain to debouch into Lake Nicaragua. In the fields between the grey lake and the Pacific, fat longhorned cattle grazed in pastures of rich grass. In this part of Nicaragua it was hard to imagine shortages of anything.

The bus was big and comfortable. Needless to say, it was not Nicaraguan: the Costa Rican bus line, the Ticabus, had an appealing reputation for reliability and comfort. Since the era of railway building had come after independence, there were scarcely any international railway connections, so the big Costa Rican buses had established a lucrative business in international transport, until first Nicaragua and then El Salvador had collapsed into civil war. Managua was now the most northerly point on the network.

The numbers of Nicaraguan soldiers in evidence increased as we drew closer to the border. Ten days earlier, a group of Commander Zero's fighters had come across from Costa Rica and occupied one of the border towns for a few hours. But the driver, wearing dark glasses and an almost plausible toupée, seemed to think the greater danger came from the potholes which had developed in the road since the Nicaraguans had

been unable to pay the bill for imported asphalt. We swerved
from one side of the road to the other, dodging between the
chasms which had opened up in the causeway.

At the border we formed the usual line to pass through
Nicaraguan emigration. Nicaraguan border-posts were unique
in the area in having their counters at the same height as the
forehead of the official seated on the other side. Once you had
handed over your passport and immigration application, the
official, his papers, stamp and inkpad became invisible. Young
children and babies had to be lifted up to shoulder height for
their faces to be compared with those in the passports and,
since many poorer Nicaraguans were very short, the immigration official was forever jumping up and down to peer
over the counter at would-be travellers. It was a ridiculous
performance.

The first thing the Costa Ricans did when we crossed the
border was to spray the bus with disinfectant, presumably to
stop the spread of some agricultural disease. It seemed an
appropriate act: every other government in Central America
was determined to stop the revolutionary contagion spreading
out of Nicaragua.

When we reached the Costa Rican immigration post the
Nicaraguan passengers made a rush for the sales kiosk. There,
stacked up in shiny mounds, were all the forbidden fruits of the
revolution – soap, toothpaste, chocolate bars and so on. Even,
incongruously for a tax-free store, piles of lavatory paper. I had
noticed the equivalent Nicaraguan establishment just down the
road – a wrecked and roofless building with DUTY FREE SHOP
written in fading black paint on the walls and a piglet tethered
outside.

On the evidence of her immigration formalities, Costa Rica
was efficient, easy-going and eccentric. None of the officials
carried guns, which made a pleasant enough change. But they
did seem over-anxious to preserve the cleanliness and tidiness of
the place. Having paid the tax to enter the country, I handed
over my passport.

'Show me your ticket to leave Costa Rica,' said the old man

behind the desk, seated so low that he was looking directly at my navel.

'I'm going *in*. I haven't got a ticket to leave Costa Rica.'

'Well, you can't come into the country without a ticket to leave.'

'But I'm going on to Panama.'

'Where's your ticket then?'

'I'll get one in San José.'

'We can't let you in without a ticket out.'

'Well, where can I get a ticket from Costa Rica to Panama without coming into Costa Rica?'

'I don't know. Maybe the bus driver will sell you one.'

I found the driver in the restaurant shovelling a plate of food into his mouth. He was embarrassed by my intrusion, as if I had caught him in private ritual with his hairpiece. 'I need a ticket to Panama,' I said.

'You can', chew chew, 'buy one', chew chew, 'when we get', chew chew, 'to San José,' he said, and let a lump of gristle drop on to the plate. He had managed to speak without either looking up or interrupting the rhythm of his mastication.

'But they won't let me into the country without a ticket out again. Is there anywhere I can buy a ticket out of Costa Rica?'

He paused this time, determined not to let the trouble caused by one passenger disturb his meal more than could be avoided. 'Only if you go back to Nicaragua,' he said and belched.

'The driver says I can't buy a ticket out of Costa Rica until I've been in Costa Rica,' I told the immigration officer.

'Well, in that case you can't come in,' said the old man, as if it were the most obvious thing in the world. 'Why don't you go back to Nicaragua, buy a ticket to Panama, and then you can come in.'

I wondered for a moment whether he was shaking me down for a bribe. It was too obvious, though – even in Guatemala they didn't do it in the middle of an immigration office, with everyone else standing around watching.

It was hard to resist the conclusion that I was being made to undergo some sort of test. The thought of money suggested a solution.

'Look,' I said. 'I've just paid ten colones to come into Costa Rica, and you've stuck a wodge of stamps in my passport. I won't accept the money back and anyway, you can't unstick the stamps. So why don't you give me a visa for a day so I can get to San José to buy a ticket for Panama?'

This seemed to strike my adversary as a passable answer to the conundrum; the old man grinned, stamped my passport and scrawled 'Transit only 24 hours' underneath. I hurried out to the bus where the driver was revving the engine, and scrambled up the steps. He gave me a disdainful glance, as if my success was hardly deserved.

It was mid-afternoon by the time we were on our way again: altogether the business of crossing the border had taken five hours. Once we were on the move I pulled off the stamps they had put in my passport and stuck them down over the place where the immigration official had inscribed my transit permission. They fitted well, just a couple of ballpen scribbles protruding from underneath, and I reckoned they would be good enough to convince an inspector who wanted to resume the game and didn't look too closely.

In the soft afternoon light, the hillsides of Costa Rica looked verdant. At the edge of the highway wooden tables had been set up to sell bottles of dark honey. The farms were well-kept and the roadside homes which in Nicaragua, Honduras, El Salvador and Guatemala had been mean improvised shacks of wood, tin and cardboard, looked solid and clean, as if the earth provided enough for everyone. Even the fenceposts, I saw, had sprouted leaves in the rich soil. Later I happened to meet a Costa Rican biologist, who gave eccentric examples of the generosity of his country's climate, including one hundred and thirty types of frog, and more varieties of butterfly than in the whole of Africa.

By early evening we were nearing San José, the Costa Rican capital. We passed the first highway tollbooth I had seen in Central America, and a couple of hours after dark reached the city itself. After Managua its bright street lights, neon advertising signs, and broad bustling boulevards glowed with extraordinary vividness. The vision of prosperity made Nicaragua seem poorer and more embattled than ever. But it also, perversely, emphasized the scale of its achievement. In the context of its history, the fact that it couldn't produce toothpaste seemed less than important.

Costa Rica was the first place since leaving home where I did not feel an outsider. I had read somewhere that when the Spanish arrived in Costa Rica they found five Indian tribes, but if so, they must have made short work of them, for there was scarcely an Indian face to be seen. As far as the physical appearance of its inhabitants and the pace and style of the city were concerned, San José looked like a northern Mediterranean city.

The streets were lined with department stores, restaurants, boutiques and French pastry shops. At the edge of a central square in which not a single beggar or armed policeman was visible stood the National Theatre, all colonnades, wrought iron porticos and winged statuary. It had been built as a cultural gesture in the 1890s, after an Italian prima donna had refused to visit Costa Rica on the grounds that it lacked a suitable auditorium. Smarting from the implied slur on their nationhood, a group of farmers launched a campaign to build a replica of the Paris Opéra. Designers and artisans were imported from Europe and the project was financed by a levy on every sack of coffee exported from the country. The resulting profusion of Italianate frescoes, gilded cornices, marble floors and rococo furniture would have been worth a visit even in Europe. In Central America it was a remarkable edifice.

I called at a café for a cup of coffee which tasted surprisingly good, probably a reflection of the fact that unlike her neighbours, Costa Rica didn't need to export all her best-quality beans. (Even this was only a comparative mark of prosperity. I read later that the average Costa Rican eats less beef in a year than the average American pet cat.) But the Costa Ricans had an agreeable sense of priorities. As I was paying my bill, the cooks ran out from the kitchen and started rooting around under the tables. 'They're looking for their cat,' said the man at the cash desk, handing me my change and getting down on to his hands and knees, making sucking noises through his teeth.

It was the first pet cat I had come across since leaving the Chinaman.

In an area notable for its predilection for war, Costa Rica had declared armies illegal and survived quite happily without one for nearly forty years. The Civil Guard owned a couple of helicopters, but the same pilot had managed to crash both of them. Occasionally one of the Civil Guard was to be seen wandering around town, ridiculously kitted out in jungle fatigues which had arrived in the latest donation of military uniforms from an unnamed 'friendly government'. The Guard personnel changed every time there was a general election, which meant that every four years a new bunch of recruits put on uniform and learned the job from scratch. By the time they had mastered the relevant skills it was time for another election and they all returned to their previous occupations. Their arsenal, should the threat of invasion ever arise, consisted of thirteen mortars which didn't work, a handful of broken-down bazookas and machine-guns, and thirty-two different kinds of small arms, some of which were so old that the ammunition had not been manufactured for twenty years.

I discovered later that the reason I had noticed the uniformed men on the streets was that the country was in the midst of what passed for a crisis. The Minister for Security had announced to a bemused nation that he had uncovered evidence of an imminent *coup d'état* 'from either the extreme right or the extreme left', a vague assertion that he chose not to amplify. Within hours, newspapers and television stations from all over the world were telephoning San José for confirmation of rumours that the president's family was under house arrest, tanks were on the streets and the president himself was in exile in Panama. Quite how this coup would be accomplished, since Costa Rica had no army, let alone tanks, was a mystery. After several hours of excited confusion in London, New York and Paris — which passed unnoticed in San José — the president, a roly-poly man with a passing resemblance to a young hippopotamus, appeared on television to reassure the nation and demand the resignation of the entire cabinet, senior civil servants and the ambassadorial corps. Although, as President Luis Albert Monge admitted, it was hardly an everyday occurrence in Costa Rica, it was, he said, 'frequent practice in other democracies', without specifying which ones he had in mind. Then the Minister for Security said his announcement had been a jest. Then he contradicted himself. The president accepted everyone's resignation, but by the end of the week most of them had been reappointed to their posts. Except for the security minister.

Up a slight hill I came to the building which had, until the 1948 revolution, been the main army garrison in the capital. A heavy castellated building like the forts in Nicaragua and El Salvador, its walls were still flecked by the bullet scars from Costa Rica's last coup, after which the leader of the victorious forces had handed the keys of the barracks over to the education minister, who promptly turned them into a museum. The decision was typical of the man I most wanted to meet in Costa Rica.

A fine rain was falling on the side of the volcano, and Don Pepé's little cabin with its rough brick walls and tin roof was almost invisible through the wet air. It was a surprisingly modest home for the architect of a state. Further down the volcano, in the suburbs at the edge of town, were the houses of the coffee merchants, the entrepreneurs and corrupt financiers, great rambling villas adorned with the prerequisites of status – high walls, green lawns and security guards. Don Pepé's home, by contrast, was little different to a thousand other single-storey dwellings scattered about the less affluent parts of town.

Jose Figueres Ferrer – Don Pepé as the affectionate diminutive had it – had virtually created modern Costa Rica. It was he who had led the revolution in 1948, he who had restored democracy, he who had established the welfare state and abolished the army. The effrontery, the presumption of a man who would dare, in an area notorious for dictators, to scrap his army! For thirty years, Figueres had supported the forces of revolution in Central America. He managed both to secure the protection of the United States and to supply arms to Castro to fight against Batista. He had supported the Sandinistas against Somoza, yet felt both Cuban and Nicaraguan revolutions had failed to fulfil their promises. For a while he had achieved the status of a minor international celebrity, but he was too difficult to pigeonhole, his experience too localized for him to be more than a diversion on the world stage. Now he was living in retirement.

'Let's see if The Dwarf's at home,' said the taxi-driver, and tooted his horn. I wondered in how many other Latin American countries he could treat a former president so offhandedly and expect to get away with it.

'It's cold,' said the girl who came out to answer the horn, rubbing her hands in the damp hill mist. 'You'd better come in and wait. Don Pepé is asleep now, but if you want to wait, he'll be out soon.' All manner of people called to see the former president, and it looked as if they all got the same treatment. There was a book of cartoons on her desk in the ante-room: she was teaching herself English.

She showed me into an ascetic little study, naked brick walls and unpainted wood, and returned to her English course. The damp air outside seemed to come right through the walls, and the raindrops rattled on the roof like a snare drum. Ten minutes went by, fifteen. I glanced at the books on his shelves – a volume of Pablo Neruda's poetry, Elizabeth Longford's biography of Churchill, Peter Wyden's account of the Bay of Pigs.

After an hour had passed there was the sound of a lavatory being flushed and a washbasin in use. A door at the back of the room opened and Don Pepé came in.

Costa Rica's national hero was like a leprechaun. At most he could have been no more than five feet three in height, but inside the elderly and wizened body which advanced across the floor with the shuffle of the very old, there was a young man. His nose was enormous, like a hawk's beak, the rest of his face covered in wrinkles. But his eyes danced as he spoke. His clothes were old and so ill-fitting that they looked as if they had belonged to someone else, or been bought years before his body shrank: his shirt hung on his thin chest like the hem of a loose tablecloth.

Figueres had been an engineer by training, later starting afresh as a coffee farmer. His political and philosophical education was the product of his own experience and self-discipline. He had begun his political life as a Social Democrat, but soon saw the inadequacies of the system when victory in the elections was snatched away by a president in collusion with the country's small communist party.

'You know what we had here in 1948?' He smiled a thin, cynical smile. 'We had a subtle kind of democracy. I call it the Bogota model. In Colombia they have it perfected – there's a constitutional right to hold elections, there's a Western judicial system.' He paused with a comedian's timing. 'And then the aristocracy is free to elect a government. That's the Bogota model.' And he reproduced the cynical smile.

He recalled how he and a caucus of like-minded allies had set out to do away with what passed for democracy in Costa Rica.

'It took me years to organize a force. It was hard to get guns,' he said. 'The army and the communists, they're usually the ones with the guns. We got some arms from political exiles through-out Latin America and then we had our first proper consignment from Argentina. We got it in through the Dominican Republic and Guatemala. And once we'd got guns, then people started pouring in to join us. Peasants and young intellectuals, that was my army – the organized trades unions were mainly communist. Everyone seemed to think the same thing – as long as the electoral way was open, it was better to have a bad government than a good revolution. But when the electoral right was denied, then fighting was a duty.'

I asked him how violent the revolution had been.

'For this country,' he answered, 'it was atrocious. Out of a population of eight hundred thousand people, we killed two thousand. I'm a Catalan and we're a violent people. But even for a Catalan, that was a terrible war.

'The banana companies used to bring illiterate peasants into Costa Rica from Nicaragua to work on their plantations. When the fighting started, the communists gave them a bottle of rum and a gun and told them they were fighting for social justice!

'We used to machine-gun them as if they were cattle!' He spoke softly and the drumming of the rain on the roof occasion-ally drowned out what he was saying. 'They were like cattle, you see. That's how they'd been treated. Imported by the banana companies, and when we killed them, we couldn't even trace their families. Like cattle, you see, just taken away from their families like cattle.'

He stopped and thought for a moment.

'You know,' he said, as if it had just occurred to him, 'if the aristocracy and the banana companies had had their way, we'd have an El Salvador here now, not a Costa Rica.'

After the revolution, Figueres had begun the process which turned his country into the only working democracy in the area. It was an impressive achievement, given the usual tendency of revolutionaries to consolidate their grip the moment they succeed. In Don Pepé's own experience it had happened in Cuba and now it was happening in Nicaragua.

'But isn't it inevitable', I asked, 'that revolutions around here will go the way of Cuba or Nicaragua?'

'The key', he said, 'is to have the revolution led by people inclined to read philosophy. *That* was what was significant about our revolution.' He was aware that he was in danger of sounding pompous, and added, 'If I may be presumptuous.' He paused for a second, then continued with a mischievous chuckle, 'and I am.'

'How do you categorize yourself, then?' I asked.

'Oh, I'm a Free Thinker. You know my hero? Bertrand Russell. He founded no sect, he was so undogmatic . . . Unlike Marx.'

'Where did you get the idea of abolishing the army?'

'One of your countrymen. H.G.Wells. I was a great reader of Wells, and in one of his books, *The Outline of History*, which I read in New York in 1920, he says that the societies of the future will have no armies. I became drunk with the idea, so drunk that when the war was over, we just disbanded the defeated army. Then we got rid of our own.'

It probably hadn't been such a difficult task, since neither army can have been very big, but it was an inspired action nonetheless. And in the aftermath of the revolution Figueres had made several other radical decisions, enfranchising women, nationalizing the banks, creating the permanent mechanism for free and fair elections and establishing public authorities to administer housing, trading and the public utilities. Then he stepped aside and let someone else have the presidency. He had twice been elected president since then but, in obedience to a law he had framed himself, he could not stand again.

He shuffled out to the front door to see me off. As we drove away, he stood short and stooped in the doorway and waved. 'You know,' the taxi-driver said cruelly, 'he's a good national hero. When he dies and we have to make a statue of him, at least we won't need much metal.'

The country's idiosyncratic peaceableness was under threat. It was overgenerous to Don Pepé to credit him entirely with the tranquillity of Costa Rica: had there been no sense of outrage at the denial of democracy in 1948, his revolt couldn't have succeeded. The country was 'temperamentally unsuited', as one politician put it, to anything other than popular government. But the price of peace was a massive debt to the international banks – the highest per capita in the world, by one account. Indebtedness to Washington, and the general lackadaisical atmosphere of Costa Rica were causing problems of their own.

No doubt most citizens would have preferred to keep their country out of the general turmoil enveloping the region, but it was difficult, particularly since the arrival of Commander Zero. Officially, the government had turned a blind eye to his presence: when I asked an official about his activities, he was characteristically evasive.

'Well,' he said, 'officially, Commander Zero isn't in Costa Rica, he's in Nicaragua.'

'And if I ask you unofficially?'

'It's a long border. Two hundred miles. What can we do?' He shrugged his shoulders.

'Well, you could try to find him,' I suggested. 'It can't be that hard to trace several thousand men in army uniform.'

'Ah,' said the official, 'but we haven't got an army.'

'But you have got a police force, haven't you?'

'But we only have one revolver for three,' he said, caught between embarrassment and pride. 'You know one of our biggest problems? Many times when one of them draws his gun, he shoots himself in the foot.'

I should have liked to meet Commander Zero, but his so-called Democratic Revolutionary Alliance was in disarray after a botched assassination attempt of gothic proportions. In the farrago of rumours, fantasies and outright lies in which the Nicaraguan counter-revolutionaries passed their dreamy days, some of the details of the attempted murder of Commander Zero were bewilderingly confused. But in conversations soon after I arrived, the background to the story became clear enough.

Eden Pastora had acquired his *nom de guerre* – Commander Zero – during the capture of the National Palace by Sandinista guerillas in August 1978. After the Nicaraguan revolution he had been made Vice-Minister of Defence in charge of training the local militia, a largely honorary position. Relegated 'from Henry V to Pistol', as Graham Greene put it, Pastora was a melancholic and restless participant in government. By July 1981, he had had enough. Complaining that the country was being sold to the Cubans and Russians, he left Nicaragua to wander about Mexico and Panama, talking to anyone who would listen about how the revolution he had fought for had been betrayed. Pastora undoubtedly had genuine reservations about the direction Nicaragua was taking, although he made a point of saying that he would never join forces with the exiled supporters of Somoza. In his decision to leave Nicaragua there was also, it seemed, something of the rootlessness of the prize-fighter who can't get out of the ring: civilian life in peacetime offered too few challenges. Pastora ended up in Costa Rica, where he was joined by other disillusioned revolutionaries, notably Alfonso Robelo, a one-time member of the Sandinista ruling junta.

Things started disastrously. Having raised a force to fight the Sandinistas, Pastora then had to send them all off to refugee camps because he couldn't afford to feed them. But soon guns, supplies and uniforms began to arrive, including a consignment of several hundred Soviet assault rifles captured by the Israelis during their invasion of Lebanon, and doubtless sent at Washington's request. Then more supplies began to arrive from shadowy 'anti-communist' organizations and 'benevolent individuals', meaning the CIA. Commander Zero took his men back into the hills along the border between Costa Rica and Nicaragua, and resumed the war which the success of the revolution had interrupted.

No one knew how many fighters Pastora commanded in the Democratic Revolutionary Alliance: estimates varied from about two to eight thousand, although some of the rum-punch raconteurs in San José doubted it was really more than a few hundred. They seemed reasonably well equipped and everyone believed their supplies came from the Americans. The embassy didn't even bother to deny it any more. The usual method, according to the gossip, was for planes to take off from a military airbase in San Salvador, head out to the Pacific and then down the coast of Nicaragua. Just inside the Costa Rican border, they would land on grass airstrips in the jungle. One of the less well hidden landing strips was owned by a fanatically right-wing American who had flown with the US airforce during the Second World War and was now happy to let his ranch be used in the fight against communism. The aircraft were usually unmarked, the pilots of Central American origin, hired by the CIA on short-term, deniable contracts.

A few months before I arrived, peasants near the Nicaraguan border had begun to tell stories of an aircraft which had crashed on a remote jungle-covered mountainside. By the time news of their discovery reached San José, a rescue team had already visited the scene of the accident and found the burned-out skeleton of an elderly DC3 aircraft but, strangely, no bodies. The peasants told them that they had often heard the plane passing overhead in the dark, and that on the night it had crashed there had been no fire, although the aircraft was badly damaged and incapable of taking off again. They were certain that the pilot and passengers had been killed in the impact of the crash. Soon afterwards strangers had arrived at the site of the accident and begun to pull objects from the fuselage, including ammunition and three bodies, which they loaded into jeeps and drove away. Then they set the aircraft alight and left. By the time the official rescue team reached the scene, nothing was left of the Dakota but for a charred wreck, a few shell casings and the soles of what looked like army boots.

But the relationship between Commander Zero and the Agency was a stormy one. While the Contras operating from Honduras were the direct creation of the CIA, Pastora was of an independent and mercurial cast of mind. His main value to the CIA was his name: his revolutionary pedigree was impeccable, whereas the Contras in Honduras included a good number whose pretensions to be fighting for democracy were transparently implausible. If the two forces could be brought together, not only would Commander Zero's reputation improve the status of the agency's militia in Honduras, but the Nicaraguan government would come under co-ordinated attack from both borders. And as an additional dividend, Pastora's private army would fall increasingly under American direction. However, the former Sandinista resisted the scheme, maintaining that the Honduran Contras were infested by veterans of Somoza's hateful National Guard. Since he had spent years fighting against the Guard, the plan for unity seemed destined to fail, and eventually the pressure for unification fractured the leadership of the Democratic Revolutionary Alliance. In May 1984, the majority of Pastora's political lieutenants announced that they had agreed to accept the CIA's proposal.

Two days later, the small group of foreign correspondents in San José were telephoned late at night. They should be ready to leave the following morning for a press conference at which Eden Pastora would have something important to say about the plans for a merger.

About fifteen journalists met the next morning at a hotel on the edge of town and a small convoy set off, led by a Landcruiser owned by the guerillas. After driving north for several hours, they reached one of the tributaries of the San Juan river, where the group clambered into dug-out canoes. Most of them knew each other reasonably well, although in addition to the core of reporters based permanently in Costa Rica, there were inevitably a few who were on shorter assignments. By Central American standards, Costa Rica was considered a relatively unexciting posting, a backwater whose main advantages were safety and a collection of reasonable restaurants. The trip to see Commander Zero was welcome almost as much for the break in routine it offered as for any news it might produce.

Soon they reached the San Juan river itself, the dividing line between Nicaragua and Costa Rica. The outboard motors propelled the dug-out canoes through the jungle, passing several deserted wooden houses on the river bank. By this time it was evening. Finally they stopped at a drab clapboard house which was obviously occupied. Pastora's guerillas showed them into a room, where the commander was sitting at a narrow wooden table, clean-shaven and in well-laundered combat kit. He rose to greet the correspondents, and for a few minutes the banter flew back and forth. Many of the journalists believed that Pastora had been in San José the night before, and that part of their delay in arriving at the house had been engineered to ensure that he was back in Nicaragua and dressed in his military fatigues by the time they arrived.

Pastora's meetings with the press were notorious: he could go on for hours in rambling conversations which would end long after everyone had put their notebooks and tape recorders away. Now he began to answer their first questions. One of the journalists, a Dane, went outside, leaving the camera case he had brought with him on the floor of the room. A female guerilla passed around cups of coffee.

Suddenly the room exploded in a brilliant hot flash. Some of the journalists realized as it was happening that a bomb had gone off, dimly aware that they had become part of a scene they had previously only witnessed as aftermath.

Pastora was only slightly hurt, superficial shrapnel wounds mainly. But several of his guerillas were dead or dying, and so were three journalists. The most acutely injured, including a Costa Rican cameraman whose camera battery had been blown through his torso, would not survive long. A young American reporter, Linda Frazier, had had both legs blown off and it was obvious she would bleed to death unless she received urgent medical attention.

Tony Avirgan, one of the journalists present, told me afterwards how he had crawled to the door with a hole in his side and multiple shrapnel wounds, to see guerillas running towards the house screaming 'Commandante, Commandante', terrified that Commander Zero might be dead. The Danish journalist re-entered the room a few moments later, solicitously asking whom he could help.

To save the lives of the seriously injured, they would have to be taken to hospital quickly. The nearest medical facilities were back in Costa Rica – ahead in Nicaragua were only jungle and hostile patrols. There was one high-speed launch tied up outside, which would make the journey far more quickly than any of the dug-out canoes, but the guerillas immediately commandeered it for the superficially injured Commander Zero. One of the correspondents begged them to take the legless American girl, but the boat cast off without her.

The wounded journalists and guerillas were left lying in the shattered room, fragments of the camera case, wood, glass and metal embedded in their bodies. Live high-voltage electricity cables had caused further severe burns for some of the victims. When guerilla medics finally arrived they didn't seem to know what to do, and had only the crudest of supplies. Avirgan noticed that the Danish journalist was lying on the floor among the wounded, as if he was injured himself.

Hours of suffering passed before the wounded were evacuated from the scene of the explosion. By then two of the journalists and eight of the rebels were dead or dying. Linda Frazier died as they lifted her legless body into one of the boats.

The hospital at San Carlos was overwhelmed. As the local doctors and nurses struggled to cope with the wounded, other journalists arrived to interview the survivors, including the Danish journalist. Tony Avirgan's wife, Martha Honey, also turned up, anxious for news of her injured husband. As she waited outside, hospital staff emerged periodically to ask whether she was a friend of the Danish journalist: he kept asking whether a woman had come to collect him. No woman arrived, and as soon as he could do so he discharged himself from the hospital and took a taxi to San José.

The bombing plunged the Costa Rican authorities into confused paralysis. Although the explosion had technically occurred on foreign soil, it had obviously been planned and executed from Costa Rica. Yet it was four days before the police began an investigation. The government ordered that Pastora be shipped out of the country on a stretcher at once, but journalists, including those who needed urgent medical treatment abroad, were forbidden to leave.

Those reporters who were not too seriously injured, and those who by good fortune had not accepted the invitation to the press conference, began their own investigation. Almost certainly the bomb had been planted by the Danish reporter, who had used the name Per Anker Hansen. It emerged that he had spent several weeks in Costa Rica, staying at a second-rate hotel in San José, not an establishment normally patronized by the press. He had entered the country with a woman travelling on a French passport, although none of the journalists could recall seeing him with her.

Martha Honey discovered that Hansen had made several attempts to interview Commander Zero, although all had failed. Finally, he had teamed up with a Swedish television journalist shortly before the trip to the border to plant the bomb. The Swede recalled that Hansen had sought him out at the hotel, suggesting that someone might have engineered their meeting to provide an unwitting accomplice. The two men had spoken English together, Hansen explaining his odd accent by saying that although he had Danish nationality, he had been brought up in Latin America. Other journalists recalled that he spoke excellent Spanish, although it seems curious in retrospect that a Swede did not notice that a fellow Scandinavian was an impostor.

The name Hansen was false, of course, and when the Costa Ricans revealed their findings, the Danish authorities disclosed that the passport had been stolen. There was no doubt he had fled Costa Rica, and the few other traces he had left were equally unfruitful: the photographic agency for which he said he worked did not exist, and at the address he gave in Paris, no one had heard of him.

But there was plenty of evidence as to the physical appearance of the bomber: pictures taken at the press conference and during the interview in hospital afterwards, when he was pretending to be wounded, showed a thin-faced man with dark hair and a dark beard. When the photograph was released to the press, a man in Panama recalled having been involved in a traffic accident with a man named Hansen of similar appearance, though nothing came of that line of inquiry. A check by Interpol suggested that Hansen might be a well-known member of ETA, the Basque separatist organization, which caused great excitement. American officials unofficially confirmed the ETA connection, but when the Costa Ricans went public with the name of the suspected bomber, the French police revealed that the Basque in question had been under surveillance in France for the previous month, and could therefore not have been involved.

At this point the trail gave out. The investigation, such as it was, had been bungled from beginning to end. The suspect's hotel room had never even been tested for fingerprints.

The explosion had obviously been the work of a professional: his calm in spending all day cradling the bomb on his lap in the jeep and then the canoe, his composure in walking back into the room after the explosion, passing the night in hospital and giving interviews – all testified to his expertise. And there was no shortage of people willing to suggest that the Costa Ricans had deliberately messed up the case because the Americans had asked them to do so, that the bombing had been planned by the CIA because Pastora was the biggest stumbling block in their plans to unite the Contras. According to this theory, the bombing had come at the end of an ultimatum period from the Agency, and Pastora had probably only been saved from death by the body of the woman with the coffee. As an explanation it made a certain amount of sense.

But equally, the Sandinistas had good reason to want Commander Zero dead, and they or their friends in Eastern Europe might easily have organized the incident. It could even have been the work of malcontents within Pastora's own Democratic Revolutionary Alliance who wanted to see the merger go ahead. At any event, with his picture splashed all over the newspapers, the assassin's anonymity was gone.

The Costa Rican police were still notionally working on the case, however. I had arranged to meet Mark Baillie, the Reuters reporter in San José, to try to learn more than I would from official sources. In theory, he was head of the Reuters team covering the Central American crisis, but wherever Central America was in crisis, it was certainly not in Costa Rica. Although under thirty, Mark had the mannerisms of a nineteenth-century foreign correspondent, languid, urbane and a little unworldly.

We had arranged to meet on the terrace of San José's best hotel, an elegant building whose appearance and style both testified to an age of infinite leisure. He arrived late. His experience of the latest police initiative in the hunt for the bomber was illuminating. He had been driving home when five plain-clothes policemen armed with rifles had jumped out, surrounded the car and produced a warrant entitling them to search the house of 'a presumed English journalist'.

The decision to arrest a squat Englishman with fair hair, thin lips and a clean-shaven appearance when photographs showed the suspect to be thin, thick-lipped, dark-haired and bearded was bizarre, to say the least. Eventually the police admitted their mistake: they had been alerted in an act of revenge by the Reuters gardener whom Mark had recently fired for attacking him while drunk.

At least no one had been shot in the foot, but the chances of finding the would-be assassin seemed more remote than ever. In the meantime, Pastora had returned to the hills, with the promise that the war would continue 'to final victory'.

There was a bus which left San José in the early evening and reached Panama City the following afternoon, assuming no problems en route. I found a seat near the front and scanned the newspaper. Twenty-two earth tremors in the first week of August ... three ambulancemen in hospital after their vehicle had run off the road ... the banana workers still on strike ... a poll showing that seventy-nine per cent of Costa Ricans disapprove of the Sandinistas.

'Are you going far?' A youth – he looked like a student – had sat down in the seat next to me.

'To Panama.'

'Be careful in Panama.' He knotted his face into an expression of concern. 'It's full of thieves. They'll steal the shirt off your back if you give them the chance.'

So it had happened again. Six international borders to be crossed, and at five of them worried warnings about my safety. Nicaraguans had thought Costa Rica safe enough, but Costa Ricans had a lesser degree of confidence in their neighbours. The young man smoothed the bottom of his moustache down into his mouth, chewing at the ends. He was silent for a moment, then continued proudly.

'How do you like my country?' It was something to be said for Costa Rica that ordinary citizens felt they had a share in 'their' country.

'It seems very peaceful,' I said. Not a profound observation, but it came easily to mind.

'We're pretty civilized, you see,' said the student. 'Have you had a tour of San José?'

'No, not an official one.'

'You see that house there?' said the student, seizing the opportunity presented by my ignorance. 'The one with the bougainvillea climbing over the security fence? It belongs to the richest man in Costa Rica. He's Spanish. They sent him to the United States during the Spanish Civil War to buy guns to fight Franco. But he kept the money and came here instead.'

There was no disapproval in the boy's voice: to him it was as conventional a way of making a living as being an engineer or a teacher. There were some aspects of Costa Rica's neutrality which came close to the moral vigour of a Swiss bank.

'Hey! look over there!' he said. I glanced out of the window at the direction in which he was pointing.

'You see that house with the television cameras on top of the stone walls? That's where Robert Vesco lived when the government gave him asylum here.'

The house was hidden behind tall grey walls, the sort of

ostentatious hideaway gangsters can afford when they know the government won't move a finger against them.

Beyond the suburbs we climbed into the hills, past Don Pepé's little shack, and on up the side of the volcano. The light was fading fast.

'Funny thing about the volcanoes here,' said the student. 'Seems to be a connection between natural disasters and the American president. The last time this volcano erupted, President Kennedy was on a visit here. Then, when President Johnson came, he'd got halfway down the aircraft steps and there was an eruption at one of the other volcanoes. The last president to visit was Reagan. Three days after he'd gone, we had the worst earthquake in the country's history.' It was an appropriate enough metaphor for the relationship between Central and North America. The drowsiness I had felt earlier began to overwhelm me.

'And over there . . .' But the words were remote.

7

Balboa's Bequest

Panama seemed empty by comparison with places like El Salvador. Swathes of hillside and marshy pastureland rolled by outside the bus. Beyond the verges of the road, any sign of human life was soon swallowed up in the trees. In the early morning light the Pacific was a dull grey, but as the day wore on and the heat rose its colour deepened until by midday it looked like old pewter.

The border formalities had passed in a sleepy haze and I had even forgotten about doctoring my visa until the official nonchalantly handed it back to me on the Panamanian side of the frontier.

The Pan American Highway went as far as Panama City and a little way beyond, but then, in the impenetrable mountains and jungles of Darien, it suddenly stopped, only beginning again south of the border with Colombia, from where it ran down through South America. There had been frequent talk of bridging the break in the road and fulfilling the dream of a highway through the Americas, but the lack of action emphasized the fact that the Central American isthmus, connected to the United States, was politically and culturally distinct from the rest of Latin America.

The United States had, in effect, created the state of Panama by giving breath to the gigantic enterprise of the canal. Without the activities of American financiers, engineers and political meddlers, the country would have remained a pestilential jungly irrelevance. As a consequence, although Panama had never been a formal colony, it was, fundamentally, a colonial country. A Great Power had exploited and blessed a poor backwater, in the process bequeathing a sense of dependence which informed not merely political and economic relations, but their entire cultural identity as well. Even the form of Spanish they spoke, the vocabulary liberally peppered with words like 'El flashlight',

'El lipstick', 'El cheesecake', was a bastard hybrid. In Panama it was not, as in the case of many former French or British colonies, that administrative and judicial systems had been grafted on, while most people lived on in squalor relatively untouched by the Europeans. The very essence of Panamanian society was the result of imperial ambition.

We approached Panama City across The Bridge of the Americas, a majestic metal arch spanning the entrance to the canal. It was hot and muggy, the sun shut out behind a furnace-grey sky. In the bay beyond the mouth of the canal, twenty ships lay at anchor in the haze, opaque outlines on a beige sea.

'Panama! The name conjures up visions of the Spanish Main, pirates and gold,' declared the little guidebook I had bought, seizing and embellishing what little picture any visitor might have of the country. My own expectations, such as they were, came from a poem I had learned as a child – 'Drake's Drum', the ode to that great Elizabethan sea-captain. After a lifetime of raiding Spanish treasure trains, circumnavigating the world and defeating the Armada, Drake had finally succumbed to dysentery on the Atlantic coast of Panama, from whence 'slung atween the round shot in Nombre Dios Bay', he might be summoned in the hour of England's need.

> Call him on the deep sea, call him up the Sound,
> Call him when ye sail to meet the foe;
> Where the old trade's plyin' an' the old flag flyin'
> They shall find him ware an' wakin', as they found
> him long ago!

Panama had been important then for the same reason it was important now – as the narrowest stretch of land between two oceans. Initially it wasn't even administered by the Spanish as part of the rest of Central America, but acquired a critical significance once they discovered a bountiful source of silver at Potosi in what is now Bolivia. It was via Panama and Portobelo, its principal port on the Atlantic coast, that the silver was shipped back to Spain.

By the end of the sixteenth century the Spanish had transported across the Atlantic three times as much gold and silver

as had been in circulation in all of Europe one hundred years
earlier, and within Spain a massive bureaucracy developed
merely to keep track of the precious metals arriving from Latin
America. Crafts and trades were allowed to die in order that
manpower might be released to monitor the movement of gold
and silver and the main business of the country became the
administration of the Empire.

Panama was the key to the success of Spain's newfound
trading activities. From Potosi, silver was transported by pack
animal to the Pacific, and then by ship up the coast to Panama.
From there, mule trains carried the cargo across to the Atlantic
for shipment back to Europe. Panama consequently became an
attractive hunting ground for buccaneers who soon took to
attacking either the mule trains or the cargo fleets as they
loaded up on the Atlantic coast. In 1668, Henry Morgan,
perhaps the most infamous of the British pirates who stalked
the Spanish Main, plundered Portobelo. Three years later he
crossed to the Pacific coast and burned Panama City to the
ground. Towards the end of his lifetime of nautical robbery, he
was rewarded with a knighthood and the governorship of
Jamaica. The history of Panama made it seem a place of
romance and history.

The centre of Panama City dashed illusions in moments. The
main street was a mass of grey concrete, having been colonized
by American banking corporations, hotels and other depressing
examples of the work of a thousand second-rate architects. The
bay upon which the town was built, sweeping and protective,
was overshadowed by armies of twenty-floor office blocks. The
neon signs of the Holiday Inn and the Hilton winked at each
other across the city.

After eighteen hours on the bus, I was tired and dirty and
decided to treat myself to a room at a hotel across the street
from the Hilton. It was hideously expensive and rather tatty.
For the sixty dollars it cost I could have spent three weeks in
some of the other hotels I had used. After a shower I took a
walk down towards the seashore. As I left the hotel, the fat
little man on the Wurlitzer organ, 'Panama's second biggest

tourist attraction, once played in the United States', was playing 'Yankee Doodle Dandy'.

In the stores, although the goods were nominally priced in the national currency, balboas, the Panamanians had never got around to printing paper notes. Thus the only paper money in circulation was American, another indication of the semi-colonial history of the country.

According to local gossip, Panama was currently awash with dollar bills. One young banker, in an immaculate blazer and well-polished shoes and reeking of expensive aftershave, explained why. Under Panamanian law, customers could open secret accounts which would never be exposed to police or other investigators, a guarantee that could no longer be promised by the Cayman Islands or Switzerland. As a result, American drug dealers were shipping in cash by the planeload, attracted also by the fact that Panama was conveniently situated between Colombia, which produced the cocaine, and the United States, its principal market. Better still, since many of the drug smugglers were of Hispanic descent, Panama was Spanish-speaking.

The confidentiality of the banking system meant that nearly one hundred and forty banks had set up in business in Panama, and many of them would take deposits 'no questions asked', the young man told me with a hint of pride. The cash surplus was such that the banks didn't have sufficient storage space and monthly consignments had to be shipped back to the United States Treasury. In the course of a year these cash shipments amounted to nearly two billion dollars. Where once thieves had come to steal gold en route to Spain, they now came to bank it.

'It's much more than just a canal,' several Panamanians said when they talked about their country, aggravated that it should be known for nothing else. But the plain fact was that without the canal Panama would not exist as a nation.

The Panama Canal was the grandest achievement of the emerging American empire: a feat of science, engineering and medicine so impressive that it set the tone for a century in which the power of the American foundries would drive the economy of the rest of the world. In digging the channel which bisected the Americas and linked the Atlantic with the Pacific, the United States affirmed Manifest Destiny and established Yankee suzerainty. Although the Suez Canal had been built by the French, in 'East of Suez' it became the emblem of the British Empire. By contrast, the building of the Panama Canal was an early signal of the decline of the European powers and the emerging strength of the United States. The Americans succeeded where the French failed.

The idea of building a canal linking the two oceans, and thereby saving the expense, time and danger of a voyage around the Horn, had been tossed about as fanciful speculation almost from the moment that Balboa's conquistadores first hacked their way across the isthmus and gazed in wonder at the expanse of the Pacific. King Charles V even commissioned a survey of possible routes for a canal in 1524. But although Panama was the narrowest point in the sliver of land connecting the two Americas, as the potential site for a canal it had a number of disadvantages, not least its appalling record as a breeding-ground for tropical fevers and the fact that any engineer would have to find some way of cutting through the central spine of mountains. Numerous other routes were considered, through Mexico, Costa Rica and Nicaragua. The plans were all re-examined when the Californian Gold Rush began, but none of the proposed canals could be built in time. For a while the Nicaraguan route, which had been advocated by the German explorer Alexander von Humboldt, seemed the favourite choice. Vanderbilt's transit company was making handsome profits from the journey via Lake Nicaragua, until it was put out of business by the building of a railway across Panama in 1855. Completed twenty years before any coast-to-coast line was operating within the United States, and built at staggering cost, a one-way ticket on the forty-seven and a half miles of the Panama Railroad cost $25, payable in gold.

The railway was a prodigious success. Profits averaged over one million dollars per annum and Panama Railroad shares became the most sought-after on the New York Stock Exchange. But a canal capable of carrying ocean-going vessels would, it was argued, be inestimably more valuable, though the problems were enormous. It was well known that conditions for the gangs of imported railway construction workers had been so harsh that each morning the trees around the labourers' camps were decorated with the corpses of those who had sneaked out to hang themselves during the night rather than face another day toiling in the heat of the jungle. Epidemics of malaria, dysentery and tropical fevers had swept through the work gangs with such lethal results that it was said that each sleeper had cost one human life. Whilst this particular fact is probably an exaggeration, it is true to say that so many of the Irish, West Indian and Chinese labourers died without leaving word of their next-of-kin that the Railroad Company was able to finance its own hospital by selling their corpses to medical schools overseas.

If anyone was capable of overcoming the difficulties, it was likely to be the man who had driven a canal one hundred miles through the sands of Suez, and in 1880 the elegant figure of the seventy-four-year-old Viscount Ferdinand de Lesseps arrived in Panama. Money to begin work on the canal had easily been raised from the sale of shares in Paris, an issue so popular that it was subscribed twice over: the Panama project had the dangerous and deceptive attraction of being only half the distance of the Suez Canal. But while in France there was boundless enthusiasm for the new canal, in Panama the practical problems were huge — poisonous snakes, wild animals, mosquitoes, the enveloping, oppressive walls of matted jungle, and the debilitating epidemics of malaria, yellow fever and cholera. The gangs of engineers and labourers had to work in thunderous torrential downpours which could wash slides of earth down to fill up the tediously dug channel in seconds, and deposit an inch of rain in an hour.

Yet the attractions of well-paid employment on the greatest engineering project in the world outweighed the difficulties and dangers and thousands of hungry workmen poured into Panama from every corner of the globe. In their wake came drink, disease and despair, and battalions of prostitutes. The labourers' settlements in Panama City and Colon were filthy fetid swamps alive with vermin and vice, and at least twenty thousand people died in the waves of sickness which swept through their miserable homes. The most popular verse produced was the poetry of suffering:

> You are going to have the fever,
> Yellow Eyes!
> In about ten days from now
> Iron bands will clamp your brow;
> Your tongue resemble curdled cream,
> A rusty streak the central seam;
> Your mouth will taste of horrid things,
> With claws and horns and fins and wings;
> Your head will weigh a ton or more,
> And forty gales within it roar!

De Lesseps became known as The Great Undertaker.

But the greatest obstacle was that the Viscount's scheme of a canal at sea level, modelled on the Suez Canal, was simply not feasible in Panama, where it was impossible to cut through the mountains in the centre of the country. A scheme involving a series of locks, designed to raise vessels across the hills, might have been a viable alternative, but the great engineer was unwilling to announce a change of plan, allowing confidence in the company to evaporate. Money began to run out. Share prices crashed. Desperate to restore faith, the company bribed Parisian newspapers to paint a brighter picture, but to no avail: inevitably and spectacularly, the whole scheme eventually collapsed, engulfed by the biggest financial scandal France had ever witnessed. A belated inquiry found senior company officials guilty of grotesque malpractice and condemned de Lesseps to five years' gaol. A broken old man, too weak to be removed from his home, he died in December 1894.

The canal conceived by the elderly French adventurer was ultimately delivered by a young American politician. Theodore Roosevelt, only forty-two when he entered the White House and possessed of apparently inexhaustible energy, became obsessed by the project. Not only was it indispensable if America was to become the greatest naval power in the world, but construction and possession of the canal would constitute a potent imperial talisman. Though contemporary historians like David McCullough (in his epic account *The Path Between The Seas*) are inclined to play down the suggestion that the canal was the work of one man, the completion of the project was pre-eminently the achievement of Teddy Roosevelt. Less bombastic men might have worried over political or diplomatic niceties such as the fact that approval would be needed from the government through whose territory the big ditch would run. But in a speech to California students, Roosevelt was to boast, 'I took the isthmus, started the canal and then left Congress not to debate the canal, but to debate me.' Perhaps it was a case of the hour creating the man, for Roosevelt's aggressive behaviour was typical of the new American attitude to its growing empire. Later, when the Attorney General was asked by Roosevelt to evolve a legal defence for America's high-handedness, he is said to have answered, 'Oh Mr President, do not let so great an achievement suffer from any taint of legality.'

In November 1906, Roosevelt himself arrived in Panama to inspect the work in progress, the first occasion on which an American president had left the country while in office. He had deliberately chosen the wettest time of the year and spent three days tramping about the excavations in his high-buttoned white suit and straw hat, sitting in the pouring rain to be photographed at the controls of one of the great steam shovels scraping the mud out of the canal basin. His bull-like appearance, as he strode through the crowds of wet labourers, jabbing out questions to his entourage, nodding understandingly when answered, provided physical expression of the fact that here, in the stinking, sweaty jungles of a foreign land, the American empire was being forged. It was, he told Congress on his return, 'a stupendous work'.

The most pressing legal problem had been raised by the government of the Republic of Colombia, who controlled the land through which the canal would pass. The canal company distrusted the Colombians, believing their avarice to be rivalled only by their capacity for prevarication and mischief-making. When they delayed over signing the agreement allowing the

Americans to begin work, Philippe Bunau-Varilla, the dapper little Frenchman who had finally scotched the Nicaragua Canal scheme, fanned the glowing coals of incipient rebellion in Panama, where there were plenty of people who stood to benefit if the project went ahead. First he supplied a group of discontented Panamanians with a draft constitution, a proclamation of independence and a new national flag hastily stitched together by his wife. Then the United States, who had discreetly been endorsing his efforts, sent a gunboat to stand offshore and protect the revolution from the Colombian army. When the Colombian government attempted to move what troops they had in Panama from their barracks on one side of the country to the scene of the rebellion on the other, the gunboat commander ordered the railroad company not to carry them. The insurrection was an immediate success. Washington gave its official blessing by immediately giving the new nation diplomatic recognition.

Having persuaded the rulers of the newly independent state to let him act as their agent in Washington, Bunau-Varilla promptly signed a treaty with the American Secretary of State, John Hay, granting the United States the right to build and manage a canal 'in perpetuity'. By the time Panamanian representatives arrived in Washington, the business had been concluded. In return for a payment of $10,000,000 and an annual fee of $250,000, not only did America have the right to build a canal, she was also entitled to establish a settlement ten miles wide along the banks of the canal from which Panamanians would be excluded. The United States could not have hoped for a more favourable arrangement: the newly independent state would be neatly divided by a piece of territory unalterably a part of America for all time.

The opening of the canal in August 1914 marked the first great endeavour of the emerging American empire and demonstrated the indomitable spirit which, over fifty years later, would put the first man on the moon. The diseases which had initially jeopardized the success of the project were eradicated. The engineering achievements were remarkable, involving the design and creation of the most extensive lock system and the biggest dam to date. Even the organization of the labour force was a feat equivalent to the construction of two new towns. While America celebrated, European powers embarked upon the convulsive struggle which was to mark the beginning of their decline.

Out in the bay, two boys were riding the breakers. Behind them half a dozen ships were lying at anchor at the point where the grey Pacific met the leaden sky. I could see the circular tower of the Holiday Inn and the new concrete blocks in which Panama's squadrons of bankers and lawyers had their offices. The corniche running along the edge of the bay was faintly reminiscent of how Beirut must have looked before the civil war blew holes in most of the landmarks. From where I was standing Panama City looked clean, affluent, modern. Yet it was a superficial impression – the previous evening I had been warned not to walk along the seafront after dusk because of the danger of robbery. Behind me in the sea wall was a shrine-cum-monument commemorating the heroes of the canal from the conquistadores to de Lesseps and the Americans. There was not a sign of any other visitor: evidently not many people came to inspect the tribute to the men who had given Panama its *raison d'être*.

Inland, the narrow streets ran downhill, overhung by the wooden balconies of buildings erected at the time the canal was being built. Washing-lines ran across the street from every balcony, indicating that each house might well be home for a dozen different families – often the sky was entirely blotted out by yards of washing hanging to dry. The shutters of most of the houses were open and inside there were men and women of every race. In one, a European in a grubby white singlet had fallen asleep watching a beauty contest on television. (It was only eleven in the morning, but the Panamanians are apparently obsessed by these events.) In the next window a black woman was scrubbing shirts. Further on, a Chinaman was sewing in a sweatshop. At the end of the street was an Indian pawnshop. The variety of nationalities testified to the thousands who had flocked into the country to work on the canal and the numbers since then who had fetched up in the city after their ships had passed through. As a consequence of their country being a racial melting-pot, the Panamanians seemed indifferent to strangers.

I cut down a side alley between the rows of wooden houses. The stink of rotting household waste was heavy and cloying. A brown rat ran across my path carrying what might, at best, have been a piece of sausage. I looked at the pile of garbage to my right and saw it was alive with long smooth tails.

The Colonial Hotel, an impressive white mansion, looked as if it might have a bar. Like most places in Old Panama, it had seen better days. There was an old Indian sitting in a tattered wicker chair in the hall; when I asked him if they had anything to drink, he pointed wordlessly to the kitchen, as if customers came infrequently and when they did their needs were effort-lessly predictable. I walked across to the doorway above which someone had scrawled 'kitchen' in charcoal. The door-jambs were grey and greasy and a tattered curtain was hanging halfway across. Inside, there was a single large pot stewing on a range. The stench of rancid cooking fat and rotting meat made my stomach heave.

Further down towards the waterfront, the slums came to an end. At the water's edge was the presidential palace, an elegant white villa with herons in the courtyard fountain, and four soldiers in dark glasses on the street outside. A young seaman with so many tattoos on his arms that they were almost solid blue was sitting on a bench between the palace and the sea. Incongruously, he was bouncing a baby up and down on his knees. He turned to stare at me, a little curious. I wished him 'Good morning' in Spanish, then in English, then French, before I realized from the grunting noises he was making to the child that he was deaf and dumb.

In the afternoon I took a taxi up to the offices of the Canal Commission. It was like entering another country. In a sense the impression was accurate: after all, the canal and all its appurtenances had been designed to be American in perpetuity.

On one side of the road at the edge of the Canal Zone was a sprawling mess of tenement blocks, tatty shops, cantinas and broken-down old cars. The streets were packed with people – a confusion of walkers and workers, beggars, drunks, children and animals, looking imprisoned in their lack of space. Across the road, it was as if the authorities were halfway through a programme of slum clearance. There were bungalows neatly surrounded by expanses of well-watered lawn. Big American cars moved noiselessly along leafy suburban avenues. This was the Canal Zone and I realized that my impression on the other side of the street had been wrong. It wasn't that the poor people were imprisoned in their tenements. It was that they were excluded from the Zone.

I walked up to the headquarters of the Canal Commission, a squat, stolid block which, like every other building roundabout, had an air of unspeakable blandness about it. The Commission had only recently acquired its name – until 1979 it had been the Panama Canal Company, a subsidiary of the Pentagon which had run the canal on behalf of the United States government. Under the terms of the agreement which the Panamanians had unwittingly signed in 1903, the Canal Zone had been destined to remain American to the end of time, but this arrangement irritated the natives to the extent that the Zone seemed like a constantly suppurating wound running across the middle of the nation. In 1977 General Omar Torrijos, Panama's iconoclastic ruler, succeeded in persuading the Carter administration to sign a treaty which would hand full control of the canal to the Panamanians on 31 December 1999. In the interim, Americans and Panamanians would work side by side, with the Panamanians gradually replacing Americans. By this time, the previous exclusiveness of the Canal Zone should no longer have been in evidence.

In the public relations office to which I was directed by humourless security guards, there was a Panamanian in control. After welcoming me politely, he introduced his deputy, one Willie K. Friar.

Mrs (Wilhelmina?) Friar responded testily to my questions about the Zone. 'There *never was* a chain-link fence separating the Zone from the rest of Panama,' she said. Yet every Panamanian I met assured me it had existed. Not according to the officials.

I asked how one might go about meeting some of the Americans living in the Zone to find out how they felt about the canal passing into Panamanian control.

'You won't find any of them want to talk to you,' said Willie, wearily. 'In fact I wouldn't even be prepared to tell you where you could meet any of them. We had plenty of newspapermen come down here around the time the treaty was being negotiated, and they made us look like a lot of backwoodsmen.'

'What do you mean?'

'Oh, they wrote a lot of stuff quoting the Zonians saying they didn't think the Panamanians had any right to the canal, how they hadn't any idea how to operate it, that kind of thing.' From what I had heard, these seemed to be entirely accurate reflections of how many Zonians felt about handing over the canal, but I didn't say so. We passed a few minutes in pleasantries, exchanging interesting but unsurprising facts. The highest toll ever paid was for the *Queen Elizabeth II*, the lowest for a swimmer in 1928; the average time spent crossing from port to port was eight hours or so. By far the most fascinating aspects of the canal were the story of its construction and the battle for control; otherwise it was just a canal like any other. Perhaps that was what explained the awful dullness that pervaded the place. Everything in the Canal Zone was run by the Commission: the schools, the grocery stores, the bars. An entire community insulated from the fact that it was living in Latin America, and bound in service to a ditch filled with water. There were people who had lived in the Canal Zone all their lives: it would be surprising if they *didn't* come across as backwoodsmen.

'Look,' she said, 'I've got to go now. You'll never get a taxi – can I give you a ride down to Fourth of July Avenue? You'll be able to pick up a cab down there without too much trouble.'

I accepted her offer and we drove towards the centre through quiet and well-ordered streets which might have been in any suburb anywhere in America. She dropped me off at the point where the Zone ended and Panama began. I looked up at the Panamanian street sign on what she had called Fourth of July Avenue. It read Avenue of the Martyrs.

* * *

The lasting slight to nationhood represented by the canal eventually found its focus in the predictable question of a flag. Initially it had been of such little significance that a national flag had been stitched together in Bunau-Varilla's parlour. But as time went on, the fact that a foreign flag flew above land that was geographically part of Panama came to be interpreted as evidence of a fifth, internal, frontier. Wiser and more liberal Americans recognized that they would have to find some means of appeasing the Panamanians, and in 1958 even President Eisenhower was sufficiently disturbed by student riots provoked by the flag question that he sent his brother Milton to Panama to produce recommendations for future peace. He wrote later: 'The same oppressive conditions and gross inequalities flagrant in other Latin American republics exist in Panama – but here there is a ready-made scapegoat: the alleged profit-making owner of the canal, the United States . . . the hordes of under-privileged living on either side of the Zone see only a strip of land which represents the nation of undreamed-of riches.'

Milton Eisenhower's visit to Panama was counter-productive: his vaguely sympathetic report was interpreted as an indication that the Americans were thinking of handing over the canal, and when nothing came of it, the Panamanians took to the streets again. A wire fence went up around parts of the Zone to keep the troublemakers out. The tension continued. Eventually the Kennedy administration conceded that the Panamanian flag might be flown alongside the American flag at certain points within the Canal Zone, as 'evidence of Panama's titular sovereignty'. Enter Jimmy Jenkins.

Jenkins was one of six sons of a driver of one of the locomotives which pulled vessels through the locks on the canal. His school, Balboa High School, was an American school like any other, but for the fact that it was in Panama and that many of the pupils shared the small-minded obsessions of their parents. In December 1963, the governor of the Canal Zone (in terms of its system of government, the Zone had more in common with company towns than with cherished notions of democracy) ordered that in future certain flagpoles would fly the Panamanian flag. Balboa High School was one of the sites at which the red and blue rectangles and stars of Panama were to be displayed. One day in early 1964 Jimmy Jenkins and his friends raised the Stars and Stripes instead, and stood guard at the flagpole to prevent anyone trying to implement the governor's order. It was a small-minded little protest, no more problematic than the demonstrations of high school students anywhere, but in the highly charged atmosphere of Panama it soon assumed enormous dimensions. Parents supported the actions of their children while Panamanian students at the National Institute, known locally as 'The Eagle's Nest', saw the whole episode as another demonstration of the high-handed arrogance of a contemptuous colonial power.

On 9 January a group of Panamanian students marched on Balboa High School, determined to remove the American flag and hoist their own. A Canal Zone police captain met the march at the school and told them they would not be allowed to raise the flag. Behind the police line a group of Zonians started to jeer at the students and soon there developed a melee of rock-throwing, punching and shooting. In the pushing and shoving the students' Panamanian flag was torn. When finally they marched away they were chanting in English, 'You'll die for this.'

Within an hour, rioting had begun. In an orgy of anti-American violence, Molotov cocktails flew, snipers shot on unarmed crowds, American cars – easily distinguishable by their Canal Zone registration plates – were wrecked, and all manner of American establishments from offices to Masonic temples were looted and put to the torch. The Panama government seemed deliberately to delay calling out the National Guard to tackle the rioters, sensing that the longer American soldiers were seen shooting at Panamanian students, the better the propaganda. Sure enough, when Yankee troops were deployed on the streets of Colon, anti-American feelings rose still further. One bar displayed the sign 'We are open to dogs but not Americans.' Within three days, twenty-four Panamanians and three American soldiers had died. They were the Martyrs commemorated on what the Zonians called Fourth of July Avenue.

Later, in the library at the Canal Commission, I looked through some of the contemporary accounts of the riots. Relations between the Zonians and the Panamanians could never have been worse. Implicit in many of the Zonian accounts was the belief that the Panamanians were lazy, dirty good-for-nothings, while part of the Panamanian press was even more vituperative about Jimmy Jenkins. Under a photograph of the boy, one newspaper commented, 'The face you see here caused 22 Panamanian deaths . . . a seed of evil and cruelty . . . his soul is filled with pus and covered in incurable pustules . . . Jenkins is a cruel monster who has inherited all the viciousness of the Zonians. His is the arrogance of the southern slaver.'

The passions which had been stirred by the riots, unedifying and unwholesome though they might have been, had done nothing but good to the Panamanian cause. Not only had martyrs been created, but the American government calculated there was now a need to balance their rights under the 1903 treaty against the damage which continued, potentially violent, opposition might do. Diplomatic relations between the two nations were broken, and the price of restoring amity was serious negotiation about ownership of the canal. Talks began during the Johnson administration, were suspended under Nixon and resumed again under Ford. By that time General Torrijos had realized the strength of the student riot weapon, and when negotiations were progressing too slowly, he threatened to provoke another riot himself.

In 1977 Torrijos and Carter signed the treaty under which the canal would – eventually – pass into Panamanian control. There had been predictable opposition both from the Zonians, who claimed the Panamanians were too incompetent to manage the canal without it all silting up, and from the right wing at home who saw no need to hand over the fruits of American enterprise to a bunch of Latin thugs. Ronald Reagan even claimed that the Canal Zone was as much a part of the United States as Texas. However, Congressional support was given only in exchange for certain provisions, one of which stated that even after the canal was handed over to the Panamanians in the year 2000, the United States would have the right to send in troops if they felt it was in danger.

The implementation of the new treaty was appropriately signalled: on the lawn outside the administration building, the Stars and Stripes was transferred to the shorter flagpole and the Panamanian flag run up the taller one. Now, on the green bump of Ancon Hill at the Pacific entrance to the canal, a huge red and blue Panamanian flag hangs as a sign of restored sovereignty. The canal itself and the dozen military bases in the Zone continue under American control until midnight on 31 December 1999. Hardly wholesale decolonization, but as close as feasible.

There had been an election in Panama that summer. It had been touted as another breakthrough for democracy, like the elections in Guatemala and El Salvador (although not, of course, Nicaragua), but it was hard to comprehend exactly how the alchemy of the ballot slip was supposed to have transformed the nation.

Everyone agreed that it had been a fraud. The voting ended, the ballot boxes were collected. It was obvious from the canvassing returns that Arnulfo Arias had won. Then an electoral tribunal was called in to count the vote. By the astonishingly slim majority of one thousand seven hundred votes in a total poll of six hundred thousand, Nicolas Barletta was declared the victor. It came as little surprise to learn that Mr Barletta enjoyed the support of the National Guard, Panama's sinister army. More remarkable were the reactions of diplomats from Western democracies, who instead of denouncing corruption simply said it was better for the country that the army candidate had won. 'He's a technocrat, he understands how to sort out the country's financial problems,' they'd say. And in due course, the Secretary of State arrived to attend his inauguration.

It was the third time that 'Fufo' Arias had been cheated of the presidency. Having reached the age of eighty-two, he was obviously an accomplished political survivor. Fifty years ago, at the beginning of his political career, he had been said to bear a vague resemblance to Errol Flynn, something which had obviously contributed to his tremendous popular appeal among the poor. Certainly the charisma of his gut nationalism bestowed upon him the air of Central America's last caudillo, yet he had never managed to survive a term in office. After being elected in 1940, he initiated a series of anti-gringo measures, becoming in effect a Nazi fellow-traveller. The United States wouldn't stand for it and assisted in his forcible removal from office. In 1949 he was elected again, only to be dragged off to gaol by the National Guard. He was in and out of prison so often over the next few years that a cell was permanently set aside for him. Then, in 1968 he was elected for the third time, but deposed in a coup eleven days later.

One evening I talked to an Englishman who had been living in Panama for thirty years, having answered a newspaper advertisement for young men prepared to live as the managers of remote banana plantations in Central America.

'I remember that election in 1968,' he said. 'It was quite a nasty one.'

'What constitutes a nasty election in Panama?' I asked.

'Oh, well, there were machine-gun battles across the street, the National Guard were going round seizing ballot boxes, that kind of thing,' he said, as if they were the sort of difficulties he could dimly remember one might encounter in elections for an English parish council.

'Come to think of it,' he went on, 'those were the last elections we had here, until this summer.'

The 1968 coup had been carried out by a group of National Guard officers led by Omar Torrijos, then a young lieutenant-colonel. Arias had recognized the danger and tried to forestall a Putsch by sending Torrijos abroad as military attaché, and cutting back on some of the Guard's less popular privileges. Predictably, they reacted by deposing him, with the justification that he was about to establish a dictatorship: whatever nonsense might be uttered about Arias representing the will of the people, the Guard were the true protectors of democracy. Arias took refuge in the Canal Zone and for a while both he and the National Guard tried to run separate governments within a mile or so of each other. But eventually he boarded an American airforce cargo plane and went to Washington, where he managed to break into the Panamanian Embassy and attempted – unsuccessfully – to establish a government in exile. Torrijos soon emerged as the real power in the land, however, and everyone settled down to acquiesce in the new status quo.

'Even before the coup he'd got quite a reputation,' said the old ex-pat. 'If one of the colonels captured an armoury, or tried to stage a coup, it was Torrijos they sent to put it down. In the riots in 1964, when the looters heard he was being sent to put the lid on things, they started taking things back to the shops.'

After Torrijos seized power, the newspapers started to call him 'the strongman of Panama', as if he were just another Latin American despot in padded shoulders and gold braid. But for a military dictator, he had a surprising facility for cultivating the friendship and respect of distinguished literary figures like Graham Greene and Gabriel Garcia Marquez, despite – or perhaps because of – the fact that he fitted no easily labelled political category. By the time of his death in August 1981 he had become the third longest-lasting military ruler in Latin America (after Stroessner in Paraguay and Castro in Cuba). Yet despite his longevity in office, he was still defying easy assessment. Within the space of three years, President Reagan managed to describe him both as 'a tin-horn dictator' and 'one of the outstanding figures in Panama's history'.

The spirit of Torrijos was still brooding over Panama, even though he had been dead for three years. Urgent little epitaphs spray-painted on walls exclaimed 'Omar lives', or 'Omar, your life inspires the nation'. But it was hard to know for sure exactly what form this inspiration took since Torrijo's political views had been something of a mystery. One minute he was friendly with Colonel Gaddafi, the next he was offering refuge to the exiled Shah of Iran. In *Getting to Know the General*, an account of his friendship with Torrijos published shortly after I returned from Panama, Graham Greene argued that he was a 'lone wolf', a 'patriot and an idealist who had no formal ideology, except a general preference for Left over Right and a scorn for bureaucrats'. In a country where elections meant almost nothing, and where the only constituency which mattered was the leadership of the National Guard, Torrijos was lionized by liberals who saw him as the best form of government available.

I suspected that many of them really liked him because of his struggle with the Yankee empire, for in the end his greatest achievement was to enable his country to crawl part of the way out from under the shadow of its history. There was no denying that in negotiating the handover of the canal, even with the reservations insisted upon by the Americans, Torrijos had accomplished more than any other ruler under United States suzerainty. For this, if for no other reason, he appealed to figures like Greene and Garcia Marquez.

But although Torrijos would doubtless have recoiled at the suggestion, it occurred to me that his political views sprang from much the same source as those of the pro-fascist Arias, whom he affected to despise. Both men's ideas had been shaped by the American presence in their country. Panama had been the closest thing to an American colony in Central America, and even after achieving a measure of independence, its involvement with the United States meant that it viewed the conventional political landscape from a distance, like a submariner through a periscope.

Born of country schoolteachers, Torrijos was thirty-nine when he took power. Over the next thirteen years, his political attitudes swung from the semi-fascist to the quasi-revolutionary. At one time he was throwing communists into gaol, at another he supplied arms and men to the Sandinista forces in Nicaragua. It was he who established the no-questions-asked banking system, and yet the same man stomped about peasant villages in jungle hat and military uniform, chewing on the monogrammed cigars sent by Castro. The contradictions were understandable only in the context of the pervasive influence exerted by the United States over Panama. Torrijos's overriding objective was to get control of the canal, and every other concern was secondary. He believed that the very existence of the great ditch had changed the natural order of things, that the canal was now the *raison d'être* of the isthmus. And if the conflicts in Central America were to be resolved in a way which would benefit the native peoples, control of the most important object in the area had to be in their hands. His strength was in knowing how far he could push the Americans. 'I pull the monkey's tail,' he'd say, 'but I don't hit the monkey.' And when Washington needed a favour done, like a temporary refuge for the deposed Shah, Torrijos was happy to oblige, knowing that one good turn would merit another.

Getting a measure of control of the canal was Torrijos's greatest obsession, and once the treaty was signed and the Somoza dictatorship had collapsed, he became an increasingly withdrawn figure. The stories of his melancholy Saturday night drinking-bouts became commonplace.

In July 1981, Torrijos set out in a light aircraft to visit a country retreat deep in the jungle. There was a torrential Panama downpour and visibility was appalling, but it seems he insisted that the pilot take off. It was only a short flight – fifteen minutes or so – but the pilot drifted off course as a result of the bad weather.

They found the remains of the plane the next day, scattered across the side of a jungle-covered mountain. American Special Forces medics, called out from their base in the Zone, recovered the bodies of the general, his female companion, his bodyguards and the two pilots.

Panama suffered deep shock: Torrijos had so dominated the nation that life without him seemed unimaginable. They gave him a theatrical farewell, as if the occasion would conceal the confusion into which the country had been plunged. The cortège was led by a riderless horse in whose stirrups the general's well-polished boots had been turned backwards. His coffin, with his bush hat and water bottle on top, followed on an orange fire truck and Torrijos's widow, Raquel, walked behind, her eyes hidden by dark glasses. Helicopters passed above the procession, scattering chrysanthemum petals over the mourners. It was the most impressive affair that the little country could mount.

Rumours about Torrijos's death had already begun to circulate. On the face of it, there seemed no reason to disagree with the official version of events – that his aircraft had crashed into a mountainside in bad weather. In an essay about the general,

Graham Greene had described how he always preferred to use young pilots who didn't know the risks they were taking. But Greene concluded his memoir, published three years after the crash, by wondering whether he had 'been perhaps unduly sceptical of any part played by the CIA in the death of Omar Torrijos'. The theory went that a bomb had been smuggled on to the aircraft, hidden inside a tape recorder.

By happy accident I managed to meet the general's bodyguard, the man around whom Graham Greene had based his account of the life of Torrijos. His name was José de Jesus Martinez, or 'Chuchu' for short. His short, powerful body and cropped white beard gave him the weathered and worldly appearance of a petty criminal, an enforcer for hire perhaps. The white singlet he wore revealed a skull and crossbones tattooed inside his left forearm. To my surprise, I discovered that he had been a professor of philosophy and mathematics until he had been seized by a quixotic impulse and joined the National Guard. Initially they had rejected him as too old and unfit, but he had appealed directly to Torrijos, who had ensured first that he was accepted and then hired him as his bodyguard. By the time of the general's death he had become his closest confidant in the Guard.

We met over coffee early one morning just off the Avenida Balboa. He had just returned from a visit Graham Greene had asked him to make to the South of France to read the manuscript of his book about Torrijos. I was going to ask him his theories on the general's death, but before I could frame the question he had begun to tell me about the relationship between the two men.

'Torrijos didn't speak English, and Graham Greene didn't speak Spanish, so I was the interpreter. But often I felt I was unnecessary – they communicated directly with each other without any common language.'

Greene and other friends of Torrijos had tried to suggest that his form of government was a possible model for the rest of Central America. In a nation with no history of democracy, the general, Greene suggested, dreamed of 'a social democratic Central America which would be no menace to the United

States, but completely independent'. Greene found it an enticing prospect. Almost at the end of my journey, I hoped for a moment I might have found a possible way out of the Central American quagmire. Chuchu disagreed.

'I think Graham Greene is wrong about the general. He's a Catholic. He *wanted* to believe that he was a social democrat. I knew Torrijos for seven years. He was no social democrat.'

'What was he then?' I asked.

'In the beginning, he was just a national revolutionary. But by the end, he had become an international revolutionary. He saw that everywhere in Central America – Nicaragua, El Salvador, Guatemala – would have to have radical change if we were going to make any progress.'

'Why did he change his mind?'

'He learned a lot when he was in power. One son-of-a-bitch asked me, was he a communist? I said no . . . not yet. But I'm quite convinced he was a genuine revolutionary. He always felt things here.' And Chuchu patted his heart with his tattooed hand.

'I remember one time, we were down in Penonomé. We found a little boy who, just out of hunger, had eaten part of his right hand. The general made them get a big bowl of rice and meat and put it in front of the little boy. He was too weak to eat it. Hunger gets you like that – you can sound a bell right by the ear of a starving child, and he won't hear it. And when children are really starving, they cannot feel pain. That's how they can eat their own body.

'We had over one hundred banks in the country, but there were children who had forgotten how to eat. When you see things like that little boy, you just want to get a machine-gun and kill somebody. You see, that's how I know Torrijos was becoming a revolutionary. I was with him. You cannot see things like that and not be changed.' It sounded an unlikely tale, but why should he be bothering to lie?

'Do you believe his death was an accident?'

'Well, just remember what the Americans said about him. They said he was a drunkard, a visceral anti-American, they said he would destroy the canal. If you add these together, you've got enough reason to kill him.

'He'd supported the Sandinistas, and he still supported them, whatever people say. Four days before his death he was talking with Tomas Borge. In fact, the thing that makes me convinced he was killed was that that week, the week before his death, all the revolutionary movements in Central America were here in Panama. He had decided, you see, to give practical support to the revolutionary groups in El Salvador and Guatemala. That was why they killed him.'

'When was the last time you saw him?'

'He'd sent me out to help fix up another secret meeting between Eden Pastora – Commander Zero – and Pepé Figueres. I telephoned Torrijos. The general answered the phone himself, and there was a silence. I knew it was because he hadn't put his false teeth in. He didn't like to talk without his teeth. I suggested that I make some arrangements and the general just said, "Yes, please do that", and that was our last conversation.'

So that was it. The last time the old sergeant-professor spoke to the hero of Central America, there was silence because he hadn't got his teeth in. The incident had an appropriate bathos.

'I never saw him alive again,' he went on. 'But I'm absolutely sure he was murdered. He was too much of a threat.'

As a murder theory it at least had a motive if not much more. No doubt had the CIA wanted to murder the general, they could have done so: after all, compared with running clandestine wars, it would have been a relatively simple task. And in view of the escalating obsession with controlling the guerillas in El Salvador and Guatemala, they might well have thought it was worth tinkering with the engine or the controls of his plane.

There would never be an explanation to satisfy everyone. It suited a good number of people to believe he was murdered. Whether the theory was true or not, it demonstrated the way in which the influence of the gringos pervaded everything in Central America. Even after death.

There was a dirty old four-coach train standing at the single platform in Panama City station. The line to Colon was a single track, so the same set of rattly old coaches did the journey there and back four times a day. The ticket booth advertised seats in two classes, air-conditioned and non-air-conditioned, but since the equipment had broken down, there was no difference any more. For $1.25 I got a seat by an open window instead. I was early, and the rest of the carriage was empty.

Colon would give me my first sight of the Atlantic since leaving Belize, and a trip across Panama seemed a suitable way to end my journey. I had no idea what to expect when I arrived.

A black youth kicked open the door into the carriage, sauntered down the aisle and, ignoring all the empty seats, sat down next to me.

'You going to Colon?' He asked the question with artificial indifference.

'Yes.'

'It's a mistake.' He said it almost to himself, shook his head and then turned to look me in the face. 'You'll lose everything you have.'

'What do you mean?'

'Colon is a bad city. It's full of bad people. They'll rob you.'

'But I want to see the city,' I said.

'OK Look, I have a car. Let me take you.' So that was the reason for his concern. A taxi-driver touting for business.

'No thanks. I want to go by train.'

'You are alone. Anyone could do anything to you. Believe me, Colon is a dangerous place.' His tone was no longer casual, there was a distinct undercurrent of menace. If this was a way of drumming up customers for his taxi, it was tantamount to intimidation and probably the more productive for all that. The man had moved closer, blocking the way out of the seat.

'Look, I want to go on the train,' I said, looking out of the window. There was no one on the platform either.

'You will regret it,' he said. His voice was indifferent again, as if he was only giving me advice for my own good which I could accept or reject as I chose.

Three things happened at once. The man put his left hand on my shoulder, and reached into the pocket of his jerkin with his other. I was convinced he had a gun or a knife inside. At the same instant the door to the carriage opened and another passenger entered the compartment. As he did so, I said 'Leave me alone,' as loudly and firmly as I could manage.

The man stayed where he was for a moment, glared at me, and then glanced at the other passenger coming towards us. He took his hand out of his pocket and turned away. His face assumed an expression that was part anger and part disdain. The other passenger was shuffling towards us from the front of the carriage. The youth got up and made for the back of the coach with purpose but no urgency. As he opened the door to get out he spoke again.

'You'll be sorry.' The same flat, indifferent tone of voice. He turned around as if to leave, and then looked back. For an awful moment I thought he might be returning, but he just shot another baleful glance, then pushed on the dirty doorhandle. The door slammed behind him.

I looked across at the passenger who had perhaps saved me from a mugging. He was short, bald and bespectacled, hardly cast in the heroic mould. I grinned at him in thanks. He sat down without seeming to see me.

As soon as I was sure that no one was watching, I took my wallet and passport out of my pocket and shoved them inside the front of my trousers. The train moved off a few moments later. I looked out of the window. The man in the jerkin was leaning against a wall. There was the suggestion of a smile at the edge of his mouth.

The first stop, a couple of minutes later, was Balboa. The terminus had been for Panamanians; this station was for canal employees. The Panama City station had consisted of a single platform and a few benches. Balboa had a newsstand, a new coat of paint and, behind, the lawns and villas of middle America in the tropics. A fat blonde woman in tight shorts boarded the train with her teenage daughter and they sat at the front of the coach.

We passed sidings jammed with old rusting freight cars. The incessant sun and rain had turned the legend WORLD FREIGHT ON THE MOVE a dismal shade of brown. Many of the waggons were covered over by creepers, as the jungle reclaimed its territory.

Soon we were moving through deep jungle and grass which grew taller than the train. Without the daily passage of the dilapidated carriages, the track would be entirely overgrown in no time. It was easy to understand how the building of the railroad had cost so many thousands of lives – merely to hack through the heavy undergrowth in the hot static air, let alone make any attempt to level ground or lay track, would have been shattering. Now it seemed the little train had outlived its utility, was slower and less convenient than the canal and road which had been built later. The line might almost have been kept open as a memorial to the thousands of Chinese coolies and West Indian labourers who had perished of fever, smallpox and cholera.

And then, incredibly, the jungle cleared, giving way to a golf course with men in bright check shorts on well-tended fairways and greens looking for all the world as if it was a Sunday morning in Florida. But this vision of a suburban weekend lasted only a couple of moments before the jungle closed in again, just as suddenly, and it seemed as if it had never existed.

Sometimes the jungle would vanish altogether, and there would be an American army camp: an array of well-cut lawns and bland rows of clapboard houses, bearing ugly military acronyms and injunctions, a chain-link fencing keeping outsiders outside. There were ten or so American military bases along the canal, built originally to defend the waterway, and as good a posting for the officer with a taste for golf and sunshine as he could hope for. For years Southern Command had been a pleasant little backwater for the unambitious, the tired and the undistinguished. But now it had become the base for much of the military activity in Central America, training troops in jungle warfare, supplying the army in El Salvador and spying on Nicaragua. I found it hard to imagine the Americans would be moving out of their bases in Panama before the allotted date. The one establishment whose closure had just been announced, however, was the School of the Americas, the military training camp at which United States officers passed on their skills to successive groups of Latin students; these numbered among their alumni a good number of the more notorious dictators in the hemisphere. There was talk about moving the school to Honduras.

Up to now, the stretch of water beside the track had seemed little more than a muddy river, but no amount of forethought could have detracted from the shock of suddenly coming upon an ocean-going freighter in the midst of the jungle. One moment we were ploughing through a mass of thick vegetation; and the next, we were confronted with the towering bow and bridge of a German cargo ship, its deck piled high with multi-coloured containers destined for Latin America or the Far East. Behind the ship more trees and creepers spread up into the distant hills, but there in the middle of a small pool of water sat this great bewildered leviathan. In a moment or two the vision disintegrated so completely that I wondered whether I had seen it at all. Then we were back into the forest, where butterflies of unnatural orange and blue circulated in the lazy air. At a place called Frijoles, or Beans, a man got off the train wearing a suit and tie and carrying a smart briefcase. He disappeared down a track to the edge of the lake, looking quite as though he were off for a day at the office in London or New York. And then the train moved off and we were back among the wild banana plants, the flowering palms and the still heavy air.

At Gatun, where the locks lower the ships to the Atlantic, a group of sixty or seventy American soldiers were waiting to take the train on its return journey to Panama. They were ready for a weekend of enjoyment, and although it was only ten in the morning the floor of the station was already covered in empty beer cans. There were more American troops than Panamanian in Panama and they lived in a hermetically sealed world. Southern Command even operated its own television network, broadcasting old recordings of 'The Muppet Show' and live editions of the network news from New York. The only difference was the absence of commercials, which were replaced by announcements of the next meeting of the Cheerleading Squad, and warnings to steer clear of pot.

Once I'd recovered from the shock of seeing ships where they were not expected, the canal itself, even the locks, the most elaborate part of the business of moving vessels from one ocean to another, was strangely unimpressive. The statistics by which it was glorified – fifty-two million gallons of water discharged to raise and lower each vessel eighty-five feet – were so idiosyncratic that there was nothing to which they could be related. It was imposing only for the fact that it existed at all, as testament to the vision and enterprise which had made it possible. Precisely because the whole operation was carried out with efficiency, it had lost its capacity for surprise. The only thing which seemed to excite people was the endless talk about plans to replace it with a new canal at sea level, an idea which had been mooted some time back, but which was unlikely to come to fruition for lack of funds.

Colon was at the end of the line; the train would wait there for several minutes before setting off back to Panama City. The carriage was empty but for the bald man who had unwittingly come to my rescue. He was standing in the doorway, holding a copy of *The South America Handbook* and peering myopically out at the city. I slid past him.

'Are you getting off here?' I asked. It was a silly question. The train didn't go any further.

'No,' he said, not moving from the doorway. He sounded French.

'No,' he said again, 'I think I will go back on the train.' He was fingering his yellow return ticket.

'The train will be here again in four or five hours,' I said. 'Why don't you wait till then? I'd be glad of the company if you feel like looking around the town.'

'No. I will go back on the train. I have read the guidebook. It says this is a very bad town. They rob people here in the middle of the street in the middle of the day. It's too dangerous to leave the train.' And he hugged the book to his chest, as if it were a Bible.

'You know, you saved me from getting mugged back there in Panama,' I said.

'What?'

'That guy who was sitting next to me when you got on the train. He was going to rob me.'

'Oh, I didn't notice anyone with you,' he said. 'I'm a bit shortsighted.'

'Sure you don't want to come to look around Colon?'

'No, it's too dangerous,' he said, turning back inside the train.

Colon was notable for nothing apart from the canal. But as much as the canal was evidence of achievement, the town was a testament to failure. It had been built by the railroad company to accommodate the thousands of roustabouts who had flooded in to construct the line which had carried me here from Panama City. Since vast numbers of them had come from the British West Indies, the poor areas were predominantly black. The company had chosen to construct the town on a coral flat in the bay, with the consequence that when the place wasn't flooded by an abnormally high tide, it was awash in garbage, excrement and the corpses of animals. It had originally been intended as a camp to accommodate the workforce who, it was assumed, would all go home once the railway was built. But the landlords who were making a living from renting out property were anxious not to lose this new source of income and the town survived as a ghastly mistake. With the railway completed there was nothing for the men to do and the place sank into decline, recovering only when work began on the canal. Since completion of that project, the Panamanian government had produced various grandiose schemes to inject new life into the place, including the establishment of a free trade zone, but all had failed. Nowhere deserved seventy years of hopelessness, and the town reeked of poverty, misery and crime.

Near the station was the worst collection of shanty dwellings I had seen since leaving El Salvador, a sprawling mass of tin-roofed shacks with an air of almost tangible despair. Occasionally, in whatever shade they could find from the oppressive stinking heat, a man or a woman would be sprawled half asleep. Not one of them gave any greeting or returned a smile.

I walked on towards the centre of town, past shabby concrete apartment blocks, stinking of urine, with lines of threadbare washing hanging from the windows. In a corner between two walls a thin whimpering dog was tethered on a tight length of wire. There was a smell of raw sewage in the air. The area was called, inevitably, 'Pueblo Nuevo', New Town.

Closer to the centre, the buildings were older, made of wood, visibly crumbling, their numerous inhabitants spilling into the streets. They spoke of the dashed hopes of those who had come seeking work and wealth. Materially they were better off than many of their fellow countrymen, but so many of their faces wore mean, blank expressions.

On the water's edge was an elegant white building, the Hotel Washington. It was the only place with a fresh coat of paint in the town, and had been there since the railway was built. I looked inside for a moment. The cavernous hall was empty and smelt of ancient cooking.

I wandered further. After half an hour or so, I was addressed by an old black woman. She was sitting with a bowl of dried brown fish on her lap.

'You'd better leave here,' she said, with no preamble.

'What do you mean?'

'You'd better go back where you came from.'

'Why?'

'Because somebody's gonna rob you.'

'Who'd want to rob me?'

The old woman looked serious, slightly exasperated to find someone questioning her well-intentioned advice.

'You know,' she said, summoning the most potent example she could think of, 'when the ships are waiting outside to come into the canal, even the sailors don't come into town any more. Maybe one or two, like you, but most of them don't come. You seen any policemen? I tell you, they don't like to come down-town. They stay in the barracks and look after the generals. It's safer.'

'But I don't have any money on me, anyway,' I said, glad I had put my wallet out of sight.

'You don't understand, man.' A note of annoyance had entered her voice. 'It used to be that they'd rob you in this town. But it's getting uncivilized now. The kids will cut you with a knife. I'm telling you, you'd better leave.'

Four other people, all of them elderly, had gathered round. An old man with hair like a wire brush echoed her words.

'She's right. This is a bad town. You'd better go back where you came from. It's uncivilized.'

I thought for a moment what an unusual word it was for him to choose, yet it was the second time I had heard it. It was as if the town had left its ethics behind with the families of the men who had come here to find riches and a new life. They had failed to fulfil their ambitions. Their sense of hope had gradually been eroded.

'You'd better go back where you came from,' said the old woman once more.

Index

Index

Anthropology in Paladin Books

Humankind £2.95 ☐
Peter Farb
A history of the development of man. It provides a comprehensive picture of how we evolved to reach our present state, and analyses the remarkable diversity of human beings.

Shabono £2.95 ☐
Florinda Donner
'A masterpiece . . . It is superb social science because in describing her experiences among the Indians of the Venezuelan jungle Florinda Donner plummets the reader into an unknown but very real world'
Carlos Casteneda

The Mountain People £2.50 ☐
Colin Turnbull
A remarkable and gripping account of two separate periods in which Turnbull lived with a declining African tribe, the Ik, in a mountain area on the borders of Uganda and Kenya.

The Forest People £2.50 ☐
Colin Turnbull
A fascinating study of the Pygmies of the Ituri Forest – a vast expanse of dense, damp and inhospitable forest in the heart of Stanley's 'Dark Continent'.

Lucy: The Beginnings of Humankind £2.95 ☐
Donald C Johanson and Maitland A Edey
'A riveting book that is at once a carefully documented report, an exciting adventure story, and a candid memoir of a brash young palaeoanthropologist . . . What Lucy suggests about our forebears will keep palaeoanthropologists arguing for years' *Publishers Weekly*.
Illustrated

History in Paladin Books

Africa in History   £2.95 ☐
Basil Davidson
Revised edition of 'one of the most durable and most literate guides to
contemporary knowledge of Africa' *Tribune*

A Higher Form of Killing   £2.50 ☐
Robert Harris and Jeremy Paxman
The escalating nuclear capabilities of the superpowers have been
extensively publicized. Less well documented has been the revival of
interest in chemical and biological weaponry. Drawing extensively
on international sources, this book chronicles for the first time the
secret history of chemical and germ warfare. Illustrated.

Decisive Battles of the Western World (Vols 1 & 2)   £3.95 ☐
J F C Fuller   each
The most original and influential military thinker Britain has ever
produced: his major work.

The Paladin History of England – the first three titles of the series are

The Formation of England   £2.95 ☐
H P R Finberg
This volume deals with Britain in the Dark Ages between Roman and
Norman conquests.

The Crisis of Imperialism   £3.95 ☐
Richard Shannon
England in the realm of Victoria. A time of development, expansion,
colonisation, enormous social upheavals and reform.

Peace, Print and Protestantism   £3.95 ☐
C S L Davies
C S L Davies' book deals with the period 1450–1558 encompassing
the reign of the Tudors and the breakaway from the Church of Rome.

To order direct from the publisher just tick the titles you want
and fill in the order form.   **PAL7082**

All these books are available at your local bookshop or newsagent, or can be ordered direct from the publisher.

To order direct from the publishers just tick the titles you want and fill in the form below.

Name _____

Address _____

_____

Send to:
Paladin Cash Sales
PO Box 11, Falmouth, Cornwall TR10 9EN.

Please enclose remittance to the value of the cover price plus:

UK 55p for the first book, 22p for the second book plus 14p per copy for each additional book ordered to a maximum charge of £1.75.

BFPO and Eire 55p for the first book, 22p for the second book plus 14p per copy for the next 7 books, thereafter 8p per book.

Overseas £1.25 for the first book and 31p for each additional book.